Societal Impact on Aging Series

Series Editor

K. Warner Schaie, PhD
Director, Gerontology Center
College of Health and Human Development
The Pennsylvania State University
University Park, PA

K. Warner Schaie, PhD, is the Evan Pugh Professor of Human Development and Psychology and Director of the Gerontology Center at the Pennsylvania State University. He has previously held professional appointments at the University of Nebraska, West Virginia University, and the University of Southern California. Dr. Schaie received his BA from the University of California–Berkeley and his MS and PhD degrees from the University of Washington, all in psychology. He is the author or editor of 26 books and over 200 journal articles and chapters related to the study of human aging. Dr. Schaie is the recipient of the Distinguished Scientific Contributions Award of the American Psychological Association and of the Robert W. Kleemeier Award for Distinguished Research Contributions from the Gerontological Society of America. He was awarded the honorary degree of Dr. phil. h.c. by the Friedrich-Schiller-University of Jena, Germany.

Martin Pietrucha received his Bachelor of Science degree in civil engineering from the New Jersey Institute of Technology. He also holds a Master of Science degree in civil engineering from the University of California at Berkeley and a Doctor of Philosophy degree in civil engineering from the University of Maryland. He has over twenty years experience in transportation engineering specializing in highway traffic operations, highway safety, and human factors issues for a variety of public and private institutions.

He is currently an associate professor with the Civil and Environmental Engineering Department at the University Park Campus of the Pennsylvania State University where he teaches courses in highway operations and highway safety. He has been Principal Investigator or Co-principal Investigator on several research projects for the Federal Highway Administration (FHWA), the National Cooperative Highway Research Program (NCHRP), and the Pennsylvania Department of Transportation (PennDOT) dealing with topics such as: delineation devices, pavement markings, and object markers for older drivers, older pedestrians, roadway signing, highway geometric design, and road safety audits.

Dr. Pietrucha is a member of Chi Epsilon, Tau Beta Pi, Sigma Xi, the Institute of Transportation Engineers, the Transportation Research Board, ITS America, the American Society of Civil Engineers, and the American Society for Engineering Education. He is also a licensed Professional Engineer in New Jersey and Virginia.

Mobility and Transportation in the Elderly

K. Warner Schaie, PhD
Martin Pietrucha, PhD
Editors

 Societal Impact on Aging

Springer Publishing Company, Inc.
536 Broadway
New York, NY 10012-3955

Acquisitions Editor: Bill Tucker
Production Editor: Janice Stangel
Cover design by: James Scotto-Lavino

00 01 02 03 04 / 5 4 3 2 1

Library of Congress Cataloging-in-Publication Data

Mobility and transportation in the elderly / K. Warner Schaie and
    Martin Pietrucha, editors.
        p.   cm.—(Societal impact on aging series)
    Includes bibliographical references and index.
    ISBN 0-8261-1309-5
    1. Aged—Transportation.   2. Aged automobile driver.
3. Traffic accidents.   I. Schaie, K. Warner (Klaus Warner, 1928-
II. Pietrucha, Martin.   III. Societal impact on aging.
HQ1063.5.M625   2000
305.26—dc21   99-054280
                                                                      CIP

Printed in the United States of America

Contents

Contributors

Karlene Ball, Ph.D.
Department of Psychology
University of Alabama-
  Birmingham
Birmingham, AL

Thomas E. Bryer, P.E.
PA Dept. of Transportation
Bureau of Highway Safety and
  Traffic Engineering
Harrisburg, PA

Jon E. Burkhardt, President
Ecosometrics Inc.
Bethesda, MD

Thomas A. Dingus
Center for Transportation
  Research
Virginia Technical University
Blacksburg, VA

Allen Dobbs, Ph.D.
University of Alberta
Dept. of Psychology
Edmonton, Alberta Canada

William J. Evans, Ph.D.
Nutrition, Metabolism, and
  Exercise Laboratory
Donald Reynolds Department
  of Geriatrics
VA Medical Center
North Little Rock, AR

James Fozard, Ph.D.
Director of Geriatric Research
Florida Geriatric Research
  Program
Morton Plant Mease Health
  Care
Clearwater, FL

Katherine Freund, Ph.D.
Independent Transportation
  Network
Portland, ME

Richard Hanowski, Ph.D.
Center for Transportation
  Research
Virginia Technical University
Blacksburg, VA

Paul P. Jovanis, Ph.D.
Head, Civil and Environmental
  Engineering
The Pennsylvania State
  University
University Park, PA

Richard Marotoli, M.D.
Adler Geriatric Center
New Haven, CT

D. Alfred Owens, Ph.D.
Franklin and Marshall College
Whitely Psychological
  Laboratories
Lancaster, PA

Cynthia Owsley
Department of Psychology
University of Alabama-
  Birmingham
Birmingham, AL

Frank Schieber, Ph.D.
University of South Dakota
Department of Psychology
Vermillion, SD

Loren Staplin, Ph.D.
Scientex Corporation
Kulpsville, PA

Harvey Sterns, Ph.D.
Institute for Life-Span Develop-
  ment and Gerontology
University of Akron
Akron, OH

Ronni Sterns, Ph.D.
Institute for Life-Span Develop-
  ment and Gerontology
University of Akron
Akron, OH

Thomas Swigart
Ford Motor Company
Human Factors Engineering
  and Ergonomics
Northville, MI

Sherry L. Willis, Ph.D.
Pennsylvania State University
University Park, PA

Preface

This is the eleventh volume in a series on the broad topic of "Societal Impact on Aging." The first five volumes of this series were published by Erlbaum Associates under the series title of "Social Structure and Aging." The present volume is the sixth published by Springer Publishing Company. It is the edited proceedings of a conference held at the Pennsylvania State University, October 13–14, 1997.

The series of Penn State Gerontology Center conferences originated from the deliberations of a subcommittee of the Committee on Life Course Perspectives of the Social Science Research Council chaired by Matilda White Riley in the early 1980s. That subcommittee was charged with developing an agenda and mechanisms that would serve to encourage communication between scientists who study societal structures that might affect the aging of individuals and those scientists who are concerned with the possible effects of contextual influences on individual aging. The committee proposed a series of conferences that would systematically explore the interfaces between social structures and behavior, and in particular to identify mechanisms through which society influences adult development. When the second editor was named director of the Penn State Gerontology Center, he was able to implement this conference program as one of the center's major activities.

The previous ten volumes in this series have dealt with the societal impact on aging in psychological processes (Schaie & Schooler, 1989); age structuring in comparative perspective (Kertzer & Schaie, 1989); self-directedness and efficacy over the life span (Rodin, Schooler, & Schaie, 1990); aging, health behaviors, and health outcomes (Schaie, Blazer, & House, 1992); caregiving in families (Zarit, Pearlin, & Schaie, 1993), aging in historical perspective (Schaie & Achenbaum, 1993), adult intergenerational relations (Bengtson,

Schaie, & Burton, 1995), older adults' decision making and the law (Smyer, Schaie, & Kapp, 1996), the impact of social structures on decision making in the elderly (Willis, Schaie, & Hayward, 1997), and the impact of the work place on older workers (Schaie & Schooler, 1998).

The strategy for each of these volumes has been to commission six reviews on three major topics by established subject-matter specialists who have credibility in aging research. We then invited two formal discussants for each chapter—usually one drawn from the writer's discipline and one from a neighboring discipline. This format seems to provide a suitable antidote against the perpetuation of parochial orthodoxies as well as to make certain that questions are raised with respect to the validity of iconoclastic departures in new directions.

To focus the conference, the editors chose three topics of broad interest to gerontologists. Social and behavioral scientists with a demonstrated track record were then selected and asked to interact with those interested in theory building within a multi-disciplinary context.

The purpose of the conference reported in this volume was to examine the effects of social structures on mobility in the elderly. Particular emphasis was given to the problems and barriers facing the older driver. For better or worse private automobiles still represent the primary access to services and social networks for a large part of the North American population. Hence, maintenance of the ability of older persons to continue driving to advanced ages is a major variable in avoiding social isolation and maintaining full participation in their communities. Reduced mobility also impairs the ability of individuals to use mass transportation systems in urban settings. Reduction in mobility, therefore, results in a substantial reduction of the quality of older persons' lives, and is often a major precursor of institutionalization.

Reduced mobility usually occurs as an interactive function of intrinsic changes (sensory, cognitive and physiological) occurring with normal and abnormal aging processes, hazards posed by increasingly complex environments, as well as vehicular designs that are less than optimal for older persons. This volume examines intrinsic and extrinsic factors that lead to reduced mobility with increasing age. It then proceeds to examine a broad spectrum of possible interventions that include cognitive and strength training, as well as the introduction of assistive devices that may make it possible for aging individuals to extend their mobility and quality of life without creating hazards for others.

The volume begins with an examination of sensory and cognitive changes that normally occur with advancing age and that are particularly relevant to understanding reduced mobility and increased risks of accidents as pedestrians, drivers, or users of mass transportation system. Next, the reader will find a review of those physiological age changes that interfere with mobility, such as muscle strength, aerobic capacity, and motor skills. These physiological changes are examined in the context of the role of exercise as it impacts body composition and functional capacity of older persons.

The second topic addresses environmental hazards that reduce mobility in the elderly. Here we consider the limitations of mass transportation and individual vehicle systems that create increasing barriers to effective use by older individuals. Social structures and processes in public and private transportation are considered and some speculations are offered on the future direction of transportation systems that impact older persons. The environmentally based causes of accidents related to age are then examined from the point of view of the safety engineer, with extensive statistics for the sample case of accident patterns in the Commonwealth of Pennsylvania.

The third topic deals with approaches that have been used or could be developed to improve the mobility and reduce accidents of older persons. Here will be found discussion of interventions to improve the relevant cognitive and sensory skills and capacities of older persons by cognitive psychologists and vision researchers, who have developed relevant training interventions. Also considered is the concordance of subjectively perceived and actual mobility outcomes, and the issue of person and environment fit for driving competence. Finally, there is a detailed review of issues involved in the development of assistive devices that would improve driving skills in the elderly or ameliorate the impact of environmental hazards. Special emphasis is given here to the development of intelligent transportation systems that might be helpful to older drivers, including viewpoints from the scientific community and the auto industry.

Our emphasis on understanding the impact of broad societal trends impacting the welfare of individuals and their development into old age brought together scientists interested in individual development, and those interested in traffic safety, mass transportation systems, and adaptation of personal transportation systems to the needs of older persons. It is hoped that the resultant interplay of views from various disciplines will contribute to our theoretical understanding of basic and applied issues regarding the maintenance of mobility in the elderly. We also hope that the in depth review of the literature provided here can inform policy development and practice.

We are grateful for the financial support of the conference that led to this volume which was provided by conference grant AG 09787-06 from the National Institute on Aging, and by additional support from the Vice-president for Research and Dean of the Graduate School of the Pennsylvania State University. We are also grateful to Judy Hall and Alvin Hall for handling the conference logistics, to Anna Shuey for coordinating the manuscript preparation, and to Rebecca Reed for preparing the indexes.

K. Warner Schaie
September, 1999

REFERENCES

Bengtson, V. L., Schaie, K. W., & Burton, L. (1995). *Adult intergenerational relations: Effects of societal changes.* New York: Springer.

Kertzer, D., & Schaie, K. W. (1989). *Age structuring in comparative perspective.* Hillsdale, NJ: Erlbaum.

Rodin, J., Schooler, C., & Schaie, K. W. (1991). *Self-directedness and efficacy: Causes and effects throughout the life course.* Hillsdale, NJ: Erlbaum.

Schaie, K. W., & Achenbaum, W. A. (1993). *Societal impact on aging: Historical perspectives.* New York: Springer.

Schaie, K. W., House, J., & Blazer, D. (1992). *Aging, health behaviors, and health outcomes.* Hillsdale, NJ: Erlbaum.

Schaie, K. W., & Schooler, C. (1989). *Social structure and aging: Psychological processes.* Hillsdale, NJ: Erlbaum.

Schaie, K. W., & Schooler, C. E. (Eds.). (1998). *Impact of the work place on older persons.* New York: Springer.

Smyer, M., Schaie, K. W., & Kapp, M. B. (1996). *Older adults' decision-making and the law.* New York: Springer.

Willis, S. L., Schaie, K. W., & Hayward, M. (1997). *Impact of social structures on decision making in the elderly.* New York: Springer.

Zarit, S. H., Pearlin, I., & Schaie, K. W. (1993). *Social structure and caregiving: Family and cross-national perspectives.* Hillsdale, NJ: Erlbaum.

CHAPTER 1

Sensory and Cognitive Changes with Age

James L. Fozard

Three facts about aging have been documented in many contexts and situations. The first is that at older ages, speed of behavior becomes slower; the slowness affects sensory function, mental activities, and motor activities such as walking, controlling a vehicle, and making other skilled manual movements. The second is that with older age (70+), the interrelationships among sensory and cognitive performance increase. This is reflected in higher correlations among measures of sensory and cognitive tasks. The third is that with older age, skilled performance requires relatively more sensory information from the environment than is the case in younger adulthood; such as, the relatively greater importance of high quality lighting for visual guidance or adjustment of walking or manual maneuvers or the greater interdependence of postural and visual information for maintaining balance.

These facts about aging provide the basis for interventions. Accordingly, the present chapter selectively summarizes some research on age-related behavioral slowing and age-related increases in dependence on environmental information for the performance of complex behavior involved in cognitive activity and physical activities of walking, maintenance of posture, falls, and stumbles. Some interventions involve adapting the physical environment to the abilities of the older person—compensation for diminished capacity. Others involve improving the capacity of an older person to adapt to a challenging environment—prevention or retarding of age-associated losses in capacity. The two approaches are not mutually exclusive, and both may be applied to personal mobility as well as to transportation, particularly driving.

At present, there is no strong scientific basis for interventions that prevent age-associated behavioral slowing. Hence, intervention focuses on compensation for consequences of slower sensory and mental activities, emphasing task redesign and changes in the working and living environment. Ergonomics and task analyses are the appropriate tools for designing interventions. Established approaches have been reviewed by Charness and Bosman (1990) and Vercruyssen (1996). Secondarily, ergonomic attention to the interface of people and modern equipment will also enhance the usefulness of computers and high technology communications equipment for older persons.

Age-associated difficulties in personal mobility—walking indoors and outdoors, climbing stairs, and so forth—have multiple causes, as is the case for most age-associated limitations in carrying out activities of daily living and instrumental activities. Most interventions emphasize compensation for limitations in personal mobility. Improved information, such as, lighting of stairs, warning signals, and so forth, and improved infrastructure, including design of surfaces, stairs, and walking apparel, are particularly relevant in considering situations that place people at risk for falls and stumbles. Another approach emphasizes prevention, largely through improving the strength of aging people. The scientific basis for prevention of age-associated limitations in walking is currently emerging. In general the focus of this intervention approach is more on the person than the physical environment. The present chapter will review strength training in elderly persons. Personal transportation most commonly involves driving, and some approaches to maintaining or improving this complex skill in older age will also be considered.

ANALYZING PERSON-ENVIRONMENT INTERACTIONS

Aging is a very individual matter. Intrinsic variability in aging resulting from genetic influences are amplified by environmental factors such as differential exposure to diseases, environmental pollutants and carcinogens, lifestyle variations, and variability in the manmade environment. All contribute to the uniqueness of the aging experience among people who might have the same calendar age. Because of the variability in person-environment situations, it is useful to have a systematic approach to describing and analyzing them. Accordingly, an adaptation of a standard analytic tool used by ergonomists and human factors scientists was developed (Fozard, Graafmans, Rietsema, Bouma, & van Berlo, 1996; Graafmans, Fozard, Rietsema, van Berlo, & Bouma, 1996). The major parts of this analytic aid are illustrated in Figure 1.1.

A specific interaction of a person and his or her environment may be characterized as an exchange of information and action; it is shown as the interface dividing the upper and lower halves of Figure 1.1. Information such as from visual displays, sounds, and so forth is received by the person from the environment, named the technical operating system in Figure 1.1. Events within the person, called the human operating system in Figure 1.1, result in actions that adjust or modify the controls of the technical operating system such as a vehicle, a device at work, or a climate control system in the home. An analysis of the interface between the person and the operating system is made to determine the assignment of function to the person or equipment and the optimization of the person-environment system.

Individual differences among people including those associated with age complicate the analysis: as shown in the inner box of Figure 1.1, age differences in sensitivity to the visual, acoustic, and thermal environments directly affect the quality of information available to the person in the system. In turn, age-associated differences in strength, reaction time, cognitive abilities, and so forth directly affect the way in which the system is controlled. Behind these factors are age differences in organs and physiological systems.

The aging or temporal dimension of person-environment interactions adds the dynamic aspect of the person-environment systems

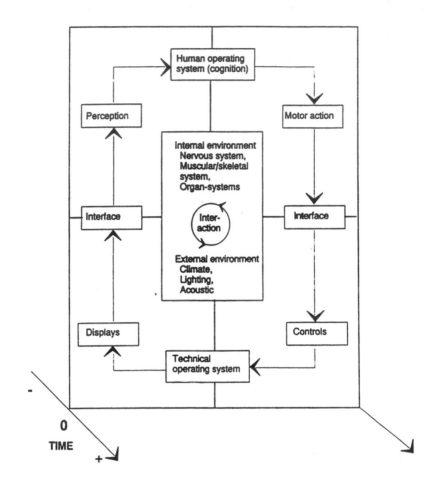

Figure 1.1 Schematic diagram showing age-related differences and changes in exchange of information and action between a person, the human operating system, and a machine or control device, the technical operating system. The interface represents the point of person/environment interaction. Age differences affecting quality of interaction are indicated in the inner box; age-related changes in people or the environment that could affect the interaction are represented by the time tracks at the bottom of the diagram where 0 represents the present. Figure adapted from Fozard, Graafmans, Rietsema, Bouma, and van Berlo (1996).

concept. This is illustrated in the time lines at the bottom of Figure 1.1, which show that the contribution of age differences in person-environment interactions reflect events earlier as well as later in time. Both people and the environments in which they work and live change during the time when people are aging so personal aging and the time period during which a person ages are interdependent. Technology introduced at the present time may differentially affect how young and old persons adapt to it, and in turn, it may alter the course of aging over time. The analysis of person-environment interactions just presented is a specialized variation of many developed in gerontology, such as by Fozard and Popkin (1978), Lawton and Nahemow (1973), Riley (1986), Riegel (1976), and Schaie (1965).

The most interesting implication of the developmental version of the analysis of person-environment interactions is that adaptability as a design principle should be considered in planning products and environments. In housing for example, the interface between equipment and appliances and their users may change over time even though the function and utilization of the equipment does not. Over time, the requirements for space utilization may also change either because of age changes in the needs of the occupants or because of the desire to accommodate to newly introduced products. The adaptability principle would now be reflected in changes in form, such as movable interior walls. I anticipate that machines that learn will be a major future development in adaptable technology that will increase the potential for environmental accommodation to human capacities and needs that change with aging.

The developmental view of person-environment interactions adds options for interventions related to age differences in sensory, cognitive, and motor functioning. In particular, prevention of age-associated limitations in function may be addressed by monitoring of physiological variables related to strength and endurance, both of which may affect personal mobility and ability to use transportation systems. Information and a challenging and stimulating environment may do much to increase the person's ability to cope with task demands. The flexibility of the visual, acoustic, and thermal environment to adapt to individual differences in responsiveness to sights, sounds, and other sensations increases the range of possibilities for compensation for age-associated declines in sensory function and speed of behavior. The potential for enhancing the quality of life of older persons by technological innovation is a third option. Aging brings with it a variety of new opportunities for learning, work, social relations, and leisure. A dynamic approach to person-environment analysis can do much to increase the options for meaningful life for older persons (Fozard et al., 1996).

BEHAVIORAL SLOWING WITH AGE—HOW MUCH DEPENDS ON TASK REQUIREMENTS

While behavioral slowing with age is universal, it is not uniform; the degree to which it occurs and how much it affects performance is task specific. Behavioral slowing is evidenced by studies of age differences and changes in sensory processes, cognitive and memory processes, and motor skills including walking and driving. Literature in these areas will be selectively reviewed to identify basic findings in each area and secondarily to studies that deal with interventions related to personal mobility and driving. Because the literature in each area is substantial and goes beyond the scope of this review, one or more relevant reviews will be cited for persons wanting more information than can be provided in this chapter.

AGE-RELATED SLOWING OF SENSORY PROCESSES

Visual sensory memory refers to the storage and initial translation or encoding of environmental information into a form of which we are conscious. The capacity of sensory memory is estimated by the amount of time needed to name a briefly presented array of unrelated letters or numbers—usually six or seven. The time available to name the letters is determined by the time the letters are actually presented plus the time the information is available as a positive visual afterimage. To control the amount of time the information is actually available, a visual mask is presented that interrupts the afterimage.

Although it is uncertain if the capacity of sensory memory becomes smaller with age (Kausler, 1994), there is little question that the time required to retrieve information from it becomes slower with aging. Cerella, Poon, and Fozard (1982) used a 7-letter array and 11 presentation times ranging from 10 to 200 ms. The mean number of letters correctly identified and the number of errors made are shown in the upper panel of Figure 1.2 for a group of young adult men (mean age 21 years) and a group of older volunteers in the Department of Veterans Affairs Normative Aging Study (mean age 64 years). The data of both groups adjusted for guessing were well fit by two component linear functions as shown in the lower panel of Figure 1.2. The average time required per letter in the first component was 27 ms per letter for the younger and 35 ms per letter for the older men. The ratio of the difference is about 1.3. The corresponding times in the second component were 142 ms and 153 ms per letter, respectively, for the two groups. This two-phase relationship between letters identified and presentation time is typical and is believed to reflect two parallel processes in iconic memory, a fast process that acts on the first letters and a slower process that operates on the later ones at a rate that is approximately equal to the speed of subvocalization of the letters (See Walsh, 1976). The same age differences in sensory memory have been obtained using other procedures as summarized by Kline and Schieber (1985, pp. 319–321).

If sufficiently long presentation times were used, the number of letters identified by all subjects in the study of Cerella et al. (1982) would increase to seven, which is about the limit for primary or short-term memory. Performance in such a situation then reflects other cognitive processes (including rehearsal of the items to be named) in addition to sensory memory. With long presentation times, secondary attributes of the stimulus materials become more important, such as the meaningfulness of the letters or other patterning.

With longer presentation times, visual search tasks reveal age differences in the accuracy of target identification that increase with complexity and size of the field to be searched. In some situations, greater susceptibility to distractors in a noisy visual field (See Kline & Scialfa, 1996 for a recent review). In these kinds of tasks, age differences may be reduced by practice and task redesign but seldom eliminated. As discussed by Karlene Ball (this volume), the age differences in visual search are of critical importance in driving, and

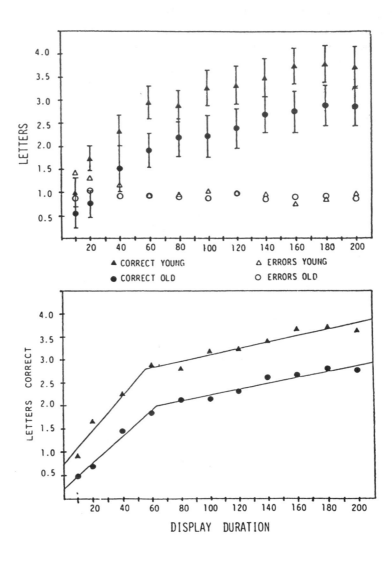

Figure 1.2   Upper panel: number of letters reported from displays of seven unrelated letters for stimulus durations ranging from 10 to 200 ms. Circles represent data from 16 men with average age of 64; triangles are data for 16 men with average age of 21 years. Lower panel: best fitting two segment linear functions fitted to data of upper panel after adjustment for errors. Reprinted with permission from Cerella, Poon, & Fozard (1982, Figure 1).

some of the age deficits in these complex processes are modifiable by training.

When target motion is included in the task requirements, the age differences in performance increase, such as dynamic visual acuity and contrast sensitivity differences are greater than static acuity or contrast sensitivity. Pursuit eye movements show declines in gain, presaccadic acceleration, and postsaccadic velocity (Morrow & Sharpe, 1993). The significance of these findings is that older persons require more catch-up saccadic movements while tracking a moving target than younger adults (Hutton, Nagel, & Loewenson, 1983). Scialfa, Thomas, and Joffe (1994) found that when a target search occurred in a noisy background, older adults were more likely than younger ones to make a saccade prior to centering on a target located away from the center of the field of view.

Similar results hold for audition. Temporal discrimination of sounds requires more separation between successive sounds for older individuals. Understanding speeded speech is poorer with increasing age. See Fozard (1990) or Kline and Scialfa (1996) for reviews.

MEMORY SPEED AND COGNITIVE PROCESSES— CONTEXT AND PRACTICE

The magnitude of age differences in the speed of retrieval of information from memory is governed by the requirements of the memory task. Imagine recalling names in a receiving line at a party. Age differences speed of retrieval are nonexistent or very small when recalling a familiar name of a good friend or family member. (Example: "Hi, Bill!"—retrieval from lexical or tertiary memory.) Age differences are larger when retrieving the name of someone just after having heard it. (Example: "Mother, this is Bill"—repeating his name just after hearing it—retrieval from primary memory.) Age differences in retrieval time are still larger when retrieving familiar names, such as, "Bill," from an arbitrary collection of names, the name of someone who had passed your place in the reception line eight persons previously. (Example: Tom, Mary, Jane, Harry, . . . Bill).

To estimate age differences in speed of retrieval from memory in the laboratory, it is important to use a task in which age differences in the quality of memory do not complicate the results. In the receiving line example above, for instance, it is likely that few people would be able to recall Bill's name at all if it were heard once in a sequence of names. One of the early studies that met that requirement was performed by Waugh, Thomas, and Fozard (1978) using male volunteers in the Normative Aging Study. The materials used in the study were 12-word pairs arranged in alphabetical order, ace–boy; cat–dog . . . yam–zoo. Speed of retrieval from *lexical memory* (LM) was measured as the time between presentation of a word pair and the initiation of the reading of the second word of a pair, dog when the pair cat–dog was presented. Speed of retrieval from *primary memory* (PM) was measured as the time to begin saying the second member of the word pair that was the last of a short sequence of pairs, yam–zoo; cat–dog; ace–boy; ace–? Speed of retrieval from *secondary memory* (SM) was measured as the time required to begin saying the second member of a word pair with the first member as a cue in an unpredictable string of word pairs, eel–fox; ink–jar; yam–zoo; ace–boy; eel–?; eel–fox; yam–zoo; ink–?; and so forth. The separation of the test pair from the first presentation of the word pair was large enough so that the retrieval was from SM, not PM. The response latencies were measured only after subjects had successfully memorized the 12 word pairs.

The results are summarized in Figure 1.3, which shows the cumulative frequency distributions of the logarithms of the latencies for the LM, PM, and SM tasks, respectively, for four age groups with the median ages shown. The age differences in the shapes of the distributions increased from LM, filled circles; to PM, filled triangles; to SM, open circles. The results were replicated in a second study in which the number of word pairs in the SM and PM tasks was held constant.

The results of the study just summarized make it easier to understand other studies of age differences in speed of memory. They are smaller when the clues or prompts provided related the item to be recalled are good (positive priming), thereby changing retrieval from secondary to primary memory, and longer when the clues are irrelevant or misleading (neutral or negative priming). In recalling unrelated items, older persons are more susceptible to proactive interference effects such that the probability of recalling an item decreases more rapidly as the number of intervening serially pre-

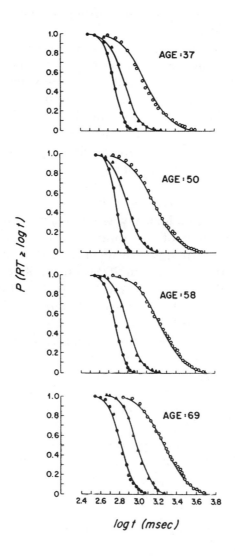

Figure 1.3 Cumulative frequencies of logarithms of response latencies for retrieval times from lexical memory (filled circles), primary memory (filled triangles), and secondary memory (open circles) for four groups of men with median ages shown. Reprinted with permission from Waugh, Thomas, & Fozard (1978, Figure 1).

sented items increases, thereby shifting retrieval from primary to secondary memory.

Age differences in speed of problem solving and learning activities vary according to the same kinds of variables. Learning a concept or rule is relatively harder for older persons when the materials are arbitrary or abstract than when they are familiar. The age differences are revealed by longer response times by elderly learners and by more repetitions of incorrect approaches to solving the problem. Memorizing the items on a shopping list takes more effort for older than for younger persons. Reviews of this research are provided by Reese and Rodeheaver (1985), Fozard, (1981), and Smith (1996).

What about age differences is the time required to retrieve the name of an object from lexical versus primary memory? When measurements were made of the time required to name pictures of familiar objects shown singly, it was found that the time increases systematically with age by about 200 ms from 30 to 70 years. Experimental analysis of the age difference shows that older adults require more time to carry out the mechanical, perceptual, and motor processes required to produce the name of the pictured object, such as car, rather than the time required to search for the name in long-term memory (Thomas, Fozard, & Waugh, 1977). In contrast, when retrieving the name of that object from memory when it is part of a collection of newly memorized unrelated words, the time required to retrieve that item is markedly longer for older adults, as described above.

The importance of context on speed of memory processes was vividly demonstrated in a study in which persons were required to say "yes" whenever a single letter presented was from a previously memorized list of six letters and "no" if it were not (Thomas, Waugh, & Fozard, 1978). In an unfamiliar condition requiring retrieval from secondary memory, an unalphabetized list of six letters—p,t,g,k,r,i—was memorized. In a familiar condition requiring retrieval from lexical memory, the memorized list consisted of the first six letters of the alphabet in their natural order—a,b,c,d,e,f. In control conditions the memorized list consisted of either one letter or none at all. The major results are summarized in Figure 1.4. Age differences in the time required to decide if a test letter was in the memorized set was minimal for the familiar set, but markedly longer for older participants as opposed to the younger in the unfamiliar list.

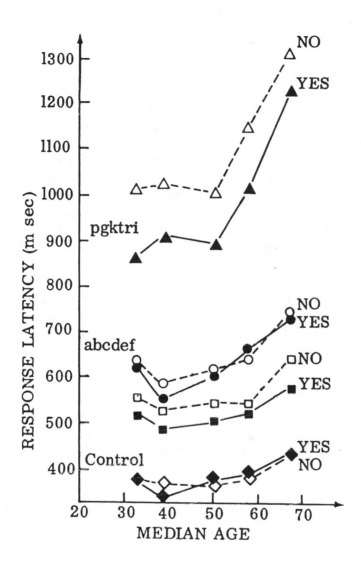

Figure 1.4 Mean times required to decide if a single letter from the memorized lists indicated was presented. Responses of no were to items from unmemorized lists of equal length. Reprinted with permission from Thomas, Waugh & Fozard (1978, Figure 1).

When the memorized list used in research such as that of Thomas et al. (1978) is the same from trial to trial, the task is referred to as consistent mapping. When the memorized list changes on every trial, the task is referred to as variable mapping. In both variable and consistent mapping tasks the age difference in decision time increases with the number of items in the list as first demonstrated by Anders, Fozard, and Lillyquist (1971) for variable mapping and by Anders and Fozard (1973) for variable and consistent mapping, results replicated and expanded on many times since. Madden and Nebes (1980) and later Fisk and colleagues (Fisk & Rogers, 1991; Fisk, Rogers, & Giambra, 1990) have shown that practice attenuates but does not eliminate age differences in speed of decision making in consistent mapping. On the basis of their literature review, Kline and Scialfa (1996) suggest that one reason age differences are not completely eliminated is that older persons are less able to inhibit processing of distractor items.

Practice does not eliminate age differences in speed of decision making in variable mapping tasks in which the list of items changes on every trial. Other research suggests that the ability to remember the items in the list may account in part for the observed age difference. Kliegl, Smith, and Baltes (1989), and Baltes and Kliegl (1992) used a mnemonic training procedure—the method of loci—to study the improvement possible by young and old adults to immediately recall lists of unrelated concrete nouns in the order they were presented. All the adults were able to learn to use the mnemonic strategy and significantly improved their ability to recite correctly lists of words after the training. However, even with very extensive practice, the age difference in the ability to recall the words was not eliminated.

Finally, when conventional signals for action are reversed, such as, push the brake when the light is green; push the accelerator when the signal light is red (e.g., Simon, 1967), reaction time increases for all persons, but relatively more for older people (see Vercruyssen, 1996 for a review).

Collectively, the examples given show that with increasing age the speed of responding is affected relatively more by the context of the task. The study by Simon shows that age-related slowing is relatively greater when the signal for action is contrary to expectation based on familiarity or experience. Behavioral slowing with age is relatively less when the context is most appropriate to the experience and expectation of a person. By inference, the speed and perhaps the ability to carry out even a familiar and over learned task by an older as compared to a younger person is compromised when the usual or expected context for carrying out the task is disrupted. In referring to this phenomenon, researchers often say that the older person has less reserve capacity than a younger one, meaning that the younger person can adapt more easily to the unusual context or can more easily ignore the unusual context while carrying out a task. (One approach to measuring reserve capacity was described in the review of Baltes and Kliegl (1992) given earlier; I will discuss other ways to measure reserve capacity later in this chapter.) The main implications of these findings is an emphasis on compensation for slower behavioral speed, usually through ergonomics. The goal should be to minimize unusual task requirements, particularly when they run counter to the experience or expectation of older persons. It should not be assumed that an older person will be able to quickly adapt to an unusual context for carrying out a familiar task (Fozard, 1981).

AGE DIFFERENCES IN MOTOR PERFORMANCE SPEED

Slowing of response times with age is evident in both continuous performance tasks, such as tracking, pursuit rotor, and tasks requiring discrete responses (Spirduso, 1995; Vercruyssen, 1996). In both, the magnitude of the age differences increase with task difficulty. Recent longitudinal data confirms the cross-sectional findings (Fozard, Vercruyssen, Reynolds, Hancock, & Quilter, 1994).

The interaction between age and task difficulty is illustrated in a reciprocal tapping task devised by Welford to evaluate Fitt's law (Brogmus, 1997; Welford, Norris, & Shock, 1969). Difficulty was varied along two dimensions—three separations between targets (travel distance) and three target widths (accuracy requirement)— making nine levels of difficulty ranging from the shortest separation combined with the widest target to the largest separation combined with the narrowest target. The function relating movement speed (based on the time required to make 50 pairs of alternating taps between the two targets) increased with age in both men and women (Brogmus, 1997). Analyses of longitudinal changes in men who were measured repeatedly over 16 years indicated that speed first increased, then decreased with age (Vercruyssen, Brogmus, Welford, & Fozard, in press). The variability of placement of responses within the target increased with repeated testing.

Age differences in skilled motor performance are most evident in tasks that require dividing attention among multiple inputs and in situations that require carrying out dual tasks. Studies with pilots and other skilled performers show that some of the challenges of these tasks that are most evident in laboratory studies are offset by long established skills of older persons. The literature in this complex area is large and in the present chapter will only address the concept of reserve capacity, which is widely used to explain the age differences in these complex tasks and give examples of the application of the idea to walking, postural sway, and driving.

RESERVE CAPACITY IN RELATION TO WALKING AND DRIVING

It is sometimes argued that an older person uses relatively more physiological or cognitive capacity to carry out a well-rehearsed and seemingly automatic activity such as walking. They may be at greater risk for accidents, falls, or stumbles while walking because they have less reserve to deal with unexpected circumstances that could arise. How is this idea evaluated and what are its practical implications?

One way to test for differences in reserve capacity is to give a person a secondary task to be carried out while engaged in the primary task, walking in the present case. If the primary task continues to be carried out but the time required to carry out the secondary task is longer or it is less well performed by older persons, then it is argued that the older person has less reserve capacity than the younger one. If the requirements of the secondary task are so demanding that performance on the primary task is compromised, then the limits of reserve capacity have supposedly been exceeded. The notion of age differences in reserve capacity were used as an agist joke against the former American president Gerald Ford in his election race with a younger challenger, Jimmy Carter. According to the joke, Mr. Ford was said to be unable to walk and chew gum at the same time. When, after his election, Mr. Carter collapsed during a long distance run, the joke was turned on him, saying that he couldn't run in footraces and be president at the same time.

There are conceptual problems in the assessment of reserve capacity, particularly in behavioral research. The basic approach is similar to that used in engineering tests of systems in which some safety factor is added in the hopes of providing additional assurance that the system being stressed will give reliable performance. If the supports for a bridge are twice as strong as that needed for its intended use, then the bridge is judged to be safer than if the strength of the supports were closer to the calculated load requirements. A significant practical problem in both the case of bridges and people is how to estimate reserve capacity without altering or destroying the system being tested.

Reserve Capacity and Walking

Lajoie, Teasdale, Bard, and Fleury (1996) investigated age differences in reserve capacity in a number of tasks related to posture and walking. Two groups of about 15 men and women in their twenties or their seventies performed a reaction time task (the secondary task) under several conditions of the primary task graded in difficulty: sitting, standing with legs at the person's preferred width, standing with feet together, and walking. During walking, the administration of the secondary task was timed to coincide with various phases of the stride cycle, such as when both feet were on the ground, when only one was in contact with the ground, and so forth. Since it is already known that older people have longer reaction times than younger ones, the evidence for diminished reserve capacity was the relative change in reaction times as the tasks became more difficult. Overall, the results were as expected. The age differences in reaction time were smallest when the participant was sitting, larger when the person was standing with feet together, then apart, and even larger when the person was walking. There were no age differences in the quality of the gait at various phases of the stride that could be associated with the requirement to perform the secondary task. Whether the person with relatively long reaction times on the secondary task would actually be at greater risk for accidents, falls, or stumbles is of course unknown in this study because no attempt was made to make the secondary task sufficiently demanding to cause disruptions in the components of the primary walking task that was measured.

Reserve Capacity and Postural Sway

The effect of carrying out a secondary cognitive task on maintaining postural balance while standing on firm or compliant (foam rubber) surfaces was investigated by Shumway-Cook, Woollacott, Kerns, and Baldwin (1997). They found that postural sway was greater in a group of elderly adults with a self-reported history of falls than in a group of age peers and a young control group without a history of falls. The requirement to perform either of two secondary cognitive tasks while standing increased the differences among the groups, particularly on the compliant surface. The anticipated difference in postural sway associated with the two tasks, a sentence completion task and a perceptual judgment task, was not found; the most important finding was that the requirement to carry out a secondary task was associated with greatest increase in postural sway in the older group with a self-reported history of falls. The time required to adaptation to the task demands was not studied in either the studies by LaJoie et al. (1996) or Shumway-Cook et al. (1997). The latter paper has an excellent list of references of research in this area.

Reserve Capacity and Driving

Another approach to investigating reserve capacity is to alter the conventional way that a man-machine system is controlled and study age differences in adaptation to the novel control system. Korteling (1994) took this approach in a study of age differences in controlling a car in a driving simulator task. The primary task in one study was keeping the simulated vehicle being controlled a constant distance behind another vehicle shown in the simulator; in the other it was steering the vehicle accurately. A foot-operated pedal controlled the speed of the vehicle operated. In the control condition, depressing the accelerator increased the speed of the vehicle; in the experimental condition, depressing the accelerator slowed the vehicle—just the reverse of the usual driving situation. The fundamental task difficulty of the driving task was adjusted for each driver, so that young and old drivers had basically the same level of performance at baseline.

The effects of reversing the outcome of depressing the accelerator pedal was dramatically different in the older and younger simulator drivers in both steering accuracy and maintaining the proper distance in the car following task. For example, the variability in following distance increased about 70% in the older group when the polarity of the accelerator pedal was reversed; the corresponding figure was about 10% in the young group (Korteling, 1994, pp. 151–153).

Korteling's research also showed that adaptation to the reversed polarity of the control system was quite rapid in the younger persons and slow or nonexistent in the older persons.

Baldwin and Schieber (1995) studied age differences in steering a vehicle in a driving simulator. Their secondary task was performing mental arithmetic. They found that under a difficult steering task, the speed of mental arithmetic was slower in the older, but not the younger adults. As in the study of Lajoie et al. (1996), they concluded that the steering task required relatively more capacity on the part of the older adults.

The importance of age differences in reserve capacity for design or engineering applications needs to be critically evaluated on a case-by-case basis, depending on how the age difference in reserve capacity is determined. A slower reaction time on a secondary task does not necessarily mean the same as a failure to control a mechanical system. The finding that stands out most clearly from all the studies is that older persons either take longer to adapt to novel task requirements or sometimes fail to adapt to them at all.

HIGH CORRELATIONS BETWEEN SENSORY AND COGNITIVE TASKS IN OLD AGE

Because of the pervasive nature of age-related slowing, researchers have sought out and found some evidence that speed-dependent tasks in apparently different domains of abilities are more highly correlated in old age than in younger age. The notion of reserve capacity sometimes has been invoked to understand these findings.

Schieber (1992) has shown a high degree of relationship between age differences in vision, audition, and smell. The high correlations are not restricted to sensory measures or to tasks that require speed. Lindenberger and Baltes (1994) have shown that in a group of men and women with an average age of 85 years, there is a high correlation between nonspeeded measures of pure tone thresholds and visual acuity and measures of cognitive performance. They found that the sensory measures accounted for about half the variance in the cognitive tasks used and 93% of the age-related variance in the cognitive tasks. They explain the high correlation on the basis of diminished physiological integrity of the brain, which adversely affects both the sensory and the cognitive tasks. An alternative but not mutually exclusive explanation is that the lowered sensory functioning results in under stimulation, which in turn adversely affects cognitive functioning. Their results are the most definitive to date in relating cognitive and sensory functioning in old age.

AGING AND PERSONAL MOBILITY AND DRIVING

Heikkinen, Jokela, and Jylha (1996) reported that in several study populations about 37 to 53% of women and 16 to 36% of men aged 80 to 84 years had difficulties or were not able to move outdoors. The increase of the difficulty with age in moving outdoors has been documented in longitudinal studies. In the Tampere Longitudinal Study on Aging (Jylha et al., 1992) it was found that among people aged 70 to 79 years and not reporting difficulties in moving outdoors at baseline, 29% of men and 46% of women had difficulties moving outdoors in the 10-year follow-up study. In another longitudinal study among people aged 80 years at baseline, the proportion of those who needed help in moving outdoors increased from 9 to 11% among men and from 11 to 34% among women during the 5-year follow-up among the survivors (Heikkinen, Heikkinen, & Ruoppila, 1997).

The ability to negotiate stairs also decreases with age. Women more often experience difficulty than men. In a survey among 65- to 84-year olds, 17.9% of women and 13.6% of men reported difficulties in climbing one flight of stairs at the age of 65 to 74 years. The corresponding figures among the 75- to 84-year olds were 33.8% for women and 23.3% for men (Rantanan, Era, & Heikkinen, 1996). When the ability of stair mounting of 75- and 80-year olds was measured in the laboratory, it was observed that about 22% of women and about 9% of men were not able to mount the step height of 20 cm (Sakari-Rantala, Heikkinen, & Ruoppila, 1995).

For the general adult population a good deal is known about the requirements for safe and easily used stairs (e.g., Templer, 1995); the degree to which these requirements should be further modified for old people is not known. In older buildings there are often major difficulties in creating the proper rise and step dimensions because the space available for retrofitting stairs necessitates more rapid ascent than is desirable.

Other abilities involved in carrying out basic (ADL) and instrumental (IADL) activities of daily living decrease with age. Chronic conditions, the process of aging, and unhealthy life styles (in particular, insufficient physical activity) are the most important underlying factors leading to disability (Heikkinen, 1995; Verbrugge & Jette, 1994). Some predictors of limitations in ADLs reflect chronic medical conditions that are probably secondary to aging. Others, such as strength and stiffness of joints may reflect intrinsic aging effects or they may be secondary to medical conditions that result in a diminished ability to exercise and use muscle groups important in mobility, thereby exacerbating the effects of normal age-related losses of strength and flexibility. There is substantial literature on the use of technologies to assist the carrying out of home tasks, including personal assistive devices (See Ferma, 1997 for a review) and adaptations of the home (See Czaja, 1997 for a review), so we will not include a discussion of this material in the present chapter.

MULTIPLE FACTORS CONTRIBUTE TO AGE DIFFERENCES IN GAIT AND WALKING SPEED

The list of predictors of limitations in ADLs and IADLs is long. Some factors reflect chronic medical problems secondary to aging while others, such as strength and stiffness of joints, may reflect intrinsic aging effects. Potentially modifiable determinants include gait and walking speed.

In healthy adults, walking speed decreases with age. In a summary of several studies, Vandervoort and Hill (1990) estimated about 1.42 ms for 20-year-old men and women and 1.21 and 1.16 ms, respectively, for men and women 60 to 79 years old, a decrease of about 15%. When in the adult lifespan slower speed of walking begins is unknown. Unpublished results of an ongoing study of age differences in walking speed in the Baltimore Longitudinal Study of Aging indicates that when men and women participants ranging in age from the twenties through the nineties are asked to walk a prescribed course rapidly, measurably slower speeds occur in participants who are in their fifties.

Spirduso (1995) cites Chao's (1986) analysis showing that in comparison to young adults in their twenties, healthy persons over 65 on average have shorter and wider strides and lower swing-to-stance ratios in the stride so that the relative time on double support in the stride cycle is greater. In short, " . . . Old adults take more steps to cover the same distance, and the time when both feet are on the ground is longer" (Spirduso, 1995, p. 170). In studies where stride length is equalized (e.g., Winter, Patia, Frank, & Walt, 1990) gait patterns are very similar across age. When older adults increase their speed, they typically increase the number of strides as opposed to young adults who typically increase stride length. A slower gait increases adaptability with respect to stride and support, postural control, and responsiveness to unexpected changes in the walking environment.

INTERVENTION STRATEGIES FOR PERSONAL MOBILITY

Many factors contribute to what Vandervoort and Hill (1990) call requirements for safe, normal confident mobility: neural, muscular, skeletal, and environmental. For the present discussion of interventions, muscular and neural factors may be considered together. Neuromuscular interventions are oriented more toward prevention of loss of strength; as we will see, many current interventions are based on the fact that leg and ankle strength can be increased by resistive strength training at any age. The major part of the following discussion concerns age differences in strength, issues involved in modifying strength by training, and the potential roles of technology in strength training.

There are important environmental interventions that are directed at compensating for age-associated difficulties in personal mobility. These include improved footwear or walking surfaces that decrease stress on the bones, increase the quality of base of support, and eliminate dangerous obstacles. Visibility of the environment used in walking or maintaining posture is especially important for older persons; this will be reviewed in the following discussion.

Strength Training and Mobility

Some of the material to be discussed is reviewed in detail by Evans (this volume). Recent reports have shown that high intensity strength training considerably increases muscle performance in older adults after a relatively short (2 to 3 months) period of training (Charette et al., 1991; Evans, 1995; Fiatarone, Marks, et al., 1990; Fiatarone, O'Neill, et al., 1990; Fielding, 1995; Frontera, Meredith, O'Reilly, Knutgen, & Evans, 1988). In particular, the dramatic strength training effects observed by Fiatarone et al. (1990) that increased mobility of very old residents of a nursing home have prompted interest in the use of strength training to improve mobility of older persons in a variety of situations. High intensity strength training has also appeared to be feasible and safe in selected patients with well-controlled rheumatoid arthritis, leading to significant improvements in strength and reductions in pain and fatigue without exacerbating disease activity (Rall, Meydani, Kehayias, Dawson-Hughes, & Roubenoff, 1996).

How much, how often, and which muscle groups to train require research to establish guidelines (Hakkinen, 1995). On the basis of their review of the available literature and experience, Pendergast, Fisher, and Calkins (1993) speculated that people need about 40% of their muscle strength—measured in various ways—that they had at age 20 to carry out activities of daily living at age 70. A recent effort at establishing training goals was reported by Schroll, Avlund, and Davidsen (1997). We can anticipate a substantial increase in research activity in this area.

In contrast to high intensity strength training, dynamic strength training programs and low-intensity resistive training produce significantly smaller changes in strength (Agre, Pierce, Raab, McAdams, & Smith, 1988; Aniansson & Gustafsson, 1981; Brown & Holloszy, 1991; Grimby et al., 1992). The study of Sipila, Multanen, Kallinen, Era, and Suominen (1996) indicated that in elderly women the effects of physical training on muscle strength and walking speed occur after endurance as well as strength training. (See also Larsson, Grimby, & Karlson, 1979; Sipila & Suominen, 1995.)

The lower muscle strength of the elderly population is purported to be related to a decrease in muscle mass (Vandervoort & McComas, 1986), but age-related changes in other modalities such as neural factors and muscle composition also affect strength (Brown, Strong, & Snow, 1988; Metter, Conwit, Tobin, & Fozard, 1997; Sipila & Suominen, 1994). Recent studies have shown that leg extension power is significantly correlated with maximal walking speed in healthy and frail elderly people (e.g., Bassey et al., 1992; Rantanen & Avela, 1997; Skelton, Grieg, Davies, & Young, 1995; Sipila & Suominen, 1994). Maximal knee extension strength is also associated with stair-mounting ability among 75- to 85-year-old men and women (Rantanen, Era, & Heikkinen, 1996).

Rantanen and Avela (1997) found that 80-year-old women exhibited 66% of the power of men the same age; in 85-year olds the ratio was 54%. Because elderly women have lower average leg extension power than men, they are more vulnerable than men to develop mobility difficulties. A slow customary walking speed has been shown to predict subsequent disability in mobility (Guralnik, Ferrucci, Simonsick, Salive, & Wallace, 1995).

Practical Issues in Implementing Strength Training Interventions

Population-based estimates of the age-specific prevalence of resistive strength training activities are not available, but there is a general consensus that involvement in such activities is low in older persons. There are several reasons. Resistive strength training is considered a body-building sport engaged in mostly by young men and usually not by women. The equipment used is complex and, to many, forbidding. The specificity of strength training effects in muscle groups makes it difficult to set goals for training. Unlike walking, running, cycling, or swimming, the beneficial effects of strength training of particular muscle groups are specific to those groups. There is a fear that resistive strength training may lead to injury in old people.

Most studies focusing on sports injuries in elderly people are related to elderly men still active in competitive sports (See Kallinen & Alen, 1995, for a review). Exertional injuries are common among them and are mostly connected with degenerative aging processes. A large proportion of injuries occur in the lower extremities. They are usually mild and cause only a brief cessation of training.

Contraindications for the assessment of physical functional capacity among elderly people are fewer for strength assessments compared to the assessment of aerobic capacity. In a population-based study 94% of men and 93% of women aged 75 years were regarded as being able to perform isometric strength tests of five major muscle groups. The corresponding figures for 80-year olds were 82 and 84%, respectively (Era, 1994). The bicycle ergometer test was interrupted before exhaustion in 57% of men and 41% of women among 75-year olds. In the 80-year olds, these figures were 69% for men and 40% for women.

Results of studies of the compliance with a prescribed regimen of strength training among volunteer adults also indicate that strength training is feasible and safe for older people. Among older adults, the percentage of persons completing strength training programs is equal to or higher than those completing programs of cardiovascular training. In such studies it is often observed that completion of aerobic training programs is halted frequently by injuries, a problem that is much less frequent in strength training (e.g., Pollack, et al., 1991). The information from these studies is of limited value for this discussion because they focus on persons who have responded to offers to participate in training programs. Studies in which persons from known populations at risk are randomly assigned to treatment conditions have yet to be conducted.

A study focussing on the determinants of isometric muscle strength in men of different ages (Era, Lyrra, Viitasalo, & Heikkinen, 1992) showed that in the youngest group, the manual workers tended to have higher strength in all muscle groups than the lower and higher status white collar workers, whereas among the middle-aged and oldest men, the manual workers tended to have the poorest performance. Ilmarinen, Louhevaara, Korhonen, Nygard, and Hakola (1992) have found that continuous performance of heavy physical labor into middle age does not protect the older worker from muscular and skeletal injuries. From studies of the age changes in the strength of middle-aged workers performing strength-demanding tasks as part of their work, that the daily performance of such activities on the job are not by themselves protective against injuries (Nygard, Luopajarvi, & Ilmarinen, 1991). One of their recommendations is that older workers engage in a regular program of strength training outside of their work or as part of a fitness program conducted at the workplace.

Another approach to increasing participation in strength training is public education and personal education and persuasion by health professionals, particularly the personal physician. Physicians are regarded as gatekeepers of health services (e.g., Heikkinen, 1989), but other health professionals also play an important role in this respect due to the commonness of chronic conditions among elderly people. Poor health is reported by elderly persons to be the main factor limiting physical exercise (Heikkinen & Kayhty, 1977; Ruuskanen & Heikkinen, 1995). The knowledge and skills of the health professionals necessary to counsel elderly people about physical exercise is lower in physicians and public health nurses—those most likely to be in contact with older persons—than in specialists in physical training.

It has also been argued that for a variety of reasons, health promotion efforts to increase physical activity levels in older populations need to move from the level of elderly individual to the level of public health policy (McKinley, 1995). The points of intervention range from patient education to training clinicians to do activity counseling and further to changing of the environment to facilitate activity and tax incentives for physically active people (Jette, in press).

Improving preparation of health professionals in physical exercise counseling is necessary to get them more involved in this service domain. For professional specialists in physical activity, a major curriculum development would be required for aging (Jones & Rikli, 1994); up to this time, training in physical activity for elderly persons has been minimal or nonexistent in most physical education departments in higher education.

Another approach to motivating people to engage in effortful resistive strength training is to use feedback from the equipment to encourage performance or increase safeness of use. This approach is widely used in equipment used for cardiovascular training. Stationary bicycles, stairclimbers, rowing machines, and treadmills have a variety of ways of presenting motivational information to the exerciser. Devices are available that manipulate task difficulty, keep track of time used, caloric expenditure, and on some bicycles, the effort required to maintain a given heart rate over a period of time. The information can be carried over from one type of machine to another. In some expensive pieces of equipment, visual and auditory displays are added to make the activity more realistic, such as, showing curving roads and hills on a display linked to a stationary bicycle. Because the activity is repetitive, a person can listen to music, stories, or watch television or movies while carrying out the exercise.

These approaches are not easily transferred to resistive strength training equipment. Strength training episodes are short, intense, and involve moving among many pieces of equipment. There is no simple and valid way to combine indices of accomplishment across muscle groups involving different pieces of equipment. At present, an exerciser is encouraged to keep a record that reflects increases in load and perhaps number of repetitions of the maneuvers accomplished with each piece of equipment. Training with a partner or using a coach is helpful in promoting and maintaining interest in the activity. Approaches to building motivational factors into strength training equipment include improving aesthetics of the apparatus used and in providing information that enhances safety are being considered; no such devices are commercially available at present.

The previous discussion has emphasized the importance of strenuous resistive strength training. However successful efforts may be to increase the use of resistive strength training, it is unlikely to become a widely accepted activity in older persons at least for several years. Accordingly, more emphasis should be given to the potential strength training benefits of everyday activities including walking, housework, and training with simple equipment.

IMPROVING VISUAL INFORMATION TO REDUCE AGE-RELATED DIFFICULTIES IN MOBILITY

Personal Mobility

Some age-associated behavioral slowing may result from relatively poor stimulus information available to older persons when carrying out even well-practiced tasks. For example, a variety of studies dating back to the 1950s have indicated the importance of higher illumination levels for older persons carrying out office type tasks (See Schieber, Fozard, Gordon-Salant, & Weiffenbach, 1991, for a review). The normal age-associated changes in visual functioning include poorer contrast sensitivity, particularly in the higher spatial frequencies; poorer dynamic acuity; slower adaptation to changes in illumination levels; and increased glare sensitivity. Most of these phenomenon occur because in older age there is less adaptability of pupil diameter to changes in light intensity. Often, these changes can be compensated for by environmental manipulations of illumination levels, contrast, design of visual images, control of glare sources, and so forth. For example, laboratory studies show that the illumination requirements for optimal acuity in older adults are higher by as much as log unit than that required for young adults. When planning improvements in the visual environment, it is important to consider the interactions among the various interventions, such as changes in one aspect (illumination level) should not create other unwanted problems (greater glare).

The importance of good lighting for everyday visual tasks is evident in many situations—finding the right button to press to activate or turn off a television set using a remote control, reading a cookbook while preparing a meal in the kitchen, driving, and so forth (Kline et al., 1992; Kosnick, Winslow, Kline, Rasinske, & Sekuler, 1988; Rubin, Roche, Prasada-Rao, & Fried, 1994). Charness and Bosman (1990) point out that most home environments do not meet the current recommendations for illumination recommended for young adults by the (USA) Society of Illuminating Engineers.

Falls and stumbles in older adults have received considerable research attention in the past 20 years. In their review of 52 studies that examine risk factors for falls, Myers, Young, and Langlois (1996) found that about a third of the studies included one or more measures of visual function—usually acuity or contrast sensitivity—as a potential risk factor. The causes of falls are multifactorial, and the relative contribution of visual problems to risk for falling varies substantially depending on the situation in which falls are measured and what other risks are assessed.

In their analysis of age differences in posture, gait, and falls, Simoneau and Leibowitz (1996) emphasize the need to consider the many sources of sensory information that contribute to age differences in these behaviors. When comparing younger and older adults, they conclude: first, the interdependence of vestibular, visual, and proprioceptive information is relatively greater in older persons; and second, the importance of visual information about the environment is relatively more important for older persons in avoiding falls and stumbles.

In the studies reviewed by Myers, Young, and Langlois (1996), visual function was measured mostly by acuity, contrast sensitivity, or differences in postural sway when eyes were closed or open. Post and Leibowitz (1986) distinguish between two types of visual information processing—focused attention on visual scenes versus information processing relative to one's location in space, particularly when moving. Common measures of visual function address the first type better than the second.

The sensory-motor correlates of postural balance were studied among representative samples of 75 year-old people living in three Nordic localities (Era et al., 1996). A good performance in balance tests was associated with good visual acuity, low vibrotactile threshold, high psychomotor speed, and good isometric muscle strength. The results of a multivariate analysis showed that among the men, the most important predictors of good performance in the balance tests were low vibrotactile threshold on the foot, high isometric hand grip strength, and low body stature. Among the women the most important predictors were low body stature, high body mass, high isometric body extension strength, and high psychomotor speed. Only a small percentage (11–13%) of the variance in the measures of balance could, however, be explained by these factors.

To assess the contribution of vision to postural stability, laboratory studies typically compare postural sway when eyes are closed and when they are open—sway is greater when eyes are closed, especially in older persons. The dependence on visual information for maintaining posture was dramatically illustrated in a study by Paulus, Straube, and Brandt (1987) who described a patient who had impaired proprioceptive information and vestibular information. In contrast to age-matched controls, the patient would begin to fall within 1 second after closing his eyes.

Turano, Rubin, Herdman, Chee, and Fried (1994) studied postural instability in older community-dwelling persons, some of whom were classified as fallers, nonfallers, or fearers of falling based on their responses to a questionnaire. In comparison to persons who reported no falls in the last year, fallers had measurably less stabilization of their postural sway with eyes open. The amount of stabilization of posture in the eyes open condition was the same for nonfallers and the fearers of falling. When the test platform on which the subject stood was stable, better contrast sensitivity was associated with smaller postural sway but not when the platform was unstable.

In his major studies of falls on stairs, Templer (1995) pointed out the importance of good visual information, particularly when negotiating the first step of a stair descent (Fozard, 1981). The importance of good illumination is evident. Local, automatically switched lighting of the stairs can increase the safety of stairs considerably, partly for those located in areas where the illumination levels for the staircase are different (usually lower) than in the surrounding areas. Local lighting of the floor area by the bed can contribute to greater safety of persons getting up in the night—the step to the floor from the bed is analogous to the first step on the descending staircase. Templer (1995) provides a wealth of examples of poor design of surfaces and lighting of staircases that provide insights on how to improve their safety.

Compensatory Changes in Vision for Driving

Kline et al. (1992) surveyed hundreds of participants in the Baltimore Longitudinal Study of Aging (BLSA) with respect to driving habits and visual problems associated with driving as well as in everyday static situations. In keeping with results of other studies, age of these drivers was negatively correlated with number of miles driven and driving at night and during rush hour. Responses to the questions relating visual problems to driving indicated that older age was associated with increased endorsements to statements in several areas: unexpected vehicles—merging traffic and cars entering field of view; vehicle speed—judging one's own speed and other vehicles moving rapidly; dim display—difficulty focusing on instrument panel; windshield problems—seeing in glare and seeing past haze on windshield; sign reading—reading street signs. There is a congruence between the age trends in these self-reports, previous research findings on visual aging, and the types of automobile accidents most likely to occur in older drivers. The data on merging and judging speed is consistent with findings of right of way and turning accidents that are more common in older drivers. The reduced field of view reflected in the questions about being surprised at the appearance of another vehicle is consonant with laboratory data on age-associated declines in the field of view described by Ball (this volume), who discusses the significance of the finding and interventions related to it. The problems of dim instrument panel and greater susceptibility to glare are consistent with laboratory findings. The difficulty in reading signs is consistent with data showing that older drivers on average need to be closer to a road sign in order to interpret or to read it. Figure 1.5 summarizes the average data to seven items for seven age groups of Baltimore Longitudinal Study of Aging men and women ranging in age from the twenties through the eighties. The ordinate represents the ratings from no difficulty (1) to difficulty (3) in the task.

Measures of contrast sensitivity were available on most of the research volunteers in Baltimore Longitudinal Study of Aging described above. Correlational analyses showed that peak spatial frequency, which decreased in old age groups, was significantly related to greater reported difficulty in eight of the questionnaire items; most importantly to instrument panel to dim, but also to others such as unexpected vehicles, speed of vehicles, and glare (Schieber, Kline, Kline, & Fozard, 1992).

The data in Figure 1.5 indicate that glare and reading road signs are rated the most difficult visual problems for drivers of all ages. The effect of glare on visual performance is strongly dependent on level of illumination and contrast. Schieber and Kline (1994) studied the relationship between two levels of illumination—daytime, 77 candelas/m2, and nighttime, 5 candelas/m2—and the legibility of 18 computer-simulated road signs, which were increased by 7% steps in angular size from a level to be illegible to a size that they could be correctly interpreted. A third condition was created by adding glare to the nighttime condition. The subjects were drivers in three age groups: 18 to 25; 40 to 55; and 65 to 79. The maximum simulated distance, that is, the smallest visual angle at which the signs could be read was greatest for the young adults under daytime illumination levels. Using that level as a standard, the ratio of performance under

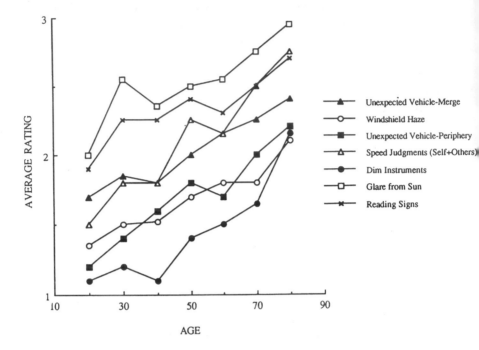

Figure 1.5 Self-reported visual difficulty in visual tasks related to driving in seven age groups of community-dwelling men and women volunteers in the Baltimore Longitudinal Study of Aging. One on the vertical axis indicates no difficulty; three indicates difficulty. Figure based on data from Kline, Kline, Fozard, Kosnick, Schieber, and Sekuler (1992).

the other conditions was determined for the three age groups under the other viewing conditions. Table 1.1 summarizes the results. The relative reduction in performance increased with age under all conditions. The addition of glare to the nighttime viewing condition reduced performance in the oldest group but not the other two.

Approaches to interventions have been thoroughly reviewed by Schieber (1994) and most of the following is taken from his evaluation. Appropriate environmental interventions include larger and simpler lettering on signs, improved headlight design, better contrast and size of road markings, and improved lighting of vehicle interiors and display panels. Many factors associated with daylight glare are

TABLE 1.1   Relative Reduction of Sign Legibility Distance in Three Viewing Conditions

| Lighting condition | Age group | | |
	18–25, $n = 12$	40–55, $n = 12$	65–79, $n = 18$
Daytime	1.00	0.88	0.80
Nighttime	0.70	0.60	0.46
Nighttime/glare	0.69	0.60	0.34

Source: Schieber and Kline (1994)

difficult to control because they change with the time of day and weather conditions. There have been some efforts made to control nighttime glare by reducing the amount of reflected headlight glare in rearview mirrors but it has proven difficult to reduce glare while maintaining visibility at the level needed by older drivers.

Interventions at a personal level include training on the useful field of view and safe-driving courses. Many states are experimenting with graded drivers licensing for older drivers, such as restricting driving to daylight hours, and so forth. The 20/40 visual acuity requirement used in 41 states for at least the first drivers's license is estimated to include about 97% of the driving population, so it is not a very effective screen for the visual problems of older adults. Other performance tests, including simulator-based assessments of driver performance, have not captured adequately the problems of older drivers. These difficulties are similar to findings regarding aging pilots. Older pilots appear to be able to use experience to overcome many of the perceptual-motor difficulties, which on the basis of laboratory tests or simulators, should negatively affect performance (Morrow & Leirer, 1997).

SUMMARY AND CONCLUSIONS

The goals of this chapter were to review selected research literature on sensory and cognitive changes with aging and discuss the implications of these findings for the ability of older adults to maintain personal mobility and to drive. Maintaining upright posture, walking, and driving include behaviors that involve utilizing and responding to complex sensory and cognitive information that changes rapidly over time. Because age-associated slowing is a common factor in sensory, cognitive, and motor behaviors, the review of the literature was organized around the implications of this general finding.

While universal, age-associated behavioral slowing is not uniform; the degree of behavioral slowing that occurs with aging is highly task specific. It was concluded that compensation for age-related slowing in sensory and cognitive processes, when necessary, usually requires task redesign and ergonomic interventions.

Since personal mobility and driving require processing of information from the environment and retrieval of information from memory, the discussion of sensory, cognitive, and motor performance was organized around speed of mental processes in these domains. Sensory or iconic memory represents the most primitive level of intake of visual and auditory information; the rate of extracting information from this very ephemeral store decreases with age, although the quality of the dual process that characterizes the activity does not. Age differences in speed of retrieval of verbal information from memory were described for three hypothetical memory stores—primary, secondary, or tertiary (or lexical) memory. The rate of retrieving information from each store decreases with age, the largest decrease being in secondary memory. There is no evidence for strategy differences in retrieval from these memory stores. Because the ability to memorize unfamiliar information decreases with age (storage into secondary memory), the discussion of age differences in speed of retrieval from memory was restricted to research in which the quality of memory was not a major determinant of performance. The analysis of research on speed of motor behavior focused on the consequences of disrupting familiar patterns of performance by changing stimulus response relationships or by adding secondary tasks to the primary one. The central concept used to explain age differences in adapting to such challenges is called reserve capacity.

Walking, performing various physical chores required in carrying out ADLs and IADLs, and avoiding falls are challenges for significant numbers of old people. Interventions based on prevention or compensation were presented. Approaches to the maintenance of strength required to carry out such activities emphasized resistive training programs, and these were discussed in considerable detail. Improvements in visibility of the physical environment were stressed as one means of reducing falls and accidents as well as in driving. Low levels of illumination and glare create the most severe visual problems for driving as well as walking and maintaining balance.

As is true in much research on age differences in abilities, the variability among sensory, cognitive, and motor skills involved in personal mobility and in driving are very substantial among elderly persons. It was concluded that task redesign and improved ergonomics can compensate for diminished sensory capacity and slower speed of mental and motor behavior, and that skill training and physical training, particularly resistive strength training, can significantly improve some skills involved in personal mobility and driving.

ACKNOWLEDGMENTS

Thanks are due to E. Jeffrey Metter and Ann Myers, Jan Graafmans, and Nicole Jones for their suggestions and critique of an earlier version of this chapter. Special thanks are due to the conference discussants of this chapter, D. Alfred Owens and Loren Staplin and to the book editor, K. W. Schaie, whose suggestions and comments resulted in significant improvements in the chapter. Some of the analysis on aging and personal mobility presented is an extension of a chapter by myself and Eino Heikkinen (in press). I learned much from Heikkinen during our collaboration, and I am pleased to share some of this with readers of this chapter. The opinions presented in this chapter do not reflect the official views of the National Institute on Aging.

REFERENCES

Agre, J., Pierce, L., Raab, D., McAdams, M., & Smith, E. (1988). Light resistance and stretching exercise in elderly women: Effect upon strength. *Archives of Physical Medicine and Rehabilitation, 69*, 273–276.

Anders, T. R., & Fozard, J. L. (1973). Effects of age upon retrieval from primary and secondary memory. *Developmental Psychology, 9*, 411–415.

Anders, T. R., Fozard, J. L., & Lillyquist, T. D. (1971). The effects of age upon retrieval from short-term memory. *Developmental Psychology, 6,* 214–217.

Aniansson, A., & Gustafsson, E. (1981). Physical training in elderly men with special reference to quadriceps muscle strength and morphology. *Clinical Physiology, 1,* 87–98.

Baldwin, C. L., & Schieber, F. (1995). Dual-task assessment of age differences in mental workload with implications for driving. *Proceedings of the Human Factors and Ergonomics Society 39th Annual Meeting* (pp. 167–171). Santa Monica, CA: Human Factors and Ergonomics Society.

Baltes, P. B., & Kliegl, R. (1992). Further testing of limits of cognitive plasticity: Negative age differences in a mnemonic skill are robust. *Developmental Psychology, 28,* 121–125.

Bassey, E. J., Fiatarone, M. A., O'Neill, E. F., Kelly, M., Evans, W. J., & Lipsitz, L. A. (1992). Leg extensor power and functional performance in very old men and women. *Clinical Science, 82,* 321–327.

Brogmus, G. E. (1997). Effects of age and sex on speed and accuracy of hand movements and the refinements they suggest for Fitt's Law. In W. A. Rogers (Ed.), *Designing for an aging population: Ten years of human factors-ergonomics research* (pp. 25–29). Santa Monica, CA: Human Factors and Ergonomics Society.

Brown, M., & Holloszy, J. (1991). Effects of low intensity exercise program on selected physical performance characteristics of 60–71-year-olds. *Aging, 3,* 129–139.

Brown, W. F., Strong, M. J., & Snow, R. (1988). Methods for estimating numbers of motor units in biceps-brachialis muscle and losses of motor units with aging. *Muscle and Nerve, 11,* 423–432.

Cerella, J., Poon, L. W., & Fozard, J. L. (1982). Age and iconic readout. *Journal of Gerontology, 37,* 197–202.

Chao, E. Y. S. (1986). Biomechanics of the human gait. In G. W. Schmid-Schonbein, S. L. Y. Woo, & B. W. Zweifach (Eds.), *Frontiers in biomechanics* (p. 226). New York: Springer-Verlag.

Charette, S., McEnvoy, L., Pyka, G., Snow-Harter, C., Guido, D., Wiswell, A., & Marcus, R. (1991). Muscle hypertrophy response to resistance training in older women. *Journal of Applied Physiology, 70,* 1912–1916.

Charness, N., & Bosman, E. A. (1990). Human factors engineering and aging. In K. W. Schaie & J. E. Birren (Eds.), *Handbook of the psychology of aging* (3rd ed., pp. 446–464). New York: Academic Press.

Czaja, S. J. (1997). Using technologies to aid the performance of home tasks. In A. D. Fisk & W. A. Rogers (Eds.), *Handbook of human factors and the older adult* (pp. 311–334). San Diego, CA: Academic Press.

Era, P. (1994). Feasibility of assessing physical functional capacity in elderly subjects. In S. Harris, H. Suominen, P. Era, & W. S. Haris (Eds.), *Toward healthy aging—International perspectives, Part 1. Physiological and biomedical aspects. Volume III: Physical activity, aging and sports* (pp. 161–168). Albany, NY: Center for the Study of Aging.

Era, P., Lyyra, A-L., Viitasalo, J. T., & Heikkinen, E. (1992). Determinants of isometric muscle strength in men of different ages. *European Journal of Applied Physiology, 64*, 84–91.

Era, P., Schroll, M., Ytting, H., Gause-Nilsson, I., Heikkinen, E., & Steen, B. (1996). Postural balance and its sensory-motor correlates in 75-year-old men and women: A cross-national comparative study. *Journal of Gerontology: Biological Sciences and Medical Sciences, 2*, M53–M63.

Evans, W. J. (1995). Effects of exercise on body composition and functional capacity of the elderly. *Journal of Gerontology: Biological Sciences and Medical Sciences, 50*, 147–150.

Ferma, G. (1997). Assistive devices. In A. D. Fisk & W. A. Rogers (Eds.), *Handbook of human factors and the older adult* (pp. 289–310). San Diego, CA: Academic Press.

Fiatarone, M., O'Neill, E., Ryan, N., Clements, K., Solares, G., Nelson, M., Roberts, S., Kehayias, J., Lipsitz, L., & Evans, W. (1990). Exercise training and nutritional supplementation for physical frailty in very elderly people. *New England Journal of Medicine, 330*, 1769–1775.

Fiatarone, M. A., Marks, E. C., Ryan, N. D., Meredith, C. N., Lipsitz, L. A., & Evans, W. J. (1990). High-intensity strength training in nonagenarians: Effects on skeletal muscle. *Journal of the American Medical Association, 263*, 3029–3034.

Fielding, R. A. (1995). The role of progressive resistance training and nutrition in the preservation of lean body mass in the elderly. *Journals of the American College of Nutrition, 14*, 587–594.

Fisk, A. D., & Rogers, W. A. (1991). Toward an understanding of age-related memory and visual search effects. *Journal of Experimental Psychology: General, 120*, 131–149.

Fisk, A. D., Rogers, W. A., & Giambra, L. M. (1990). Consistent and varied memory/visual search: Is there an interaction between age and response-set effects? *Journal of Gerontology: Psychological Sciences, 45*, P81–P87.

Fozard, J. L. (1981). Person-environment relations in adulthood: Implications for human factors engineering. *Human Factors, 23*, 3–27.

Fozard, J. L. (1990). Vision and hearing in aging. In J. E. Birren & K. W. Schaie (Eds.), *Handbook of the psychology of aging* (3rd ed., pp. 150–170). New York: Academic Press.

Fozard, J. L., & Heikkinen, E. (in press). Maintaining movement ability in old age. In J. A. M. Graafmans, V. Taipale, & N. E. Charness (Eds.), *Gerontechnology, a sustainable investment in the future.* Amsterdam, The Netherlands: IOS Press.

Fozard, J. L., & Popkin, S. L. (1978). Optimizing human development: Ends and means of an applied psychology of aging. *American Psychologist, 33,* 975–989.

Fozard, J. L., Graafmans, J. A. M., Rietsema, J., Bouma, H., & van Berlo, A. (1996). Aging and ergonomics: The challenges on individual differences and environmental change. In K. Brookhuis, D. Weikert, J. Moraal, & D. deWaard (Eds.), *Aging and human factors* (pp. 51–66). Groningen, The Netherlands: University of Groningen, Traffic Research Center.

Fozard, J. L., Vercruyssen, M., Reynolds, S. L., Hancock, P. A., & Quilter, R. E. (1994). Age differences and changes in reaction time: The Baltimore Longitudinal Study of Aging. *Journal of Gerontology: Psychological Sciences, 49,* 179–189.

Frontera, W., Meredith, C., O'Reilly, K., Knutgen, H., & Evans, W. (1988). Strength conditioning in older men: Skeletal muscle hypertrophy and improved function. *Journal of Applied Physiology, 64,* 1038–1044.

Graafmans, J. A. M., Fozard, J. L., Rietsema, J., van Berlo, A., & Bouma, H. (1996). Gerontechnology: Matching the technological environment to the needs and capacities of the elderly. In K. Brookhuis, C. Weikert, J. Moraal, & D. deWaard (Eds.), *Aging and human factors* (pp. 19–30). Groningen, The Netherlands: University of Groningen, Traffic Research Centre.

Grimby, G., Aniansson, A., Hedberg, M., Henning, G-B., Grangard, U., & Kvist, H. (1992). Training can improve muscle strength and endurance in 78- to 84-year old men. *Journal of Applied Physiology, 73,* 2517–2523.

Guralnik, J., Ferrucci, L., Simonsick, E., Salive, M. E., & Wallace, R. B. (1995). Lower extremity function in persons over 70-years as a predictor of subsequent disability. *New England Journal of Medicine, 332,* 556–561.

Hakkinen, E. (1995). Neuromuscular fatigue and recovery in women at different ages during heavy resistance loading. *Electromyography and Clinical Neurophysiology, 35,* 403–413.

Heikkinen, E. (1995). Epidemiologic-ecological models of aging. *Canadian Journal on Aging, 14,* 82–99.

Heikkinen, E., Jokela, J., & Jylha, M. (1996). Disability and functional status among elderly people: Cross-national comparisons. In G. Gaselli, & A. D. Lopez (Eds.), *Health and mortality among elderly populations* (pp. 202–220). Oxford: Clarendon Press.

Heikkinen, E., & Kayhty, B. (1977). Gerontological aspects of physical activity—Motivation of older people in physical training. In R. Harris & L. E. Frankel (Eds.), *Guide to fitness after fifty* (pp. 191–205). New York: Plenum Press.

Heikkinen, E., Heikkinen, R-L., & Ruoppila, I. (Eds.). (1997). Functional capacity and health of elderly people—The Evergreen Project. *Scandinavian Journal of Social Medicine, 53*(Suppl.), 1–106.

Heikkinen, R-L. (1989). Primary care services for the elderly in six European areas at the beginning of the 1980s. In E. Heikkinen & W. E. Waters (Eds.), *Health, life styles and services for the elderly. Continued data analysis within the Eleven Country Study* (pp. 75–98). Copenhagen, Denmark: World Health Organization, Public Health in Europe 29.

Hutton, J. T., Nagel, J. A., & Loewenson, R. B. (1983). Variables affecting eye tracking performance. *Electroencephalography, Clinical Neurophysiology, 56,* 414–419.

Ilmarinen, J., Louhevaara, V., Korhonen, O., Nygard, C. H., & Hakola, T. (1992). Aging and physical capacity to work: A four-year follow-up. In W. J. H. Goedhard (Ed.), *Aging and work* (pp. 78–98). The Hague, The Netherlands: CIP Gehevens Koninklijke Bibliotheek.

Jette, A. (in press). Designing and evaluating psychosocial interventions for promoting self-care behaviors among older adults. In M. Ory, G. DeFries, & A. Duele (Eds.), *Proceedings of the national invitation conference on research issues related to self-care and aging.*

Jones, C. J., & Rikli, R. E. (1994). The revolution in aging: Implications for curriculum development and professional preparation in physical education. *Journal of Aging and Physical Activity, 2,* 261–272.

Jylha, M., Jokela, J., Tolvanen, E., Heikkinen, E., Heikkinen, R.-L., Leskinen, E., Lyyra, A.-L., & Pohjolainen, P. (1992). The Tampere Longitudinal Study on Aging: Description of the study. Basic results on health and functional ability. *Scandinavian Journal of Social Medicine, 47*(Suppl.), 1–58.

Kallinen, M., & Alen, M. (1995). Aging, physical activity and sports injuries: An overview of common sports injuries in the elderly. *Sports Medicine, 20,* 41–52.

Kausler, D. H. (1994). *Learning and memory in normal aging.* San Diego, CA: Academic Press.

Kliegl, R., Smith, J., & Baltes, P. B. (1989). Testing-the-limits and the study of adult age differences in cognitive plasticity of a mnemonic skill. *Developmental Psychology, 25,* 247–256.

Kline, D. W., & Schieber, F. (1985). Vision and aging. In J. E. Birren & K. W. Schaie (Eds.), *Handbook of the psychology of aging,* 2nd ed., (pp. 296–331). New York: Van Nostrand Reinhold.

Kline, D. W., & Scialfa, C. T. (1996). Sensory and perceptual functioning: Basic research and human factors implications. In A. D. Fisk & W. A. Rogers (Eds.), *Handbook of human factors and the older adult* (pp. 27–54). San Diego, CA: Academic Press.

Kline, D. W., Kline, T. J. B., Fozard, J. L., Kosnick, W., Schieber, F., & Sekuler, R. (1992). Aging and driving: The problems of older drivers. *Journal of Gerontology, 47*, P27–34.

Korteling, J. E. (1994). Multiple-task performance and aging. Thesis Rijkuniversiteit Groningen. (pp. 150–156). The Hague, The Netherlands: CIP Data Koninklijk Bibliotheek.

Kosnick, W., Winslow, L., Kline, D., Rasinske, K., & Sekuler, R. (1988). Visual changes in daily life throughout adulthood. *Journal of Gerontology, 43*, P63–70.

Lajoie, Y., Teasdale, N., Bard, C., & Fleury, M. (1996). Upright standing and gait: Are there changes in attentional requirements related to normal aging? *Experimental Aging Research, 22*, 199–216.

Larsson, K., Grimby, G., & Karlson, J. (1979). Muscle strength and speed of movement in relation to age and muscle morphology. *Journal of Applied Physiology, 46*, 451–456.

Laukkanen, P., Heikkinen, E., & Kauppinen, M. (1995). Muscle strength and mobility as predictors of survival in 75–84-year-old people. *Age and Aging, 24*, 468–473.

Lawton, M. P., & Nahemow, L. (1973). Ecology and the aging process. In C. Eisdorfer & M. P. Lawton (Eds.), *Psychology of adult development and aging* (pp. 619–674). Washington, DC: American Psychological Association.

Lindenberger, U., & Baltes, P. B. (1994). Sensory functioning in old age: A strong connection. *Psychology and Aging, 9*, 339–335.

Madden, D. J., & Nebes, R. D. (1980). Aging and the development of automaticity in visual search. *Developmental Psychology, 16*, 377–384.

McKinley, J. B. (1995). The new public health approach to improving physical activity and autonomy in older populations. In E. Heikkinen, J. Kuusinen, & I. Ruoppila (Eds.), *Preparation for aging* (pp. 87–102). New York: Plenum Press.

Metter, E. J., Conwit, R., Tobin, J., & Fozard, J. L. (1997). Age-associated loss of power and strength in the upper extremities in women and men. *Journals of Gerontology: Biological Sciences, 52A*, B267–276.

Miller, E. (1977). A note on visual information processing in presenile dementia: A preliminary report. *British Journal of Social and Clinical Psychology, 16*, 99–100.

Morrow, D., & Leirer, V. (1997). Aging, pilot performance and expertise. In A. D. Fisk & W. A. Rogers (Eds.), *Handbook of human factors and the older adult* (pp. 199–230). San Diego, CA: Academic Press.

Morrow, M. J., & Sharpe, J. A. (1993). Smooth pursuit initiation in young and elderly observers. *Vision Research, 33,* 203–210.

Myers, A. H., Young, Y., & Langlois, J. A. (1996). Prevention of falls in the elderly. *Bone, 18*(Suppl.), 87S–101S.

Nygard, C. H., Luopajarvi, T., & Ilmarinen, J. (1991). Musculoskeletal capacity and its changes among aging municipal employees in different work categories. *Scandinavian Journal of Work and Environmental Health, 17*(Suppl. 1), 110–117.

Paulus, W., Straube, A., & Brandt, T. H. (1987). Visual postural performance after loss of somatosensory and vestibular function. *Journal of Neurology, Neurosurgery and Psychiatry, 50,* 1542–1545.

Pendergast, D. R., Fisher, N. M., & Calkins, E. (1993). Cardiovascular, neuromuscular and metabolic alterations with age leading to frailty. *Journal of Gerontology, 48*(Special issue), 61–67.

Pollock, M. L., Carroll, J. F., Graves, J. E., Leggett, S. H., Braith, R. W., Limacher, M., & Hagberg, J. M. (1991). Injuries and adherence to walk/jog and resistance training programs in the elderly. *Medicine and Science in Sports Exercise, 23,* 1194–1200.

Post, R. B., & Leibowitz, H. W. (1986). Two modes of processing visual information: Implications for assessing visual impairment. *American Journal of Optometry and Physiological Optics, 63,* 94– 96.

Rall, L. C., Meydani, S. N., Kehayias, J. J., Dawson-Hughes, B., & Roubenoff, R. (1966). The effect of progressive resistance training in rheumatoid arthritis: Increased strength without changes in energy balance or body composition. *Arthritis and Rheumatism, 39,* 415–426.

Rantanen, T., & Avela, J. (1997). Leg extension power and walking speed in very old people living independently. *Journal of Gerontology: Medical Sciences, 52A,* 225–231.

Rantanen, T., Era, P., & Heikkinen, E. (1996). Maximal isometric knee extension strength and stair mounting ability in 75- and 80-year-old men and women. *Scandinavian Journal of Rehabilitation Medicine, 28,* 89–93.

Reese, H. W., & Rodeheaver, D. (1985). Problem solving and complex decision making. In J. E. Birren & K. W. Schaie (Eds.), *Handbook of the psychology of aging* (2nd ed., pp. 474–499). New York: Van Nostrand Reinhold.

Riegel, K. F. (1976). The dialectics of human development. *American Psychologist, 31,* 689–700.

Riley, M. W. (1986). The dynamics of life stages: Roles, people and age. *Human Development, 29,* 150–156.

Rubin, G. S., Roche, K. B., Prasada-Rao, P., & Fried, L. P. (1994). Visual impairment and disability in older adults. *Optometry and Vision Science, 71,* 750–760.

Ruuskanen, J., & Heikkinen, E. (1995). A community-based intervention program of physical exercise promotion and counseling for the elderly. In S. Harris, E. Heikkinen, & W. S. Harris (Eds.), *Physical activity, aging and sports* (Vol. IV, pp. 125–138). Albany, NY: Center for the Study of Aging.

Sakari-Rantala, R., Heikkinen, E., & Ruoppila, I. (1995). Difficulties in mobility among elderly people and their association with socioeconomic factors, dwelling environment and use of services. *Aging Clinical and Experimental Research, 7,* 433–440.

Schaie, K. W. (1965). A general model of the study of developmental problems. *Psychological Bulletin, 64,* 92–107.

Schieber, F. (1992). Aging and the senses. In J. E. Birren, R. B. Sloane, & G. Cohen (Eds.), *Handbook of mental health and aging* (2nd ed., pp. 251–306). San Diego: Academic Press.

Schieber, F. (1994). *Recent developments in vision, aging, and driving: 1988–1994.* Report 94-26. Ann Arbor , MI: University of Michigan Transportation Research Institute.

Schieber, F., & Kline, D. W. (1994). Age differences in the legibility of symbol highway signs as a function of luminance and glare level: A preliminary report. In *Proceedings of the Human Factors and Ergonomics Society, 38th Annual Meeting* (pp. 133–135). Santa Monica, CA: Human Factors and Ergonomics Society.

Schieber, F., Fozard, J. L., Gordon-Salant, S., & Weiffenbach, J. (1991). Optimizing the sensory-perceptual environment of older adults. *International Journal of Industrial Ergonomics, 7,* 133–162.

Schieber, F., Kline, D. W., Kline, T. J. B., & Fozard, J. L. (1992). *The relationship between contrast sensitivity and the visual problems of older drivers.* Tech. Paper 920613, pp. 1–7. Warrendale, PA: Society of Automotive Engineers.

Schroll, M., Avlund, K., & Davidsen, M. (1997). Predictors of five-year functional ability in a longitudinal survey of men and women aged 75 to 80: The 1914-population in Glostrup, Denmark. *Aging, Clinical and Experimental Research, 9,* 143–152.

Scialfa, C. T., Thomas, D. M., & Joffe, K. M. (1994). Age-related changes in the eye movements subserving visual search. *Optometry and Visual Science, 71,* 1–7.

Shumway-Cook, A., Woollacott, M., Kerns, K. A., & Baldwin, M. (1997). The effects of two types of cognitive tasks on postural stability in older adults with and without a history of falls. *Journal of Gerontology: Medical Sciences, 52A,* M232–M240.

Simon, J. R. (1967). Choice reaction time as a function of auditory S-R correspondence, age and sex. *Ergonomics, 10,* 659–664.

Simoneau, G. G., & Leibowitz , H. W. (1996). Posture, gait and falls. In J. E. Birren & K. W. Schaie (Eds.), *Handbook of the psychology of aging* (4th ed., pp. 204–217). San Diego, CA: Academic Press.

Sipila, S., & Suominen, H. (1994). Knee extension strength and walking speed in relation to quadriceps muscle composition and training in elderly women. *Clinical Physiology, 14,* 433–442.

Sipila, S., & Suominen, H. (1995). Effects of strength and endurance training on thigh and leg muscle mass and composition in elderly women. *Journal of Applied Physiology, 78,* 334–340.

Sipila, S., Multanen, J., Kallinen, M., Era, P., & Suominen, H. (1996). Effects of strength and endurance training on isometric muscle strength and walking speed in elderly women. *Acta Physiologica Scandinavia, 156,* 457–464.

Skelton, D. A., Grieg, C. A., Davies, J. M., & Young, A. (1995). Strength, power and related functional ability of healthy people aged 65–89 years. *Age and Ageing, 23,* 371–377.

Smith, A. D. (1996). Memory. In J. E. Birren & K. W. Schaie (Eds.), *Handbook of the psychology of aging* (4th ed., pp. 236–250). San Diego, CA: Academic Press.

Spirduso, W. W. (1995). *Physical dimensions of aging.* Champaign, IL: Human Kinetics.

Templer, J. (1995). *The staircase: Studies of hazards, falls and safer design.* Cambridge, MA: MIT Press.

Thomas, J. C., Fozard, J. L., & Waugh, N. C. (1977). Age differences in naming latencies. *American Journal of Psychology, 90,* 499–509.

Thomas, J. C., Waugh, N. C., & Fozard, J. L. (1978). Age and familiarity in memory scanning. *Journal of Gerontology, 33,* 528–533.

Turano, K., Rubin, G. S., Herdman, S. J., Chee, E., & Fried, L. P. (1994). Visual stabilization of posture in the elderly: Fallers vs nonfallers. *Optometry and Vision Science, 71,* 761–769.

Vandervoort, A., & Hill, K. (1990). Neuromuscular performance of the aged. In M. L. Howe, M. J. Stones, & C. J. Brainerd (Eds.), *Cognitive and behavioral factors in atypical aging* (pp. 69–101). New York: Springer-Verlag.

Vandervoort, A. A., & McComas, A. J. (1986). Contractile changes in opposing muscles of the human ankle joint with aging. *Journal of Applied Physiology, 61,* 361–367.

Verbrugge, L. M., & Jette, A. (1994). The disablement process. *Social Science and Medicine, 38,* 1–14.

Vercruyssen, M. (1996). Movement control and speed of behavior. In A. D. Fisk & W. A. Rogers (Eds.), *Handbook of human factors and the older adult* (pp. 55–86). San Diego, CA: Academic Press.

Vercruyssen, M., Brogmus, G. E., Welford, A. T., & Fozard, J. L. (in press). Longitudinal changes in speed and accuracy of hand movements. Submitted to Journal of Gerontology: Psychological Sciences.

Walsh, D. A. (1976). Age differences in central perceptual processing: A dichoptic backward masking investigation. *Journal of Gerontology, 31,* 178–185.

Waugh, N. C., Thomas, J. C., & Fozard, J. L. (1978). Retrieval times from different memory stores. *Journal of Gerontology, 33,* 352–357.

Welford, A. T., Norris, A. H., & Shock, N. W. (1969). Speed and accuracy of movement and their changes with age. *Acta Psychologica, 30,* 3–15.

Winter, D. A., Patia, A. E., Frank, J. S., & Walt, S. E. (1990). Biomechanical walking pattern changes in the fit and healthy elderly. *Physical Therapy, 70,* 340–347.

The Place of Ambient Vision in Understanding Problems of Mobility and Aging

D. Alfred Owens

S enior citizens comprise the fastest growing segment of our population. Compared to previous generations, current senior citizens are healthier, more active, and more likely to hold a motor vehicle operator's license (Department of Transportation, 1994). Of course, the process of aging takes a toll, and for many individuals effects of aging eventually interfere with normal daily activities, especially driving. A key challenge to behavioral science, as well as gerontology, is to develop conditions favorable to both the continuation of independent mobility and the optimization of public safety.

As pointed out by Dr. Fozard (this volume), efforts to compensate for the deleterious effects of age often take the form of environmental interventions, which in the context of driving could include improved visibility of signs and road delineation at night. Recent efforts also focus on methods to avoid, minimize, or reverse age-related losses of an individual's capacities. An important part of the second strategy is to advise individuals about appropriate precautions or restriction of activities in view of their changing sensory and cognitive capabilities. This sort of counseling seems especially useful for aging motorists who still desire the independent mobility afforded by a personal automobile, yet face increasing difficulty in coping with complex, dynamic situations of a busy traffic environment.

DRIVERS' RESTRICTIONS? A SEARCH FOR APPROPRIATE CRITERIA

Annually, more and more families are facing difficult questions of aging drivers. When is it no longer safe for an elder to drive alone? or to drive at all? What sorts of traffic situations are acceptable? Which should be avoided? Such questions require an answer, but the best answers are not yet clear. Some organizations currently offer helpful advice based, in the tradition of drivers' education, on common sense and experience. In an effort to address more specific personal needs, a few innovators have developed individualized advisory programs that utilize on-road driving evaluations (Platt, 1996). But such techniques are not yet standardized nor widely available.

Meanwhile, regulatory agencies seek appropriate means to evaluate the changing capabilities of aging motorists with an eye toward restricting or terminating their driving privileges. It is important to recognize the uncertain validity of such age-based license restrictions. For many years, licensing criteria have relied on qualitative assessment of vehicle control, supplemented by evaluation of the candidate's knowledge of rules of the road and a limited set of vision tests, such as resolution acuity and visual fields. While these measures seem necessary, they have not proven sufficient to predict which individuals are at risk of a mishap, nor do they provide a useful basis for individualized counseling or restriction of driving activities (Higgins, 1996; Leibowitz, Owens, & Helmreich, 1995; Waller, 1991; Wood, 1998). Indeed, recent evidence indicates that strict screening of older drivers can be counterproductive.

A Scandinavian study, which assessed the outcomes of rigorous medical screening and restriction of elder drivers in Finland in comparison with the laissez-faire system in Sweden, found no evidence for increased safety with age-related screening of driving privileges. On the contrary, the results revealed a higher incidence of fatal pedestrian accidents among the elder population in Finland that was largely prohibited from driving (Hakamies-Blomqvist, Johansson, & Lundberg, 1996). Although interpretations of such results must be tentative, there is no clear evidence of actual safety benefits from age-related restrictions of driving licenses. In my view, this reflects our limited understanding of how best to evaluate and advise (or restrict) individual motorists.

Well-grounded solutions to the problems of aging motorists, including the development of valid licensing criteria, await a fuller understanding of the basic processes required to drive a motor vehicle. This stands as a difficult and interesting challenge to psychological science. An adequate theoretic account will have to be broader than most current formulations, for it will need to incorporate multiple levels of sensory, behavioral, and cognitive processes. Then it must explain the interactive functions of these processes in the task of driving through a complex and unpredictable road environment (Leibowitz, Owens, & Helmreich, 1995).

Recent research is beginning to fill the gap. One of the more promising developments is the Useful Field Of View test (UFOV; Ball, Owsley, Sloane, Roenker, & Bruni, 1993; Owsley, et al., 1998), which measures perception of events that occur rapidly over an extended portion of the visual field (the central 30°). The UFOV has exceeded the capability of previous tests to predict increased crash involvement, and current findings suggest it may also provide a beneficial training device to ameliorate age-related losses of attention and perception (Ball, this volume). An explanation of how the UFOV fits into a broader theory of driving remains to be worked out. It seems plausible that the UFOV assesses attentional processes normally engaged in monitoring changes in the road environment. These processes may be critical for such routine maneuvers as lane changes and turns across oncoming traffic. Further research on visual attention and, more generally, age-related variations in the speed of perceptual and cognitive processing, offer promising avenues to explain the success of the UFOV test and to expand our basic understanding of cognitive and perceptual processes (Schieber, this volume).

BEYOND COGNITION: THE ROLE OF AMBIENT VISION

The importance of clear vision and alert mental faculties for complex tasks like driving is obvious. So obvious that we may tend to overlook the fact that the performance of skilled tasks also requires finely tuned coordination of sensory-motor processes that occur outside of conscious awareness. It may be useful to reconceptualize driving behavior in terms of multiple levels of control as proposed by Rasmussen (1983).

From this perspective, performance of complex tasks is characterized as involving three qualitatively distinct levels of control: knowledge-based, rule-based, and skill-based control. *Knowledge-based control* is thoroughly cognitive; it includes such functions as acquiring information, comparing options, and selecting a future path of action. In the context of driving, this level of control is exemplified by the process of planning a trip. *Rule-based control* is somewhat less abstract in nature. It depends on learned routines, acts, or conventions that can be implemented automatically after extensive practice, but although automatic, these acts can still be reported and explained by the actor. In driving, such acts might include responses to traffic signs, signals, and other vehicles; their execution may involve attentional processes of the sort tested by the UFOV. *Skill-based control* occurs outside of conscious awareness. According to Rasmussen (1983), it "rolls along without conscious attention or control. . . . sense input is not selected or observed: the senses are only directed toward the aspects of the environment needed subconsciously. . . . " This level of control sounds very much like the guidance function of ambient vision, which we believe is fundamental to the driving task (Leibowitz & Owens, 1977, 1986; Leibowitz, Owens, & Post, 1982). Before considering ambient vision, a few comments about theories of perception in general may be in order.

Historically, theories of perception and action have focused on the nature of personal experience and intentional control of behavior. From the pioneering work of philosophy (e.g., Descartes, 1637/1965) and physiology (Helmholtz, 1866/1962) through current psychological theories (Bruce, Green, & Georgeson, 1996; Gregory, 1990; Marr, 1982; Rock, 1995), perception has been treated as a process of symbolic representation, built through cognitive or computational inference. This approach rests on the presumption that sensory inputs are ambiguous and distorted—the classic example being the flatness of the retinal image. Thus, perception is deemed essentially to be one's experience of the internal representation, which is constructed on the basis of various cues (or computations), combined with knowledge of the world, its objects, and their properties. This internal representation serves as the mental stage for selecting, executing, and monitoring one's actions. From this perspective, cognitive processes like attention and decision are pivotal for complex behaviors like driving (e.g., Shinar, 1978).

In the past 30 years, research in animal behavior and neuroscience has called attention to parallel visual processes that serve to maintain spatial orientation and guide behavior. Contrary to the traditional assumption of a single internal representation, this evidence indicates that visual awareness and visuomotor coordination are served by two subsystems, referred to as focal and ambient, respectively, which are functionally and, to some degree, anatomically distinct. *Focal vision* focuses on the center of the visual field, where it serves to recognize objects and events; it fills subjective experience. *Ambient vision* utilizes information from the entire visual field to maintain postural orientation, guide locomotion, and other visuomotor acts like reaching and grasping; it is barely accessible to awareness (Goodale & Humphrey, 1998; Held, 1968, 1970; Trevarthen, 1968). Early research on animal behavior demonstrated that visual recognition and guidance processes can be selectively disrupted by lesions of visual pathways that project to different parts of the brain (Humphrey, 1974; Ingle, 1967; Schneider, 1967, 1969). Later work with primates showed that visual awareness and object recognition depend on neural pathways from the occipital to the inferotemporal cortex, referred to as the ventral stream. In contrast, visual control of posture and action depends on processing in pathways from the midbrain (especially the superior colliculus) and occipital cortex through the posterior parietal cortex, referred to as the dorsal stream (Goodale & Milner, 1992; Mishkin, Ungerleider, & Macko, 1983).

Perhaps the most renowned example of the neurologic dissociation between visual experience and visual control of action is the clinical phenomenon known as blindsight. Weiskrantz (1986) and others (e.g., Pöppel, Held, & Frost, 1973) have reported multiple cases of patients who are subjectively blind following damage to their visual cortex, yet they retain remarkable abilities to localize unseen events in the blind portions of their visual field. Interpretations of blindsight remain under dispute (Gazzaniga, Fendrich, & Wessinger, 1994) as, indeed, much remains to be learned about the organization and interactions of visual subsystems that serve perception and action (Goodale & Humphrey, 1998).

The discovery of two modes of visual processing has fundamental implications for understanding driving and the problems of aging drivers. Contrary to the traditional view, realization of multiple modes of vision means that we cannot assume that visual control of complex tasks like driving involves a single internal representation, nor can we assume that individuals have conscious access to all the visual processes involved in guidance of their behaviors (Owens & Andre, 1996). If this is true, then assessment and prediction of driving performance will have to be extended beyond current efforts, which have retained the traditional focus on focal abilities like acuity and attention.

TWO MODES OF VISION & DIFFICULTIES WITH NIGHT DRIVING

Returning to the practical difficulties of mobility and aging, we should consider a situation that is especially troublesome for older motorists, but also represents an area of great risk to the entire motoring population. This situation, night driving, is of special interest here because the study of age-related difficulties can increase our understanding of a problem faced by young drivers. As illustrated in Figure 1.6, crash data indicate that the nighttime road fatality rate, adjusted for mileage, is three to four times higher than the daytime rate (National Safety Council, 1982–1997). Although crashes occur for many reasons, most analysts agree that alcohol intoxication and degraded visibility are prominent contributing factors (Evans, 1991; Owens & Sivak, 1996). For the present purposes, I will concentrate on the latter problem, the effect of degraded visibility on road safety at night.

It is widely agreed that driving is "a visual task" (Sivak, 1996). All known jurisdictions require a vision test to obtain a motor vehicle operator's license. Yet surprisingly few, if any, require a test of night vision to obtain a driver's license. Every driver's vision, regardless

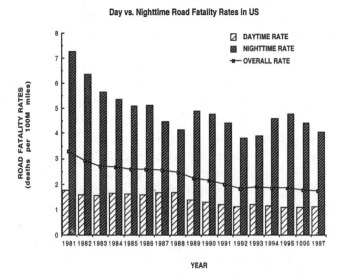

Figure 1.6 Comparison of road fatality rates in the United States under day and night conditions; overall annual fatality rates are given by the continuous line. Nighttime fatality rates are consistently 3 to 4 times higher than daytime rates. (Data from NRC, 1982–1997).

of age, is impaired in low illumination (Higgins, 1996; Leibowitz & Owens, 1991). Moreover, analyses of crash data have shown that certain classes of collisions—especially those with low-contrast obstacles like pedestrians—are more prevalent at night and are strongly associated with poor visibility (Owens & Sivak, 1996). Studies of traffic flow, however, indicate that traffic travels at the same speed at night as in daytime (Herd, Agent, & Reizenbergs, 1980). This seems irrational in view of the unavoidable limitations of vision. Why don't drivers exhibit greater caution at night by decreasing their speed? Examined closely, it seems this is not simply a matter of deliberate recklessness, for such behavior is widespread among night motorists, including prudent individuals, and it seems to be sanctioned by official designation of uniform speed limits for day and night traffic (Leibowitz, Owens, & Tyrrell, 1998). In short, there appears to be a discrepancy in our commonly held beliefs about vision and driving. While good vision is widely accepted as critical for safe driving, the actual limitations of night vision are generally overlooked or taken rather casually by individual drivers and regulatory agencies alike.

In this context, the behavior of older drivers stands out as an example of greater caution and safety than that of their younger counterparts. Anecdotal reports and survey results show that many healthy senior citizens, who are still active motorists, are reluctant or unwilling to drive at night (Kosnik, Sekuler, & Kline, 1990). The greater caution of seniors regarding night driving is borne out by crash data. Figure 1.7 summarizes the data from the US National Highway Traffic Safety Administration's records of all fatal crashes from 1980 through 1993 (Owens & Brooks, 1995). Fatal crash involvement of female and male drivers is presented as a function of age for three light conditions: Daylight (bright); Twilight (variable illumination); and Nighttime (dark).[1]

It is evident in Figure 1.7 that involvement in fatal crashes at night decreases as a function of age group for both genders. So the nighttime toll, arguably the greatest problem of traffic safety (recall: night fatality rates are three to four times higher than daytime rates), is largely a problem of younger not older motorists. While various factors may contribute to this age-related decline in nighttime crashes, it is likely that voluntary restriction of driving at night is a key factor. A recent survey of elder drivers found that, while 83% of those with good vision continued to drive, they limited night driving to less than 10% of their total mileage (Chaparro, McGregor, & Stumpfhauser, 1998).

Why are older drivers more cautious and less willing to drive at night than their younger counterparts? A good answer to this question could be beneficial in at least two respects: (a) It could strengthen the basis for individualized evaluation and advice regarding appropriate limitations of senior citizens who wish to continue driving; and (b) it might provide new insight into the reason that

---

[1]To control for differences in the number of drivers across age groupings, data are presented as the percentage of drivers within each age category who are involved in fatal crashes under each of the three lighting conditions. Because the three light conditions include 18 hours per day (75% of 24 hours), the percentages for each age category would sum to 75% if crashes were distributed uniformly over the 24 hours.

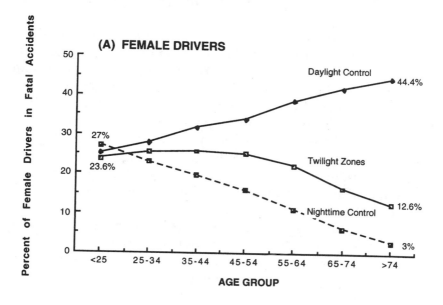

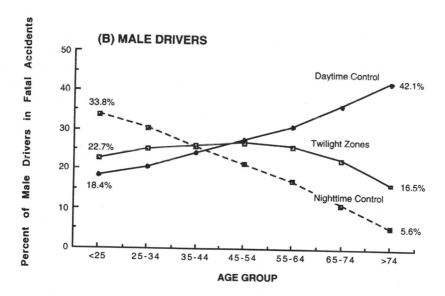

Figure 1.7 Proportions of fatal crashes in the United States under daytime (bright), nighttime (dark), and twilight (variable light) conditions for female and male drivers in seven different age groups. Involvement in fatal crashes at night declines with advancing age. (From Owens & Brooks, 1995)

younger drivers are not appropriately disturbed by their actual visual limitations at night.

One possible answer is suggested by abundant psychophysical evidence that the focal visual abilities of senior citizens (e.g., acuity and contrast sensitivity) decline more rapidly with reduced luminance (Kline & Schieber, 1985; Sloane, Owsley, & Alvarez, 1988). Therefore, older drivers are likely to experience greater difficulty than younger drivers in reading signs and in recognizing all types of objects, landmarks, and other roadway features at night. Such losses of focal vision can create difficulties in navigation in unfamiliar environments, and it could give rise to a general sense of greater risk when driving in familiar areas. But the answer appears to be more complicated.

Other evidence suggests that diminished visual acuity and contrast sensitivity are not strongly associated with increased accident involvement, nor with reduced confidence in driving. It is interesting to note that state transportation departments are currently experiencing increasing pressure from individuals with low-vision petitioning for driving privileges, and some states already offer restricted licenses for low-vision drivers. In a recent review of this issue, Higgins (1996) points out that all night drivers, including young adults with excellent vision, routinely experience reductions of acuity and peripheral vision to levels that would be classified clinically as low vision if they occurred in daylight. Moreover, the recent survey of elder drivers by Chaparro et al. (1998) found that 50% of those who suffered visual impairments in daylight (acuity worse than 20/40) that would disqualify them from driving in most states still continued to drive.

These findings suggest that driving performance and confidence depend on more than focal vision. In light of the evidence for two modes of vision, it seems plausible that ambient visual guidance functions also play an important role in driving. This hypothesis is particularly appealing in the context of night driving because the evidence shows that the ambient functions, which may be important for vehicle guidance, remain highly efficient under nocturnal conditions, at least for young adults. (As we will see, ambient vision of elders has not been tested until recently.) Figure 1.8 summarizes data showing that focal vision (i.e., acuity and contrast sensitivity) is selectively degraded over the luminance range found in twilight and darkness, whereas ambient vision (i.e., *vection*, or feelings of self

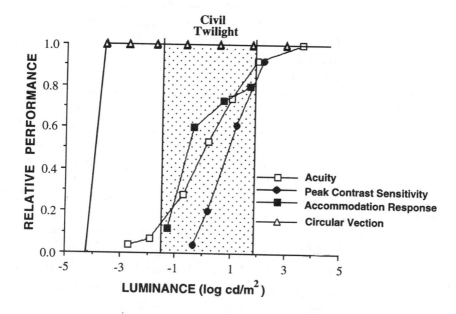

Figure 1.8 Relative visual performance as a function of luminance for three types of Recognition (focal) Vision and one type of Guidance (ambient) Vision. Shaded area identifies the range of luminances commonly encountered in civil twilight. (From Owens & Andre, 1996)

motion that arise from global motion of the visual surroundings) is unaffected by reduced luminance until light levels fall to near absolute threshold.

Twenty years ago, we proposed that the selective degradation of focal vision in low light may help to explain why many drivers seem overconfident and fail to compensate for unavoidable visual impairments at night (Leibowitz & Owens, 1977). Stated briefly, the argument asserts that many drivers (particularly younger drivers) are simply unaware of their visual impairment at night. This happens for two reasons: First, because ambient vision remains highly efficient, controlling the vehicle's speed and direction remains relatively easy at night. Second, because of the benefits of well-engineered lighting and reflectorization systems, focal vision also remains good for much of what a driver must see—there is little difficulty in seeing instruments, other vehicles, lane markings, and road signs. Consequently, most drivers tend to "overdrive" their headlights (Leibowitz, Owens, & Tyrrell, 1998). The young driver's visual deficits at night are selective, and become a problem only when the driver encounters an unmarked low-contrast obstacle on the road. Unfortunately, when that happens, the driver is likely to be caught by surprise, too late to avoid a collision. The fact that such encounters are scarce is a mixed blessing because most drivers have no opportunity to learn of their limitations until the rare occasion when recognition is too late.

Using a night driving simulator at the University of Michigan, we were able to test the selective degradation hypothesis in elderly persons as well as young and middle-aged drivers (Owens & Tyrrell, 1999). All participants were required to drive the simulator at a constant speed down a very simple night road, comprised of two edge-lines that curved unpredictably to the right and left. Tests were conducted under four luminances, which ranged from daylight (1.5 log cd/m²) through twilight to relative darkness, when only scotopic (peripheral) vision was possible (−2.5 log cd/m²). Figure 1.9 summarizes the combined effects of age and luminance on steering accuracy.

From Figure 1.9, it is evident that steering ability in low light diminishes with advancing age. The youngest subjects exhibited the smallest steering errors, which increased only slightly at the lowest luminance. In contrast, elder drivers exhibited significant and progressive increases in steering errors as luminance decreased. Middle-aged drivers showed an intermediate effect, with a nonsignificant trend toward greater steering errors at intermediate light levels and significantly greater errors at the lowest luminance. While conclusions must be tentative because of the limited number of participants and the fact that the simulator was much simpler than the actual night road environment, these results present new evidence for an important role of ambient vision in driving. Consistent with the selective degradation hypothesis, the steering ability of young adults remained highly accurate even in the lowest scotopic light conditions. But the ability to steer accurately in low light appears to diminish gradually with advancing age. These age-related differences in visual guidance abilities may be associated with the tendency of younger drivers to "overdrive" their headlights at night as well as

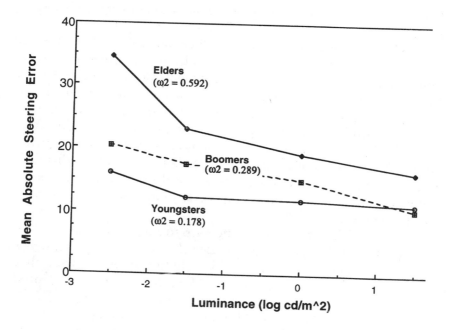

Figure 1.9 Mean absolute steering errors as a function of luminance for three age groups. Mean ages were 72 years for elders, 39 years for middle-aged, and 24 years for youngsters. Omega (ω^2) values indicate the magnitude of effects of luminance on steering accuracy for each age. (From Owens & Tyrrell, 1999)

the tendency of older drivers to feel insecure or reluctant to drive at night (Owens & Andre, 1996).

SUMMARY AND CONCLUSION

The problems of mobility and aging are both frustrating and challenging. The frustrations are probably greatest in the practical domain, where pressing difficulties of senior citizens are presently treated in a rather haphazard and sometimes arbitrary manner. Though well intentioned, such clumsy efforts seem unavoidable for lack of fundamental understanding of the perceptual, cognitive, and behavioral processes engaged in basic mechanisms of everyday locomotion.

Nowhere is this gap in understanding more evident than in the area of drivers' licensing for senior citizens. Regulatory policies aimed to restrict or repeal seniors' driving privileges, although motivated by concern for public safety, seem ineffective. Yet common sense and experience show that limitation and eventual cessation of driving will be necessary for many aging drivers. Common sense and experience also dictate that for many individuals driving activities should be restricted gradually in accordance with the individual's changing capabilities. The trouble is, we do not quite understand the capabilities involved in driving, or any other sort of locomotion for that matter.

From a scientific standpoint, the gaps in our understanding pose an important challenge, for the puzzles of mobility and aging present new opportunities for inquiry and insight. Progress in solving these puzzles will surely expand our basic knowledge, and it will surely benefit from interdisciplinary thinking and collaboration. Dr. Fozard's review has taken an admirable step toward integrating diverse research from psychophysics, perception, and cognition. The present commentary points toward further conceptual links with research from human factors, animal behavior, and neuroscience, which indicate that perception and action involve multiple parallel processes. Some important processes, like ambient vision and skill-based behavioral control, occur rapidly and efficiently without awareness or involvement of cognitive perceptual representations. A full understanding of human mobility and its age-related changes will require an account of these noncognitive as well as cognitive systems.

When considering the challenges and promise of future research, it is intriguing to note that investigations originally motivated by the practical problems of aging are apt to have far-reaching benefits. Through the process of solving these pressing practical problems, we will gain new fundamental insights to the nature of perception, action, and cognition.

ACKNOWLEDGMENTS

Research and preparation of this commentary was supported by Franklin & Marshall College and the Industry Affiliation Program for Human Factors in Transportation Safety of the University of Michigan. I also am grateful for editorial advice from Deborah A. and Justin M. Owens.

REFERENCES

Ball, K., Owsley, C., Sloane, M. E., Roenker, D. L., & Bruni, J. R. (1993). Visual attention problems as a predictor of vehicle crashes in older drivers. *Investigative Ophthalmology & Visual Science, 23*, 3110–3123.

Bruce, V., Green, P. R., & Georgeson, M. A. (1996). *Visual Perception—Physiology, Psychology and Ecology* (3rd ed.). Hillsdale, NJ: Lawrence Erlbaum.

Chaparro, A., McGregor, L., & Stumpfhauser, L. (1998). The driving habits of older adults with visual impairment. *Proceedings of the Human Factors and Ergonomics Society 42nd Annual Meeting, 2*, 1266–1270.

Decartes, R. (1637/1965). *Discourse on method, optics, geometry, and meteorology* (P. J. Olscamp, Trans.). Indianapolis, IN: Bobbs-Merrill.

Department of Transportation. (1994). *The effects of age on the driving habits of the elderly: Evidence from the 1990 national personal transportation study.* (DOT-T-95-12) Washington, DC: Department of Transportation.

Evans, L. (1991). *Traffic safety and the driver.* New York: Van Nostrand Reinhold.

Gazzaniga, M. S., Fendrich, R., & Wessinger, C. M. (1994). Blindsight reconsidered. *Current Directions in Psychological Science, 3*, 93–96.

Goodale, M. A., & Humphrey, G. K. (1998). The objects of action and perception. *Cognition, 67*, 181–207.

Goodale, M. A., & Milner, A. D. (1992). Separate visual pathways for perception and action. *Trends in Neuroscience, 15*, 20–25.

Gregory, R. L. (1990). *Eye and Brain: The psychology of seeing.* Princeton: Princeton University Press.

Hakamies-Blomqvist, L., Johansson, K., & Lundberg, C. (1996). Medical screening of older drivers as a traffic safety measure—A comparative Finnish-Swedish evaluation study. *Journal of the American Geriatric Society, 44* (June), 650–653.

Held, R. (1968). Dissociation of visual function by deprivation and rearrangement. *Psychologische Forschung, 31*, 338–348.

Held, R. (1970). Two modes of processing spatially distributed visual stimulation. In F. O. Schmitt (Ed.), *The neurosciences: Second study program.* New York: Rockefeller University Press.

Helmholtz, H. (1866/1962). *Handbook of Physiological Optics* (3rd ed., Vol. 1). (J. P. C. Southall, Trans.) Hamburg: Voss.

Herd, D. R., Agent, K. R., & Rizenbergs, R. L. (1980). Traffic accidents: Day versus night. *Transportation Research Record, 753,* 25–30.

Higgins, K. E. (1996). Low vision driving among normally-sighted drivers. In R. G. Cole & B. P. Rosenthal (Eds.), *Remediation and management of low vision* (pp. 225–236). St. Louis: Mosby.

Humphrey, N. K. (1974). Vision in a monkey without striate cortex: A case study. *Perception, 3,* 241–255.

Ingle, D. (1967). Two visual mechanisms underlying the behavior of fish. *Psychologische Forschung, 31,* 44–51.

Kline, D. W., & Schieber, F. (1985). Vision and aging. In J. E. Birren & K. W. Schaie (Eds.), *Handbook of the psychology of aging.* New York: Van Nostrand Reinhold.

Kosnik, W. D., Sekuler, R., & Kline, D. W. (1990). Self-reported visual problems of older drivers. *Human Factors, 32*(5), 597–608.

Leibowitz, H. W., & Owens, D. A. (1977). Nighttime driving accidents and selective visual degradation. *Science, 197,* 422–423.

Leibowitz, H. W., & Owens, D. A. (1986). We drive by night: and when we do we often misjudge our visual capabilities. *Psychology Today, 20,* 55–58.

Leibowitz, H. W., & Owens, D. A. (1991). Can normal outdoor activities be carried out in civil twilight? *Applied Optics, 30,* 3501–3503.

Leibowitz, H. W., Owens, D. A., & Helmreich, R. L. (1995). Transportation. In R. S. Nickerson (Ed.), *Emerging needs and opportunities for human factors research.* Washington, DC: National Academy Press.

Leibowitz, H. W., Owens, D. A., & Post, R. B. (1982). Nighttime driving and visual degradation. *SAE Technical Paper Series,* No. 820414. Warrendale, PA: Society of Automotive Engineers.

Leibowitz, H. W., Owens, D. A., & Tyrrell, R. A. (1998). The Assured Clear Distance Ahead Rule: Implications for nighttime traffic safety and the law. *Accident Analysis and Prevention, 30,* 93–99.

Marr, D. (1982). *Vision: A computational investigation into the human representation and processing of visual information.* New York: W. H. Freeman.

Mishkin, M., Ungerleider, L. G., & Macko, K. A. (1983). Object vision and spatial vision: Two cortical pathways. *Trends in Neuroscience, 6,* 414–417.

National Safety Council. (1982–1997). *Accident Facts.* Chicago, IL: National Safety Council.

Owens, D. A., & Andre, J. T. (1996). Selective visual degradation and the older driver. *International Association of Traffic and Safety Sciences Research, 20*(1), 57–66.

Owens, D. A., & Brooks, J. C. (1995). *Drivers' vision, age, and gender as factors in twilight road fatalities* (Report No. UMTRI-95-44). Ann Arbor, MI. The University of Michigan Transportation Research Institute.

Owens, D. A., & Sivak, M. (1996). Differentiation of visibility and alcohol as contributors to twilight road fatalities. *Human Factors, 38*(4), 680–689.

Owens, D. A., & Tyrrell, R. A. (1999). Effects of luminance, blur, and age on nighttime visual guidance: A test of the selective degradation hypothesis. *Journal of Experimental Psychology: Applied, 5*(2), 1–14.

Owsley, C., Ball, K., McGwin, G., Sloan, M. E., Roenker, D. L., White, M. F., & Overley, E. T. (1998). Visual processing impairment and risk of motor vehicle crash among older adults. *Journal of the American Medical Association, 279,* 1083–1088.

Platt, F. N. (1996). *Going on 80–>>II. Tune up your driving skills.* Kennett Square, PA: Fletcher N. Platt, AlphaGraphics.

Pöppel, E., Held, R., & Frost, D. (1973). Residual visual function after brain wounds involving the central visual pathways in man. *Nature, 243,* 295–296.

Rasmussen, J. (1983). Skills, rules, and knowledge: Signals, signs, and symbols, and other distinctions in human performance models. *IEEE Transactions on Systems, Man, and Cybernetics, SMC-13*(3), 257–266.

Rock, I. (1995). *Perception.* New York: W. H. Freeman.

Schneider, G. E. (1967). Contrasting visuomotor functions of tectum and cortex in the golden hamster. *Psychologische Forschung, 31,* 52–62.

Schneider, G. E. (1969). Two visual systems: Brain mechanisms for localization and discrimination are dissociated by tectal and cortical lesions. *Science, 163,* 895–902.

Shinar, D. (1978). *Psychology on the road.* New York: Wiley.

Sivak, M. (1996). The information that drivers use: Is it indeed 90% visual? *Perception, 25,* 1081–1089.

Sloane, M. E., Owsley, C., & Alvarez, S. L. (1988). Aging, senile miosis and spatial contrast sensitivity at low luminance. *Vision Research, 28,* 1235–1246.

Trevarthen, C. (1968). Two mechanisms of vision in primates. *Psychologische Forschung, 31,* 229–337.

Waller, P. F. (1991). The older driver. *Human Factors, 33*(5), 499–505.

Weiskrantz, L. (1986). *Blindsight: A case study and implications.* New York: Oxford University Press.

Wood, J. M. (1998). How do visual status and age impact on driving performance as measured on a closed circuit driving track? *Ophthalmic and Physiological Optics, 9,* 34–40.

Countering Mobility Losses Due to Functional Impairments in Normally Aging Individuals: Applying Fozard's Framework to Everyday Driving Situations

Loren Staplin

The analysis of social structures and mobility in elderly persons dictates an examination of intrinsic and extrinsic factors that lead to reduced mobility with increasing age, as well as possible interventions to extend the mobility and quality of life for older persons without creating a hazard for others. Implicit is an assumption that a major segment of the older population will reside at home and rely on private transportation. The paper presented by Fozard provides a broad framework for understanding the impact of deficits in sensory, perceptual, and cognitive functions plus a loss of strength and flexibility, which occur with normative aging, on the mobility of older drivers and pedestrians; it also guides the discussion of potential countermeasures.

The framework adopted in this paper characterizes the interaction of a person and the environment as an exchange of information and action. The individual receives and processes information—typically with an emphasis on visual information—and somehow adjusts, modifies, or otherwise acts on an operating system. In this approach, the interface between the person and the operating system understandably becomes the focus of attention in deciding how to optimize the person-environment system. Three avenues for intervention are identified: (a) prevent or restore declining functionality, where practical; (b) adapt the environment to accommodate age-related diminished capabilities; and (c) compensate for reduced mobility, and therefore reduced quality of life, through technological innovation. To date, the second avenue has been more fully explored.

Choices among intervention approaches must be tied to a specific type of functional decline on a specific task. Context is also critical, with special regard to the extent that task requirements conform to expectations based on familiarity or experience. Compensation for age-related response slowing, as discussed in this paper, provides a case in point. As supported by the work of Cerella, Poon, and Fozard (1982) and a number of other, more recent studies, an apparent system-wide degradation in the speed of processing yields robust effects; this is probably the most-often-cited cause of age-related cognitive performance decrements in the applied gerontology literature, especially for complex tasks. The speed of visual search tasks, of working memory, and of related cognitive processes are all affected, with important consequences for driving.

Consider the performance context where accident analyses consistently show older drivers to exhibit the greatest difficulty—intersections. Induced exposure analyses show older drivers to be most strongly overrepresented in left turn crashes where the older driver operates the turning vehicle (Staplin & Lyles, 1991), but many other problems at these sites have been documented in the technical literature. In virtually all cases, sensory and cognitive changes with aging are implicated.

The results of two very recent investigations are illustrative: Intersection Negotiation Problems of Older Drivers, sponsored by National Highway Traffic Safety Administration (Staplin, Gish, Decina, Lococo, & McKnight, 1998), and Intersection Geometric Design for Older Drivers and Pedestrians, sponsored by the Federal Highway

Administration (Staplin, Harkey, Lococo, & Tarawneh, 1997). Both studies yield convergent findings. The single most challenging aspect of intersection negotiation for older drivers is performing left turns across traffic during the permitted (green ball) signal phase. Other common problems include: all maneuvers at skewed (non-90°) intersections due to difficulty in turning the head to view intersecting traffic; hitting raised curbs and other barriers such as channelizing islands in the rain and at night due to reduced visibility; performing an abrupt lane-change maneuver after finding oneself positioned in the wrong lane—especially a turn only lane—during an intersection approach due to poor design, poor visibility of pavement markings, or obstruction of signs upstream intended to inform drivers of intersection traffic patterns; difficulties at the end of an auxiliary right turn lane on an arterial or acceleration lane on a freeway in merging with adjacent lane traffic due to conflicts with vehicles in the blind spot; and, of course, reading the names on street signs due to insufficient legibility distance.

The age differences documented in the Fozard paper provide clear evidence of why such difficulties should be expected to increase with normative aging. The varying types of functional deficits described in this paper also suggest that the resulting performance decrements will be interactive, if not completely additive, in their impacts on safe intersection negotiation, and they lead to varying prescriptions for—in Fozard's terms—"optimization of the person-environment system" to accommodate age differences in functional capability. The application of training and countermeasures based on innovative technologies are considered separately.

The strategy of providing "environmental support" to compensate for age-related functional decline was articulated by Craik in the early 1980s and has clear application to efforts to preserve the mobility of older persons. Many practical interventions have been described and have been—or are in the process of being—implemented. At the sensory level, interventions such as larger characters on signs support drivers who have deficits in high spatial frequencies, as do wider spacings between characters, adjustments in the height-to-stroke-width ratios, and tailored fonts, which somewhat reduce reliance on edge discrimination for legibility. Similarly, the redesign of symbols on street signs to subtract high spatial frequency information as necessary elements for their recognition offers substantial benefits.

Poorer contrast sensitivity, which can impair detection of the roadway edge—especially under reduced visibility conditions—benefits from properly maintained center- and edge-line striping, painted curbs and medians, and from the use of raised, retroreflective delineation elements.

Attentional deficits—selective attention, particularly—may be ameliorated to some extent by enhancing the attention conspicuity of priority messages on highways. Enhanced contrast between a sign and its visual surround may be achieved through a number of techniques. These include larger size signs; less eccentric sign placements, using overhead mounts wherever feasible; longitudinal separation of key sign messages from the clutter of commercial signage; and high visibility backplates or sign borders. Backplates are also commonly used, and are quite effective, in raising the conspicuity of traffic signal heads. Nighttime conspicuity depends strongly on the use of retroreflective treatments, which can be used to great benefit to draw attention to highway design features that violate a motorist's expectancy—shifts in roadway alinement; locations where one-way or wrong-way movements are possible; the presence of curbs, abutments, median dividers; and so forth.

Cognitive losses, finally, can slow reading times and lower the comprehensibility of traffic control messages; impair direction finding, route following, and other aspects of spatial cognition; and result in significantly slower vehicle control responses under conditions of information overload or where a planned action must be inhibited or changed quickly to perform an emergency maneuver. Interventions to help offset modest cognitive decline are less obvious, in many cases, but some practical countermeasures have been identified. One example is the use of redundant upstream signing conveying the decision rule for right-of-way status for left turns at an intersection; motorists' responses are primed if they have advance notice that, for example, "left turns must yield on green," instead of waiting to learn of this rule from a sign posted across the intersection, at a point when they may be already committed to a course of action. Recent guidelines for message development for variable message signs—governing abbreviations, the number of pages permissible, and required exposure durations—also take (age-related) diminished cognitive abilities into account (I-95 Corridor Coalition, 1995).

A comprehensive overview of recommended changes in highway design, operations, and traffic control for attenuating difficulties experienced by drivers with diminished functional capacity is provided in a current FHWA (Federal Highway Administration) publication: the *Older Driver Highway Design Handbook* (Staplin, Lococo, & Byington, 1998).

Turning to another avenue noted in the Fozard paper, prevention or remediation of functional deficits, there is some evidence that targeted training activities may offer a feasible approach, complementing efforts to provide environmental support as just described. For example, preattentional deficits, manifested in a reduced ability to respond appropriately to peripheral targets while satisfying the demands of a primary foveal task, are reflected in the useful field of view (UFOV). These losses are exaggerated among elderly persons and have been significantly associated with intersection crash involvement in the research of Ball and her colleagues (Ball, Owsley, Sloan, Roenker, & Bruni, 1993). It has been further hypothesized that UFOV training in an office setting can transfer to actual operating conditions and produce traffic safety and mobility benefits that persist over time.

Lastly, the avenues for intervention identified by Fozard point toward technological innovation as a means to enhance the safe mobility of individuals with functional deficits. This approach is reflected in the myriad assistive devices within the vehicle and on the highway under development, testing, and demonstration as intelligent transportation system (ITS) initiatives. Several have particular relevance as countermeasures for sensory and cognitive deficits.

The most widely known category of ITS devices are probably navigational assistance units, providing in-vehicle guidance information to a driver over an auditory as well as a visual interface. Ranked more highly by older drivers as desirable than navigational devices are vision enhancement systems; this technology, developed earlier for military applications, has been adapted by industry laboratories for use in private automobiles in the form of both near-IA (infrared) and far-IR systems, and is currently in a field evaluation stage. At the other end of the spectrum, ultraviolet (UV) systems to render highway delineation and traffic control devices more visible at night are also the subject of field demonstration and evaluation research at the U.S. Department of Transportation.

Collision avoidance systems, including intelligent cruise control (for headway maintenance) plus side and rear object detection systems, exist as options in concept vehicles and should be commercially available soon. A number of important questions remain, however, regarding the human factors requirements of the control interfaces for these technologies, such that overload conditions and interference with primary (tracking and hazard avoidance) driving tasks can be minimized or eliminated.

On the highway side, active traffic control systems represent ITS technologies that could potentially improve safety for older drivers at intersections. These systems sense the presence and closing velocities of vehicles in conflict with an individual's intended movement. Systems of this type could potentially display advisories to turning motorists when a predetermined threshold for safe clearance interval is violated. The expected benefit from this technology derives from the finding that with increasing age, judgments about gap safety at intersections depend more and more on instantaneous estimates of the distance of an approaching vehicle, without appreciation of its speed and, therefore, the time-to-collision. With an active system, a warning message or change in the traffic control device status could be effected when a conflict vehicle is approaching at excessive speed.

To close, the broad societal impact of age-related difficulties in mobility, and driving in particular, dictate a need to integrate interventions across all avenues. As such efforts proceed, parallel initiatives resulting in innovative approaches to screen the most at-risk drivers—without regard to age—will help converge on a system-wide solution. The development of a North American Model Driver Screening and Evaluation Program is now underway at the National Highway Traffic Safety Administration, with the aim of promoting standardized, reliable, and cost-effective assessment methods that are widely perceived to be fair by older and younger persons alike. Ideally, such methods will be implemented both in Department of Motor Vehicle (DMV) settings and in a variety of health and human services settings throughout the community. With improved detection and regulation of drivers at risk from functional impairment—with a special emphasis on self-regulation to the greatest extent possible—plus the gains that may be realized from training and rehabilitation of age-related performance deficits, the interventions discussed here will significantly enhance the safe mobility of seniors.

REFERENCES

Ball, K., Owsley, C., Sloane, M., Roenker, D., & Bruni, J. (1993). Vision attention problems as a predictor of vehicle crashes in older drivers. *Investigative Ophthalmology and Visual Science, 34*(11), 3110–3123.

Cerella, J., Poon, L. W., & Fozard, J. L. (1982). Age and iconic read-out. *Journal of Gerontology, 37,* 197–202.

I-95 Corridor Coalition. (1995). *VMS/HAR operations guidelines and recommended practices.* Publication No. I-95 CC 9-95-09. Washington, DC: U.S. DOT.

Staplin, L., Gish, K. W., Decina, L. E., Lococo, K., & McKnight, A. S. (1998). *Intersection negotiation problems of older drivers, Volume I.* U.S. DOT Final Report No. DTNH22-93-C-05237. Washington, DC:

Staplin, L., Harkey, D., Lococo, K., & Tarawneh, M. (1997). *Intersection geometric design and operational guidelines for older drivers and pedestrians, Volume I.* U.S. DOT Publication No. FHWA-RD-96-132. Washington, DC:

Staplin, L., Lococo, K., & Byington, S. (1998). *Older driver highway design handbook.* U.S.DOT Publication No. FHWA-RD-97-135. Washington, DC:

Staplin, L., & Lyles, R. W. (1991). Age differences in motion and perception and specific traffic maneuver problems. *Transportation Research Record, 1325,* 23–33.

CHAPTER 2

Effects of Exercise on Body Composition and Functional Capacity of Elderly Persons

William J. Evans

The capacity of older men and women to adapt to regularly performed exercise has been demonstrated by many laboratories. Aerobic exercise results in improvements in functional capacity and reduced risk of developing type II diabetes in elderly persons. High intensity resistance training (above 60% of the 1 repetition maximum) has been demonstrated to cause large increases in strength in elderly persons. In addition, resistance training results in significant increases in muscle size in elderly men and women. Resistance training has also been shown to significantly increase energy requirements and insulin action of elderly persons. Resistance training has a positive effect on multiple risk factors for osteoporotic fractures in previously sedentary postmenopausal women. This includes increased levels of physical activity. Increasing leg muscle strength in elderly men and women increases mobility as measured by total levels of physical activity.

Since the sedentary lifestyle of a long-term care facility may exacerbate losses of muscle function, we have applied this same training program to frail, institutionalized elderly men and women in a population of 100 nursing home residents, a randomly assigned high intensity strength training program resulted in significant gains in strength and functional status. In addition, spontaneous activity, measured by activity monitors increase significantly in those participating in the exercise program, while there was no change in the sedentary control group. Prior to the strength training intervention, the relationship of whole body potassium and leg strength was seen to be relatively weak ($r^2 = 0.29$, $p < 0.001$), indicating that in the very old muscle mass is an important but not the only determiner of functional status. Thus exercise may minimize or reverse the syndrome of physical frailty that is so prevalent among the oldest old. Because of their low functional status and high incidence of chronic disease, there is no segment of the population that can benefit more from exercise training than elderly person.

INTRODUCTION

A remarkable number of factors effect an individual's ability to walk, including vision, balance, cognitive function, muscle reflexes, strength, and endurance. All of these factors may change with advancing age such that walking for many of the oldest old becomes an activity to be feared rather than enjoyed. This review will focus on the effects of diet and exercise on musculoskeletal factors that may effect gait, with particular emphasis on the capacity of elderly people to adapt appropriately to exercise, both aerobic and strengthening.

MUSCLE MASS

Muscle weakness has been demonstrated to be strongly associated with advancing age. This muscle weakness is associated with decreased mobility and increasing risk of frailty and falls in the oldest old and is likely the result of age-associated decreased muscle mass. This age-related decrease in skeletal muscle mass has been termed sarcopenia (Evans, 1995; Evans & Campbell, 1993). Sarcopenia in humans has been demonstrated both indirectly and directly. The excretion of urinary creatinine, reflecting muscle creatine content and total muscle mass, decreases by nearly 50% between the ages of 20 and 90 (Tzankoff & Norris, 1978). Computed tomography of individual muscles shows that after age 30 there is a decrease in cross-sectional areas of the thigh along with decreased muscle density associated with increased intramuscular fat. These changes are most pronounced in women (Imamura, Ashida, Ishikawa, & Fujii, 1983). Muscle atrophy may result from a gradual and selective loss of muscle fibers. The number of muscle fibers in the midsection of the vastus lateralis of autopsy specimens is lower by about 110,000 in elderly men (age 70–73) than in young men (age 19–37), a 23% difference (Lexell, Henriksson-Larsen, Wimblod, & Sjostrom, 1983). The decline is more marked in Type II muscle fibers, which fall from an average 60% in sedentary young men to below 30% after the age of 80 (Larsson, 1983), and is significantly related to age-related decreases in strength ($r = 0.54$, $p < 0.001$).

MUSCLE STRENGTH

A reduction in muscle strength is a major component of normal aging. Data from the Framingham (Jette & Branch, 1981) study indicate that 40 percent of the female population aged 55 to 64 almost 45% of women aged 65 to 74, and 65% of women aged 75 to 84 years were unable to lift 4.5 kg. In addition, a similarly high percentage of women in this population reported that they were unable to perform some aspects of normal household work. Larsson et al. (Larsson, Grimby, & Karlsson, 1979) studied 114 men between the ages of 11 and 70 years and found that isometric and dynamic strength of the quadriceps increased up to the age of 30 years and decreased after the age of 50. They saw reductions in strength between 50 and 70 in the range from 24 to 36%. They concluded that much of the reduction in strength was due to a selective atrophy of Type II muscle fibers, which were 36% smaller in diameter when compared to 40-year-old subjects. It appears that muscle strength losses are most dramatic after the age of 70 years. Knee extensor strength of a group of healthy 80-year-old men and women studied in the Copenhagen City Heart Study (Danneskoild-Samsoe, Kofod, Munter, Grimby, & Schnohr, 1984) was found to be 30% lower than a previous population study (Aniansson, Grimby, Hedberg, &

Krotkiewski, 1981) of 70 year old men and women. Thus cross-sectional as well as longitudinal data indicate that muscle strength declines by approximately 15% per decade in the sixth and seventh decade and about 30% thereafter (Danneskoild-Samsoe et al., 1984; Harries & Bassey, 1990; Larsson, 1978; Murray, Duthie, Gambert, Sepic, & Mollinger, 1985). While there is some indication that muscle function is reduced with advancing age, the overwhelming majority of the loss in strength results from an age-related decrease in muscle mass. We (Frontera et al., 1991) examined more that 200 men and women between the ages of 45 and 78 years. Isokinetic and isometric strength of the upper and lower body were significantly different between men and women and were decreased with advancing age. However, when corrected for fat-free mass (estimated from hydro-static weighing) and total body muscle mass (estimated from 24-hour urinary creatinine), age-related differences disappear (Table 2.1). These data indicate that muscle of the growing weakness of advancing age is due to sarcopenia rather than alterations in the intrinsic quality of skeletal muscle with advancing age.

STRENGTH AND FUNCTIONAL CAPACITY

Bassey, Bendall, and Pearson (1988) measured muscle strength and the amount and speed of customary walking in a large sample of men and women older than 65 years. They found an age-related decline in muscle strength and a significant negative correlation between strength and chosen normal walking speed for both sexes

TABLE 2.1   Strength Corrected for Body Composition in Older Women

Age (years)	Strength (Nm)	Nm/FFM	Nm/muscle mass
45–54	108 ± 22	2.7 ± 0.4	6.1 ± 0.9
55–64	98 ± 20	2.6 ± 0.4	5.9 ± 1.2
65–78	89 ± 15[*]	2.5 ± 0.4	5.8 ± 1.1

[*]Different from age 45–54 group ($p < 0.05$).
Source: Frontera et al., 1991.

($r = 0.041$, $p < 0.001$ for men; $r = 0.36$, $p < 0.01$ for women). Bassey and coworkers (Bassey et al., 1989) measured flexibility and found that the mean value for the elderly was 30 degrees less than those accepted for younger men and women. Nearly one half of the distribution fell below the accepted threshold level of 120 degrees for adequate function. Fiatarone and colleagues (1990) observed a closer relationship between quadriceps strength and habitual gait speed ($r = -0.745$, $p < 0.01$) in a group of frail institutionalized men and women above the age of 86 years. In these subjects, fat-free mass ($r = 0.732$) and regional muscle mass estimated by computerized tomography ($r = 0.752$) were correlated with muscle strength. In the same population, we (Bassey et al., 1992) recently demonstrated that leg power is closely associated with functional performance. In older, frail women leg power was highly correlated with walking speed ($r = 0.93$, $p < 0.001$) accounting for up to 86% of the variance in walking speed (Table 2.2). Leg power, which represents a more dynamic measurement of muscle function, may be a useful predictor of functional capacity in the very old. These data suggest that with the advancing age and very low activity levels seen in institutionalized patients, muscle strength is a critical component of walking ability.

TABLE 2.2   Relations Between Leg Extensor Power and Functional Performance

	Men	Women	All (n)
Chair rising speed (s)	0.45	0.83***	0.65*** (24)
Stair-climbing speed (m/s)	0.76**	0.85***	0.81*** (22)
Walking speed (km/h)	0.58*	0.93***	0.80*** (25)
Stair-climbing power (W)	0.91***	0.86***	0.88*** (23)

*$p < 0.05$, **$p < 0.01$, ***$p < 0.001$.
Leg extensor power (W/kg, both legs together) is the independent variable. The subjects were 26 nursing home residents (men mean age 88 ± 1.6 years, women mean age 86 ± 1.5 years).
Source: Bassey et al., 1992.

PROTEIN NEEDS AND AGING

Previous estimates of dietary protein needs of elderly persons using nitrogen balance have ranged from 0.59 to 0.8 g $\cdot$ kg^{-1} $\cdot$ d^{-1} (Gersovitz, Munro, Scrimshaw, & Young, 1982; Uauy, Schrimshaw, & Young, 1978; Zanni, Calloway, & Zezula, 1979). However, the low value was reported by Zanni et al., who preceded their 10-day dietary protein feeding with a 17-day protein-free diet, which was likely to improve nitrogen retention during the 10-day balance period. Recently, we (Campbell, Crim, Dallal, Young, & Evans, 1994a) reassessed the nitrogen balance studies mentioned above using the currently accepted, 1985 World Health Organization (WHO/FAO/UNU, 1985) nitrogen-balance formula. These newly recalculated data were combined with nitrogen balance data collected on 12 healthy older men and women (age range 56–80 years, 8 men and 4 women) consuming the current recommended daily allowance (RDA) for protein or double this amount (0.8 g $\cdot$ kg^{-1} $\cdot$ d^{-1} and 1.6 g $\cdot$ kg^{-1} $\cdot$ d^{-1}, respectively) in our laboratory. Our subjects consumed the diet for 11 consecutive days and nitrogen balance (mg N $\cdot$ kg^{-1} $\cdot$ d^{-1}) was measured during days 6 to 11. The estimated mean protein requirements from the three retrospectively assessed studies and the current study can be combined by weighted averaging to produce an overall protein requirement estimate of 0.91 $\pm$ 0.043 g $\cdot$ kg^{-1} $\cdot$ d^{-1}. The combined estimate excluding the data from our 12 subjects is 0.894 $\pm$ 0.048 g protein $\cdot$ kg^{-1} $\cdot$ d^{-1}.

The current RDA in the United States of 0.8 g $\cdot$ kg^{-1} $\cdot$ d^{-1} is based on data collected, for the most part, on young subjects. The RDA includes an upward adjustment based on the coefficient of variability (CV) of the average requirement established in these studies (0.6 g $\cdot$ kg^{-1} $\cdot$ d^{-1}). Based on the CV previously established for N-balance studies, an adequate dietary protein level for 97.5% of the elderly population would be provided by an intake of 25% (twice the SD) above the mean protein requirement. Our data suggest that the safe protein intake for elderly adults is 1.25 g $\cdot$ kg^{-1} $\cdot$ d^{-1}. On the basis of the current and recalculated short-term N-balance results, a safe recommended protein intake for older men and women should be set at 1.0 to 1.25 g of high quality protein $\cdot$ kg^{-1} $\cdot$ d^{-1}. Hartz (Hartz, 1992) reported that approximately 50% of 946 healthy free-living men and women above the age of 60 living in the Boston, Massachusetts area consume less than this amount of protein and 25% of the elderly men and women in this survey consume less than 0.86 g and less than 0.81 g protein · kg^{-1} · d^{-1}, respectively. A large percentage of homebound elderly people consuming their habitual dietary protein intake (0.67 g mixed protein · kg^{-1} · d^{-1}) have been shown (Bunker, Lawson, Stansfield, & Clayton, 1987) to be in negative N balance. Inadequate dietary protein intake may be an important cause of sarcopenia. The compensatory response to long-term decrease in dietary protein intake is a loss in lean body mass.

ENERGY METABOLISM

Daily energy expenditure declines progressively throughout adult life (McGandy et al., 1966). In sedentary individuals, the main determinant of energy expenditure is fat-free mass (Ravussin, Lillioja, Anderson, Cristin, & Bogardus, 1986), which declines by about 15% between the third and eighth decade of life, contributing to a lower basal metabolic rate in elderly persons (Cohn, et al., 1980). Tzankoff and Norris (1978) saw that 24-hour creatinine excretion (an index of muscle mass) was closely related to basal metabolic rate at all ages. Nutrition surveys of those over the age of 65 years show a very low energy intake for men (1400 kcal/day; 23 kcal/kg per day). These data indicate that preservation of muscle mass and prevention of sarcopenia can help prevent the decrease in metabolic rate. While body weight increases with advancing age, an age-associated increase in relative body fat content has been demonstrated by a number of investigators. The cause of this increase in body fatness results from a number of factors, but chief among these causes are a declining metabolic rate and activity level coupled with an energy intake that does not match this declining need for calories. Meredith et al. (Meredith, Zackin, Frontera, & Evans, 1987) demonstrated that endurance-trained men between 20 and 60 years of age consumed a diet very high in calories but that body fat levels were closely related to the total number of hours spent exercising per week. Age was not found to be a covariate in this study. More recently, Roberts and co-workers (Roberts et al., 1992) examined the relationship between total energy use (using the doubly labeled water technique) and body composition in a group of sedentary young and old men and found that energy spent in daily activity accounted for 73% of the variability in body fat content.

In addition to its role in energy metabolism, skeletal muscle and its age-related decline may contribute to such age-associated changes as reduction in bone density (Bevier, et al., 1989; Sinaki, McPhee, & Hodgson, 1986; Snow-Harter, et al., 1990), insulin sensitivity (Kolterman, Insel, Saekow, & Olefsky, 1980), and aerobic capacity (Flegg & Lakatta, 1988). For these reasons strategies for preservation of muscle mass with advancing age and for increasing muscle mass and strength in the previously sedentary elderly population may be an important way to increase functional independence and decrease the prevalence of many age-associated chronic diseases.

ROLE OF AEROBIC EXERCISE

Maximal aerobic capacity has been demonstrated to decrease at the rate of approximately 1% per year. This decline is due to a number of factors, including decreased maximal cardiac output due to lower maximal heart rate and contractility, decreased muscle mass (Flegg & Lakatta, 1988), and the decreased oxidative capacity of skeletal muscle (Meredith, Frontera, et al., 1989). As tasks of every day living represent a larger and larger percentage of the maximum capacity for oxygen consumption, it is not difficult to see why many elderly persons (particularly women because of a lower fitness level at all ages) choose not to perform them. The capacity of elderly men and women to respond to increased levels of physical activity with improvements in strength or aerobic capacity depend, in large measure, on the frequency, intensity, and duration of the exercise program. With aerobic exercise training, intensity is generally reported as a percentage of the volume of oxygen consumed per minute during maximal exercise (VO_{2max}) or of maximal heart rate. Aerobic training involves high repetition muscle contractions and leads to minimal strength gains. Intensity of resistance training is generally reported as a percentage of the one repetition maximum (1 RM), the maximum amount of force that a muscle group can generate with one single contraction.

A number of studies have shown a great capacity of elderly persons to respond to aerobic exercise. A study (Seals, Hagberg, Hurley,

Ehsani, & Hollosky, 1984b) examining the effects of 6 months of low-intensity and 6 months of high-intensity exercise demonstrated that healthy 60- to 70-year old subjects increase their average VO_{2max} by 30% with a range of 2 to 40%. There was no change in maximal cardiac output as a result of the year-long intervention, however, a decrease in blood lactate levels during a standard exercise task was observed. The authors concluded that the increase in maximal aerobic capacity occurred as a result of peripheral rather than central adaptations. Our laboratory (Meredith, et al., 1989a) compared the peripheral effects of vigorous endurance exercise (stationary cycling: 45 min/day, 3 days/wk at 70% maximal heart rate reserve) in young (24 yr) and older (65 yr) men and women. The muscle oxidative capacity (from *m. vastus lateralis* biopsies) of the older subjects increased by an average of 128%, while the young subjects showed only a 27% increase. The absolute increase in VO_{2max} was not different between the two groups, however, the relative improvement in the older subjects was 20% versus 12% in the younger subjects. Kohrt and coworkers (1991) examined the adaptations of 53 men and 57 women between the ages of 60 and 71 years to 9 to 12 months of regular aerobic exercise (walk/run: 4 days/wk, 45 min/day, 80% maximal heart rate). They observed an average 24% increase in VO_{2max} with a large range (0–58%). In a subset of 23 men and women in this study, Coggan et al. (1992) observed large increases in muscle mitochondrial enzyme activity and capillary density, indicating a substantial capacity of skeletal muscle to respond to regular aerobic exercise.

It is well established that aging is associated with decreased glucose tolerance and a greatly increased incidence of non-insulin dependent diabetes mellitus (NIDDM). It is generally accepted that decreasing glucose tolerance of aging is associated with the previously mentioned age-associated changes in body composition and activity levels (Kolterman, et al., 1980). Improved fitness as a result of aerobic exercise has also been demonstrated to improve glucose tolerance in previously sedentary subjects (Holloszy, Schultz, Kusnierkiewicz, Hagberg, & Ehsani, 1986; Seals, Hagberg, Hurley, Ehsani, & Holloszy, 1984a) and exercise has been shown to prevent the onset of NIDDM. Recently, our laboratory examined the effects of 12 weeks of high- or low-intensity aerobic exercise (cycle ergometry: 4 days/wk, 45 min/day at 55% or 75% maximal heart rate) with no weight loss on aspects of muscle and whole body carbohydrate metabolism. Men and women with impaired glucose tolerance were selected for participation after an oral glucose tolerance test. No differences were seen between the low and high intensity exercise. Significant improvements in oral glucose tolerance and insulin-stimulated glucose disposal rate were accompanied by increased skeletal muscle glycogen levels and a 68% increase in muscle glucose transporter-4 (GLUT-4) levels. These data indicate that improvements in carbohydrate resulting from exercise occur primarily in skeletal muscle. Clearly, exercise can improve glucose metabolism in both subjects at high risk for NIDDM as well as those with the disease by increasing the opportunity for body fat loss as well as stimulating the adaptive response of skeletal muscle, the primary site of glucose disposal.

STRENGTH TRAINING

Strength conditioning, also termed progressive resistance training (PRT), is generally defined as training in which the resistance against which a muscle generates force is progressively increased over time. Muscle strength has been shown to increase in response to training between 60 and 100% of the 1 RM (MacDougall, 1986). Strength conditioning results in an increase in muscle size and this increase in size is largely the result of an increase in contractile protein content.

It is clear that when the intensity of the exercise is low, only modest increases in strength are achieved by elderly subjects (Aniansson & Gustafsson, 1981; Larsson, 1982). A number of studies have demonstrated that, given an adequate training stimulus, older men and women show similar or greater strength gains compared to young individuals as a result of resistance training.

Frontera et al. (Frontera, Meredith, O'Reilly, & Evans, 1990; Frontera, Meredith, O'Reilly, Knuttgen, & Evans, 1988) showed that older men responded to a 12-week progressive resistance training program (80% of the 1 RM, three sets of eight repetitions of the knee extensor and flexors, 3 days per week) by more than doubling extensor strength and more than tripling of flexor strength. The increases in strength averaged approximately 5% per training session, similar to strength gains observed by younger men. Total muscle area estimated by computerized tomography (CT) increased by 11.4%. Biopsies of the *vastus lateralis* muscle revealed similar increases in type I fiber area (33.5%) and type II fiber area (27.6%). Daily excretion of urinary 3-methyl-L-histidine increased with training ($p < 0.05$) by an average of 40.8%, indicating that increased muscle size and strength resulting from PRT is associated with an increased rate of myofibrillar protein turnover. Half of the men who participated in this study were given a daily protein-calorie supplement (S) providing an extra 560 ± 16 kcal/d (16.6% as protein, 43.3% as carbohydrate, and 40.1% as fat) in addition to their normal ad libitum diet. The rest of the subjects received no supplement (NS) and consumed an ad libitum diet. By the 12th week of the study, dietary energy (2960 $\pm$ 230 in S vs. 1620 ± 80 kcal in NS) and protein (118 ± 10 in S vs. 72 ± 11 g/d in NS) intake were significantly different between the S and NS groups.

Composition of the midthigh was estimated by computerized tomography and showed that the S group had greater gains in muscle than did the NS men (Meredith, Frontera, & Evans, 1992). In addition, urinary creatinine excretion was greater at the end of the training in the S group when compared to that of the men in the NS group, indicating a greater muscle mass in the S group at the end of the 12 weeks of training. The change in energy and protein intake (beginning vs 12 weeks) was correlated with the change in midthigh muscle area ($r = 0.69$, $p = 0.019$; $r = 0.63$, $p = 0.039$, respectively). There were no differences in the strength gains between the two groups. These data suggest that a change in total food intake, or perhaps, selected nutrients, in subjects beginning a strength-training program can affect muscle hypertrophy. High intensity resistance training appears to have profoundly anabolic effects in the elderly population. Data from our laboratory demonstrate a 10 to 15% decrease in nitrogen excretion at the initiation of training that persists for 12 weeks (Campbell, Crim, Young, Joseph, & Evans, 1995). That is, progressive resistance training improved nitrogen balance, thus older subjects performing resistance training have a lower mean protein requirement than do sedentary subjects. These results are somewhat at variance to our previous research (Meredith, Zackin, Frontera, & Evans, 1989b), demonstrating that regularly performed aerobic exercise causes an increase in the mean protein requirement of middle-aged and young endurance athletes. This difference likely results from increased oxidation of amino-acids during aerobic exercise that may not be present during resistance training.

Resistance training may be an important adjunct to weight loss interventions in elderly persons. Campbell and co-workers (Campbell, Crim, Young, & Evans, 1994b) examined the effects of high-intensity resistance training on calorie requirements of a group of 12 men and women aged 56 to 80 years. Caloric intake was titrated for body weight maintenance in a group of older men and women living in a metabolic ward. These subjects were participating in both upper and lower body resistance training (3 d/wk, three sets of eight repetitions, 80% 1 RM). At the end of 12 weeks of training, these subjects required an average 15% increase in energy intake to maintain body weight. The increased energy expenditure included increased resting metabolic rate and the energy cost of resistance exercise. The results of this study are supported by the data of Pratley et al. (1994), who also demonstrated a significant increase in resting metabolic rate with resistance training. Resistance training is, therefore, an effective way to increase energy requirements, decrease body-fat mass, and maintain metabolically active tissue mass in healthy older people. In addition to its effect on energy metabolism, resistance training has also been demonstrated to improve insulin action in older subjects (Miller, et al., 1994).

Regularly performed aerobic exercise has been demonstrated to have positive effects on bone health in healthy, postmenopausal women (Gutin & Kasper, 1992). Nelson and co-workers (Nelson, Dilmanian, Dallal, & Evans, 1991) demonstrated that a 1-year program of vigorous walking preserved the bone density of the lumbar spine when compared to a group of age-matched sedentary controls. However, no effect of exercise was seen at any other bone site or in total body calcium. Recently, we (Nelson, et al., 1994) examined the effects of a high-intensity resistance training program on bone health in a group of postmenopausal women. Forty women (aged 50–70 years) were randomized to a sedentary control or resistance training (80% of 1 RM, twice a week, 52 weeks) group. The sedentary control group demonstrated typical age-associated declines in bone density and total body mineral content while the strength training had a protective effect on the femoral neck bone mineral density (BMD), lumbar spine BMD, and total body mineral content. However, in addition to its effect on bone, the strength training also increased muscle mass and strength, dynamic balance, and overall levels of physical activity. All of these outcomes may result in a reduction in the risk of osteoporotic fractures. In contrast, traditional pharmacologic and nutritional approaches to the treatment or prevention of osteoporosis have the capacity to maintain or slow the loss of bone, but not the ability to improve balance, strength, muscle mass, or physical activity.

The very old and frail elderly population experiences skeletal muscle atrophy as a result of disuse, disease, undernutrition, and the effects of aging, per se. Muscle weakness that accompanies advanced age has been positively related to the risk of falling and fracture in these older individuals (Scheibel, 1985). For this reason we studied the effects of high-intensity, progressive resistance training on quadriceps muscle strength in a group of institutionalized elderly men and women (age range 87–96 years). Initial strength levels were extremely low in these subjects, with a mean 1 RM of 8 kg for the quadriceps. The absolute amount of weight lifted by the subjects during the training increased from 8 to 21 kg. The average increase in strength after 8 weeks of resistance training was $174 \pm 31\%$, and mean increase in muscle cross sectional area via CT was $10 \pm 8\%$ (Fiatarone, et al., 1990).

The substantial increases in muscle size and strength were accompanied by clinically significant improvements in tandem gait speed and index of functional mobility. Repeat 1 RM testing in seven of the subjects after 4 weeks of no training showed that quadriceps strength had declined 32%. Our preliminary data indicate that maintenance of the initial strength gains can be accomplished by as little as one exercise session per week at the appropriate training intensity (60–100% of 1 RM).

Fiatarone and coworkers also demonstrated (Fiatarone, et al., 1994) that increasing muscle strength in very old nursing home residents improved balance, gait speed, and spontaneous activity. In this study, the relationship between whole body potassium levels (and index of active cell mass) and lower body strength was examined in 100 subjects between 72 and 98 years old. A significant correlation of $r^2 = 0.29$ was seen. This relatively weak relationship indicates that while muscle mass is an important determiner of functional status in the very old, other factors such as overall levels of physical activity may be equally important. These studies demonstrate that frail elderly men and women, well into their tenth decade of life, retain the capacity to adapt to progressive resistance exercise training with significant and clinically relevant muscle hypertrophy and increases in muscle strength. Results from the resistance training studies performed in young, middle-age, elderly, and oldest-old participants indicate that it is the intensity of the stimulus, not the underlying fitness or frailty of the individual, that determines the magnitude of the gains in strength and muscle size.

BALANCE TRAINING

Strength training may increase balance through the improvement in strength of muscle involved in walking. Indeed ankle weakness has been demonstrated to be associated with increased risk of falling in nursing home patients (Whipple, Wolfson, & Amerman, 1987). However, balance training, which may demonstrate very little improvement in muscle strength, size, or cardiovascular changes has also been demonstrated to decrease the risk of falls in older people (Wolfson, et al., 1993). Tai Chi, a form of dynamic balance training that requires no new technology or equipment, has been demonstrated to reduce the risk of falling in older people by almost 50% (Wolf, et al., 1996). As a component of the National Institute on Aging Frailty and Injuries: Cooperative Studies of Intervention Techniques trials, individuals aged over 70 were randomized to Tai Chi (TC), individualized balance training (BT), and exercise control education (ED) groups for 15 weeks (Kutner, Barnhart, Wolf, McNeely, & Xu, 1997). In a follow-up assessment 4 months postintervention, 130 subjects responded to exit interview questions asking about perceived benefits of participation. Both TC and BT subjects reported increased confidence in balance and movement, but only TC subjects reported that their daily activities and their overall life had been affected; many of these subjects had changed their normal physical activity to incorporate ongoing TC practice. The data suggest that when mental as well as physical control is perceived to be enhanced, with a generalized sense of improvement in overall well-being, older persons' motivation to continue exercising also increases. Province et al. (1995) examined the overall effect of many different exercise interventions in the FICSIT trials on reducing falls. While each these separate interventions were underpowered to make conclusion about their effects on the incidence of falls in an elderly population, they did conclude that "all training domains, taken together under the heading of 'general exercise' showed an effect on falls, this probably demonstrates the 'rising tide raises all boats' principle, in which training that targets one domain may improve performance somewhat in other domains as a consequence. If this is so, then the differences seen on fall risk due to the exact nature of the training may not be as critical compared with the differences in not training at all." Recently, the use of a community-based exercise program for frail older people was examined (Hickey, et al., 1996). Participants were predominantly sedentary women over age 70 with multiple chronic conditions. The program was conducted with peer leaders to facilitate its continuation after the research demonstration phase. In addition to positive health outcomes related to functional mobility, blood pressure maintenance, and overall well-being, this intervention was successful in sustaining active participation in regular physical activity through the use of peer leaders selected by the program participants.

CONCLUSION

In summary, it is clear that the capacity to adapt to increased levels of physical activity is preserved even in the oldest old. Regularly performed exercise has been demonstrated to result in a remarkable number of positive changes in elderly men and women. Because sarcopenia and weakness may be an almost universal characteristic of advancing age, strategies for preserving or increasing muscle mass in elderly persons should be implemented. With increasing muscle strength increased levels of spontaneous activity have been seen in both healthy, free-living older subjects and very old and frail men and women. Resistance training, in addition to its positive effects on insulin action, bone density, energy metabolism, and functional status, may also be an important way to increase levels of physical activity in the elderly population.

REFERENCES

Aniansson, A., Grimby, G., Hedberg, M., & Krotkiewski, M. (1981). Muscle morphology, enzyme activity and muscle strength in elderly men and women. *Clinical Physiology, 1,* 73–86.

Aniansson, A., & Gustafsson, E. (1981). Physical training in elderly men with special reference to quadriceps muscle strength and morphology *Clinical Physiology, 1,* 87–98.

Bassey, E. J., Bendall, M. J., & Pearson, M. (1988). Muscle strength in the triceps surae and objectively measured customary walking activity in men and women over 65 years of age. *Clinical Science, 74,* 85–89.

Bassey, E. J., Fiatarone, M. A., O'Neill, E. F., Kelly, M., Evans, W. J., & Lipsitz, L. A. (1992). Leg extensor power and functional performance in very old men and women. *Clinical Science, 82,* 321–327.

Bassey, E. J., Morgan, K., & Dallosso, H. M. (1989). Flexibility of the shoulder joint measured as a range of abduction in a large representative sample of men and women over 65 years of age. *European Journal of Applied Physiology, 58,* 353–360.

Bevier, W. C., Wiswell, R. A., Pyka, G., Kozak, K. C., Newhall, K. M., & Marcus, R. (1989). Relationship of body composition, muscle strength, and aerobic capacity to bone mineral density in older men and women. *Journal of Bone & Mineral Research, 4,* 421–432.

Bunker, V., Lawson, M., Stansfield, M., & Clayton, B. (1987). Nitrogen balance studies in apparently healthy elderly people and those who are housebound. *British Journal of Nutrition, 57,* 211–221.

Campbell, W. W., Crim, M. C., Dallal, G. E., Young, V. R., & Evans, W. J. (1994a). Increased protein requirements in the elderly: New data and retrospective reassessments. *American Journal of Clinical Nutrition, 60,* 167–175.

Campbell, W. W., Crim, M. C., Young, V. R., & Evans, W. J. (1994b). Increased energy requirements and body composition changes with resistance training in older adults. *American Journal of Clinical Nutrition, 60,* 167–175.

Campbell, W. W., Crim, M. C., Young, V. R., Joseph, L. J., & Evans, W. J. (1995). Effects of resistance training and dietary protein intake on protein metabolism in older adults. *American Journal of Physiology, 268,* E1143–E1153.

Coggan, A. R., Spina, R. J., King, D. S., Rogers, M. A., Brown, M., Nemath, P. M., & Holloszy, J. O. (1992). Skeletal muscle adaptations to endurance training in 60 to 70-yr-old men and women. *Journal of Applied Physiology, 72,* 1780–1786.

Cohn, S. H., Vartsky, D., Yasumura, S., Savitsky, A., Zanzi, I., Vaswani, A., & Ellis, K. J. (1980). Compartmental body composition based on total-body potassium and calcium. *American Journal of Physiology, 239,* E524–E530.

Danneskoild-Samsoe, B., Kofod, V., Munter, J., Grimby, G., & Schnohr, P. (1984). Muscle strength and functional capacity in 77–81 year old men and women. *European Journal of Applied Physiology, 52,* 123–135.

Evans, W. (1995). What is sarcopenia? *Journal of Gerontology, 50A*(special issue), 5–8.

Evans, W. J., & Campbell, W. W. (1993). Sarcopenia and age-related changes in body composition and functional capacity. *Journal of Nutrition, 123*, 465–468.

Fiatarone, M. A., Marks, E. C., Ryan, N. D., Meredith, C. N., Lipsitz, L. A., & Evans, W. J. (1990). High-intensity strength training in nonagenarians: Effects on skeletal muscle. *Journal of the American Medical Association, 263*, 3029–3034.

Fiatarone, M. A., O'Neill, E. F., Ryan, N. D., Clements, K. M., Solares, G. R., Nelson, M. E., Roberts, S. B., Kehayias, J. J., Lipsitz, L. A., & Evans, W. J. (1994). Exercise training and nutritional supplementation for physical frailty in very elderly people. *The New England Journal of Medicine, 330*, 1769–1775.

Flegg, J. L., & Lakatta, E. G. (1988). Role of muscle loss in the age-associated reduction in VO_{2max}. *Journal of Applied Physiology, 65*, 1147–1151.

Frontera, W. R., Hughes, V. A., & Evans, W. J. (1991). A cross-sectional study of upper and lower extremity muscle strength in 45–78 year old men and women. *Journal of Applied Physiology, 71*, 644–650.

Frontera, W. R., Meredith, C. N., O'Reilly, K. P., & Evans, W. J. (1990). Strength training and determinants of VO_{2max} in older men. *Journal of Applied Physiology, 68*, 329–333.

Frontera, W. R., Meredith, C. N., O'Reilly, K. P., Knuttgen, H. G., & Evans, W. J. (1988). Strength conditioning in older men: Skeletal muscle hypertrophy and improved function. *Journal of Applied Physiology, 64*, 1038–1044.

Gersovitz, M., Munro, H., Scrimshaw, N., & Young, V. (1982). Human protein requirements: Assessment of the adequacy of the current recommended dietary allowance for dietary protein in elderly men and women. *American Journal of Clinical Nutrition, 35*, 6–14.

Gutin, B., & Kasper, M. J. (1992). Can vigorous exercise play a role in osteoporosis prevention? A review. *Osteoporosis International, 2*, 55–69.

Harries, U. J., & Bassey, E. J. (1990). Torque-velocity relationships for the knee extensors in women in their 3rd and 7th decades. *European Journal of Applied Physiology, 60*, 187–190.

Hartz, S. C. (1992). *Nutrition in the elderly: The Boston Nutritional Status Survey.* London: Smith-Gordon.

Hickey, T., Sharpe, P. A., Wolf, F. M., Robins, L. S., Wagner, M. B., & Harik, W. (1996). Exercise participation in a frail elderly population. *Journal of Health Care for the Poor and Underserved, 7*, 219–231.

Holloszy, J. O., Schultz, J., Kusnierkiewicz, J., Hagberg, J. M., & Ehsani, A. A. (1986). Effects of exercise on glucose tolerance and insulin resistance. *Acta Medica Scandinavica, 711*(Suppl.), 55–65.

Imamura, K., Ashida, H., Ishikawa, T., & Fujii, M. (1983). Human major psoas muscle and scrospinalis muscle in relation to age: A study by computed tomography. *Journal of Gerontology, 38,* 678–681.

Jette, A. M., & Branch, L. G. (1981). The Framingham disability study: II. Physical disability among the aging. *American Journal of Public Health, 71,* 1211–1216.

Kohrt, W. M., Coggan, A. R., Spina, R. J., Ogawa, T., Ehsani, A. A., Bourey, R. E., Martin III, W. H., & Holloszy, J. O. (1991). Effects of gender, age and fitness level on response of VO_{2max} to training in 60–71 yr olds. *Journal of Applied Physiology, 71,* 2004–2011.

Kolterman, O. G., Insel, J., Saekow, M., & Olefsky, J. M. (1980). Mechanisms of insulin resistance in human obesity: Evidence for receptor and post-receptor defects. *Journal of Clinical Investigation, 65,* 1272–1284.

Kutner, N. G., Barnhart, H., Wolf, S. L., McNeely, E., & Xu, T. (1997). Self-report benefits of Tai Chi practice by older adults. *Journal of Gerontology, 52,* P242–P246.

Larsson, L. (1978). Morphological and functional characteristics of the aging skeletal muscle in man. *Acta Physiolgica Scandinavica, 457*(Suppl.), 1–36.

Larsson, L. (1982). Physical training effects on muscle morphology in sedentary males as different ages. *Medicine and Science in Sports and Exercise, 14,* 203–206.

Larsson, L. (1983). Histochemical characteristics of human skeletal muscle during aging. *Acta Physiolgica Scandinavica, 117,* 469–471.

Larsson, L. G., Grimby, G., & Karlsson, J. (1979). Muscle strength and speed of movement in relation to age and muscle morphology. *Journal of Applied Physiology, 46,* 451–456.

Lexell, J., Henriksson-Larsen, K., Wimblod, B., & Sjostrom, M. (1983). Distribution of different fiber types in human skeletal muscles: Effects of aging studied in whole muscle cross sections. *Muscle & Nerve, 6,* 588–595.

MacDougall, J. D. (1986). Adaptability of muscle to strength training—a cellular approach. In B. Saltin (Ed.), *Biochemistry of Exercise VI* (pp. 501–513). Champaign, IL: Human Kinetics.

McGandy, R. B., Barrows, C. H., Spanias, A., Meredith, A., Stone, J. L., & Norris, A. H. (1966). Nutrient intake and energy expenditure in men of different ages. *Journal of Gerontology, 21,* 581–587.

Meredith, C. N., Frontera, W. R., & Evans, W. J. (1992). Body composition in elderly men: Effect of dietary modification during strength training. *Journal of the American Geriatric Society, 40,* 155–162.

Meredith, C. N., Frontera, W. R., Fisher, E. C., Hughes, V. A., Herland, J. C., Edwards, J., & Evans, W. J. (1989). Peripheral effects of endurance training in young and old subjects. *Journal of Applied Physiology, 66*, 2844–2849.

Meredith, C. N., Zackin, M. J., Frontera, W. R., & Evans, W. J. (1987). Body composition and aerobic capacity in young and middle-aged endurance-trained men. *Medicine and Science in Sports and Exercise, 19*, 557–563.

Meredith, C. N., Zackin, M. J., Frontera, W. R., & Evans, W. J. (1989). Dietary protein requirements and body protein metabolism in endurance-trained men. *Journal of Applied Physiology, 66*, 2850–2856.

Miller, J. P., Pratley, R. E., Goldberg, A. P., Gordon, P., Rubin, M., Treuth, M. S., Ryan, A. S., & Hurley, B. F. (1994). Strength training increases insulin action in healthy 50- to 65-yr-old men. *Journal of Applied Physiology, 77*, 1122–1127.

Murray, M. P., Duthie, E. H., Gambert, S. T., Sepic, S. B., & Mollinger, L. A. (1985). Age-related differences in knee muscle strength in normal women. *Journal of Gerontology, 40*, 275–280.

Nelson, M. E., Dilmanian, F. A., Dallal, G. E., & Evans, W. J. (1991). A one-year walking program and increased dietary calcium in postmenopausal women: Effects on bone. *American Journal of Clinical Nutrition, 53*, 1304–1311.

Nelson, M. E., Fiatarone, M. A., Morganti, C. M., Trice, I., Greenberg, R. A., & Evans, W. J. (1994). Effects of high-intensity strength training on multiple risk factors for osteoporotic fractures. *Journal of the American Medical Association, 272*, 1909–1914.

Pratley, R., Nicklas, B., Rubin, M., Miller, J., Smith, A., Smith, M., Hurley, B., & Goldberg, A. (1994). Strength training increases resting metabolic rate and norepinephrine levels in healthy 50- to 65-yr-old men. *Journal of Applied Physiology, 76*, 133–137.

Province, M. A., Hadley, E. C., Hornbrook, M. C., Lipsitz, L. A., Miller, J. P., Mulrow, C. D., Ory, M. G., Sattin, R. W., Tinetti, M. E., Wolf, S. L., & Group, f. t. F. (1995). The effects of exercise on falls in elderly patients: A preplanned meta-analysis of the FICSIT trials. *Journal of the American Medical Association, 273*, 1341–1347.

Ravussin, E., Lillioja, S., Anderson, T. E., Cristin, L., & Bogardus, C. (1986). Determinants of 24-hour energy expenditure in man. *Journal of Clinical Investigation, 78*, 1568–1578.

Roberts, S. B., Young, V. R., Fuss, P., Heyman, M. B., Fiatarone, M. A., Dallal, G. E., Cortiella, J., & Evans, W. J. (1992). What are the dietary energy needs of adults? *International Journal of Obesity, 16*, 969–976.

Scheibel, A. (1985). Falls, motor dysfunction, and correlative neurohistologic changes in the elderly. *Clinics in Geriatric Medicine, 1*, 671–677.

Seals, D. R., Hagberg, J. M., Hurley, B. F., Ehsani, A. A., & Holloszy, J. O. (1984a). Effects of endurance training on glucose tolerance and plasma lipid levels in older men and women. *Journal of the American Medical Association, 252,* 645–649.

Seals, D. R., Hagberg, J. M., Hurley, B. F., Ehsani, A. A., & Holloszy, J. O. (1984b). Endurance training in older men and women: cardiovascular responses to exercise. *Journal of Applied Physiology: Respiration, Environmental and Exercise Physiology, 57,* 1024–1029.

Sinaki, M., McPhee, M. C., & Hodgson, S. F. (1986). Relationship between bone mineral density of spine and strength of back extensors in healthy postmenopausal women. *Mayo Clinic Proceedings, 61,* 116–122.

Snow-Harter, C., Bouxsein, M., Lewis, B., Charette, S., Weinstein, P., & Marcus, R. (1990). Muscle strength as a predictor of bone mineral density in young women. *Journal of Bone Mineral Research, 5,* 589–595.

Tzankoff, S. P., & Norris, A. H. (1978). Longitudinal changes in basal metabolic rate in man. *Journal of Applied Physiology, 33,* 536–539.

Uauy, R., Scrimshaw, N., & Young, V. (1978). Human protein requirements: Nitrogen balance response to graded levels of egg protein in elderly men and women. *American Journal of Clinical Nutrition, 31,* 779–785.

Whipple, R. H., Wolfson, L. I., & Amerman, P. M. (1987). The relationship of knee and ankle weakness to falls in nursing home residents. *Journal of the American Geriatric Society, 35,* 13–20.

WHO/FAO/UNU. (1985). Energy and protein requirements. *World Health Organization Technical Report Service.* New York: Author.

Wolf, S. L., Barnhart, H. X., Kutner, N. G., McNeely, E., Coogler, C., & Xu, T. (1996). Reducing frailty and falls in older persons: an investigation of Tai Chi and computerized balance training. Atlanta FICSIT Group. Frailty and Injuries: Cooperative Studies of Intervention Techniques [see comments]. *Journal of the American Geriatric Society, 44,* 489–497.

Wolfson, L., Whipple, R., Judge, J., Amerman, P., Derby, C., & King, M. (1993). Training balance and strength in the elderly to improve function. *Journal of the American Geriatric Society, 41,* 341–343.

Zanni, E., Calloway, D., & Zezulka, A. (1979). Protein requirements of elderly men. *Journal of Nutrition, 109,* 513–524.

Exercise, Activity, and Aging: Encouraging Words

Richard A. Marottoli

In the paper, "Effects of Exercise on Body Composition and Functional Capacity of the Elderly," Evans (this volume) makes a cogent argument for the benefits of aerobic, resistance, and balance training on muscle size, strength, and daily function, as well as ancillary benefits on bone density, insulin action, and energy metabolism. A number of studies are reviewed that describe the age-associated changes in aerobic capacity, muscle size, nutrition, and balance, as well as the mechanism by which, and extent to which, exercise training can improve these parameters and other health-related outcomes. In the process, a number of observations are made about the potential clinical and societal implications of these interventions.

In his review, Dr. Evans makes a number of key points about changes associated with aging: muscle mass and strength decrease; strength is linked to walking speed; fat-free mass and basal metabolic rate decrease, while body fat and weight increase; glucose tolerance decreases and the risk of non-insulin dependent diabetes mellitus increases. While nutrition and balance interventions are discussed, the focus of the review is on aerobic and resistance training, which contribute to the following benefits: increased muscle size, strength, and aerobic capacity; improved glucose metabolism, glucose handling, and insulin action; increased bone density, energy metabolism, balance, gait speed, and physical activity. A central message is that activity and exercise can be safe and effective, even in very old and frail individuals.

A number of additional observations may help in interpreting the review and understanding its clinical and societal implications and applicability. First is the concept of a mobility continuum, ranging from simple, elemental movements and basic activities of daily living at one end to extremes of out-of-home mobility and travel at the other. What the studies described in the review suggest is that anyone can potentially benefit from exercise, and that even small increments in performance can improve mobility in meaningful ways across the continuum. Increasing variability in task performance with age is a well-established phenomenon. Thus, if one compares performance of older and younger subjects on physical ability tasks, for instance, older subjects will on average do somewhat less well (not as strong or not as fast). However, there is a substantial overlap in performance between older and younger groups, some older persons do as well or better than many of their younger counterparts, and everyone can potentially benefit from training. This review highlights that old does not equal infirm or incompetent.

Part of the problem on an individual and a societal level is our perception of older persons. The image-is-everything concept pervades the media and advertising and contributes mightily to the public perception of aging. Well-known athletes, slender young models, or generic hard bodies pitch athletic apparel, sports drinks, cars, underwear, fitness clubs, or even hot dogs, with the desired response on the part of the viewer being cool, sexy, athletic, while older persons pitch nutritional supplements, denture cream, or a different type of undergarment where the focus is more on whiling time away or avoiding embarrassment. There are exceptions, however, with a number of athletes demonstrating athletic prowess over an extended period of time or at a relatively advanced age, such as Carl Lewis (track and field), Bonnie Blair (speed skating), George Foreman (boxing), and Paul Newman (auto racing). Unfortunately, the prevailing themes feed not only the public perception of older persons, but the perceptions of many older people, who may view themselves as too old or too frail to exercise.

Dr. Evans emphasizes that the intensity of the stimulus is the key to benefitting from an exercise program, particularly resistance training. While this is likely true, it assumes that people are actually doing the exercises. In intervention trials, the first battle is getting people to do the exercises, then making sure the exercises are of sufficient intensity to provide benefit. Motivation to start participating and to stay with the program can be enhanced by a number of factors. The relevance of the program to the prospective participants must be made clear: how will they benefit? Also, safety must be emphasized, particularly in more frail populations, with emphasis on training and observation until people learn how to do the exercises and demonstrate their ability to do them correctly. There are other potential indirect benefits to exercise, including the opportunity for socialization if group sessions are conducted. This can also go a long way to making participation fun and enjoyable.

Lastly, Dr. Evans' paper helps to broaden our perspective on the value of exercise. First, as noted above, is the idea that anyone can potentially benefit, regardless of fitness level at the start. Second, expanding on the studies described in the paper, is the concept that any type of activity (physical, social, productive) may be beneficial to health and physical/psychological functioning, leading to the possibility of an activity menu from which people could select a range of activities or exercises based on their interests and abilities. Perhaps the most important implication of all this is that it gives people the opportunity to take control of their situations and to take an active rather than a passive approach to their functional states.

There are a number of potential practical applications of the findings beyond those discussed in the paper. With regard to pedestrian safety, Langlois and colleagues (1997) evaluated older pedestrians in the New Haven Established Populations for Epidemiologic Studies of the Elderly (EPESE) cohort. They found that older pedestrians' walking speed was substantially less than the time allotted for crossing a street with a walk light. This suggests both environmental changes (to the timing of the walk lights), as well as the possibility for interventions to enhance walking speed. Dr. Evans refers to the potential benefits of exercise in reducing fall risk, citing the Frailty and Injuries: Cooperative Studies of Intervention Techniques (FIC-SIT) trials. In one of the sites, a multifactorial intervention directed at a range of risk factors (postural hypotension, sedative use, number of prescriptions, arm/leg strength, range of motion, balance, transfers, and gait) demonstrated that the number of risk factors could be reduced, resulting in a decreased risk of falls in the intervention group (Tinetti et al., 1994). Lastly, a number of studies have demonstrated that the key determinants of functional recovery after hip fracture are prefracture physical and cognitive functioning, suggesting that interventions to improve prefracture function could enhance the likelihood of recovery after a fracture occurs. In addition, a recently completed trial demonstrated that aggressive rehabilitation after the fracture could also effectively restore function, at least in cognitively intact persons (Tinetti et al., 1999). In summary, there are a wide range of clinical situations where the findings described in the Evans paper could be implemented to enhance safety and well-being.

That said, there are a number of caveats that need to be kept in mind before implementing the findings described by Dr. Evans on a larger scale. First, not every intervention works for every person, and not everyone is able or willing to do every intervention. Thus, tailoring a regimen as much as possible to the needs and preferences of an individual may have the greatest benefit. More data is needed in a number of areas: (a) the effectiveness and safety of training programs in very old and frail persons; (b) a broader range of clinical outcomes (including falls and fractures); and (c) identifying what types of interventions/training programs work best for different individuals. Cognitive impairment may limit participation or benefit, but it may be possible to find other activities that would be beneficial or specialized training may be required. Safety must be ensured and emphasized throughout the program, with supervision at least early in the training until participants are comfortable with the exercise and demonstrate competence in its performance (this will also provide encouragement and support that may enhance adherence and ultimate benefit). Evans' chapter is a valuable and effective starting point and should encourage us to find ways to confirm and expand on the studies described therein to maximize the benefit for as many people as possible, enhancing their mobility and functional status.

REFERENCES

Langlois, J. A., Keyl, P. M., Guralnik, J. M., Foley, D. J., Marottoli, R. A., & Wallace, R. B. (1997). Characteristics of older pedestrians who have difficulty crossing the street. *American Journal of Public Health, 87,* 393–397.

Tinetti, M. E., Baker, D. I., Gottschalk, M., Williams, C., Pollack, D., Garrett, P., Gill, T. A., Marottoli, R. A., & Acampora, D. (1999). Home-based multicomponent rehabilitation program for older persons after a hip fracture: A randomized trial. *Archives of Physical Medicine and Rehabilitation, 80,* 916–922.

Tinetti, M. E., Baker, D. I., McAvay, G., Claus, E. B., Garrett, P., Gottschalk, M., Koch, M. L., Trainer, K., & Horwitz, R. I. (1994). A multifactorial intervention to reduce the risk of falling among elderly people living in the community. *New England Journal of Medicine, 331,* 821–827.

CHAPTER 3

Limitations of Mass Transportation and Individual Vehicle Systems for Older Persons

Jon E. Burkhardt

OVERVIEW

The rapid growth of the oldest segment of our population is creating special transportation problems in the United States. This is because our transportation systems were not designed for a high number of elderly travelers. The limitations of the two principal modes of travel for older persons—the automobile and public mass transportation—create significant problems for older adults who are attempting to maintain a desirable level of mobility as they age.

The vast majority of United States citizens, including the eldest, rely on automobiles for their transportation. There are several reasons for this:

- First, autos offer many desirable travel characteristics for many types of persons;

- Second, in many communities other forms of transportation are not extensive, not affordable, or simply not available; and
- Third, perceptions of travel by auto have become densely intertwined with basic American values, including independence, self-sufficiency, freedom, and community involvement.

Driving one's own car is the option used by most persons in the United States today to obtain the mobility necessary to maintain their connections to society.

But the aging of our society is creating greater and greater numbers of older persons who are increasingly unable to safely operate a motor vehicle. Recent medical advances have made such significant increases to life expectancy that prospects for living longer than one can safely operate an automobile have dramatically increased for many persons. This is because the usual consequences of the aging process include an increase in functional disabilities and a reduction in the skills and abilities needed to drive an automobile (Retchin, Cox, Fox, & Irwin, 1988; Transportation Research Board, 1988; Waller, 1991). At the same time, prospects for obtaining mobility by any means other than driving oneself have not markedly improved. Furthermore, many of the same problems that lead to problems with an individual's ability to continue to drive also create problems in the ability to use mass transit services.

Several issues are important. These begin with an overview of current travel patterns for older persons and then move to projections of future travel conditions. Next, it will be useful to review some of the problems and limitations of our current travel options and to investigate alternative options. Finally, we need to consider the steps necessary to actually make improvements to our current situation.

CURRENT TRAVEL PATTERNS OF ELDERS

In terms of transportation, one of the strongest implications of the aging process is a loss of personal independence. The number of persons whose usual means of transportation is their own car declines consistently and dramatically with age; this is accompanied by increasing dependence on relatives, friends, and neighbors. Ownership of the facilities and faculties for transportation self-sufficiency also declines with age; drivers' licenses, working automobiles, and driving behavior all decline substantially with age. The youngest of elderly persons leave their houses each day for trips more frequently than those who are older, and, when they go out, they take more trips. The youngest of elderly persons also more often have more income than the eldest, making trips more affordable for them.

Travel Frequency

Among persons 60 years of age or more, those of more advanced ages travel less than those who are younger. Using information derived from household surveys of older persons in Maryland, we found that those who left home the previous day for business or pleasure declines from 91.5% of those 60 to 64 to 54.5% of those 90 and older (Burkhardt, 1994). Furthermore, those who are younger take more trips per day than those who are older; 50% of those persons 90 years and older who travel take just one trip per day; less than 31% of those persons 60 to 64 years old who travel take just one trip per day.

Travel Mode

An examination of travel mode also indicates other changes that accompany aging. Data for Maryland residents (see Table 3.1) show that persons in their sixties most frequently travel by their own car, but the reliance on the personal car decreases dramatically with increasing age. Persons in their sixties seldom rely on relatives or friends and neighbors for their transportation, but this reliance increases substantially as a person ages.

Interactions Between Travel Frequency and Travel Mode

Those older persons whose usual means of travel is their own car (75% of our sample) travel more often by any relevant measure of travel frequency: they were much more likely to have traveled on the previous day, they made more trips, and those who traveled were likely to have made more than one trip the previous day. Persons who used public transportation or those who walked made the next

TABLE 3.1 Usual Means of Travel

	Mode		
Age group	Own car %	Relative's car %	Friends and neighbors %
60–64	86.8	9.3	1.1
65–69	85.3	9.9	2.6
70–74	73.9	18.0	2.8
75–79	58.8	30.6	3.3
80–84	48.4	39.8	7.8
85–89	27.6	44.8	19.0
90+	22.0	66.7	0.0
All elderly persons	74.8	18.0	3.2

Source: Burkhardt (1994).

most trips. Persons who relied on relatives, friends and neighbors, and taxis more often took only one trip or did not travel at all the previous day. These data (see Table 3.2) indicate that limitations on travel resources have strong effects on travel frequency, thus confirming the importance of auto ownership as a key to mobility under our configurations of transportation and land use systems.

DRIVING

Currently, declines in driving begin at about age 75. Questions about driving show a large separation between those persons less than 75 years old and those 75 and older. Those persons who have valid drivers' licenses, live in households with cars in working condition, or currently drive those cars are predominantly in the younger age group. Each of these factors exhibits an extremely strong correlation with age, as shown in Table 3.3. It is the 80 to 84 age group in which the proportion of older persons whose usual means of transportation is their own car falls below 50% and the reliance on others (relatives

TABLE 3.2 Effects of Travel Resources on Trip Frequency

Travel characteristics	Usual means of travel							
	Own car	Relative's car	Friends/ neighbors	Public transit	Agency transit	Taxi	Walk	Other
Percent using this mode as usual means of travel	74.8	18.0	3.1	1.2	0.6	0.7	0.5	1.0
Travel yesterday or day before? (% yes)	90.4	59.0	57.1	86.4	41.7	77.8	0.0	61.1
Of those traveling, percent taking only one trip	20.7	44.0	50.0	21.1	16.7	60.0	42.9	72.7
Of those traveling, percent using this mode	81.8	12.8	2.2	1.3	0.4	0.3	0.5	0.7
Average number of trips by those taking trips in past 2 days	2.61	1.86	1.91	2.16	2.17	1.40	1.57	1.45
Average number of trips in past 2 days (including those persons making no trips)	2.36	1.08	1.09	1.86	1.18	0.58	1.44	0.89

TABLE 3.3   Variables Related to Driving

	Factors		
Age group	Valid driver's license	Working car in household	Do you currently drive?
60–64	90.8	94.8	93.0
65–69	88.0	92.7	91.0
70–74	76.6	90.7	80.5
75–79	66.6	81.0	72.7
80–84	57.3	75.6	62.1
85–89	37.1	64.6	49.1
90+	27.2	54.5	33.3
All elderly persons	79.5	89.0	84.3

Values shown are percent yes in that age group.
Source: Burkhardt (1994).

and friends and neighbors) nearly reaches 50%. With advancing age, the overall pattern is a strong decline in self-sufficiency for fulfilling personal travel needs.

Which Older Persons Have Transportation Problems?

Overall, 9.2% of the elderly persons interviewed reported that they had problems getting around. There are significant differences by age group. The youngest, those less than 70 years of age, least often had problems: only 5.7% of those 60 to 64 and 5.5% of those 65 to 69 reported difficulties. After that, there are substantially more problems: 11.8% of those 70 to 74, 14.7% of those 75 to 79, and 18.9% of those 80 to 84 years of age reported that they had problems getting around. Interestingly, the percent of persons with problems declines after age 84: 16.7% of those 85 to 89 had problems, and none of those 90 and over reported any transportation problems. This decline is due to other demographic factors; the highest proportions of respondents living with children, grandchildren, or other relatives (not their spouse) is highest for all age groups after age 84. Another way of looking at this is that persons in their eighties are much more likely to live alone than younger or older elderly persons; 46.6% of those in their eighties live alone, versus 18.9% of those in their sixties, 31.1% of those in their seventies, and 27.3% of those in their nineties. So it would appear that other persons are often providing for the transportation needs of the oldest elderly persons.

Which older persons have transportation problems? They are most often those persons who are in the upper age brackets, female, lacking their own transportation resources, socially isolated, in poor health, and in the lower income brackets. Persons who are already involved in social support systems more often have transportation problems; they are, presumably, obtaining some relief for their problems through the social services network.

PROJECTIONS OF FUTURE TRAVEL

As we have seen, most older Americans now travel by car to fulfill their local travel needs. Many older people drive, and most of the remainder travel as auto passengers. Current trends suggest that we may soon see significant changes in the numbers of persons who are elderly, the percent of persons who are elderly, the number of older drivers, the percentage of drivers who are older, and the amount of driving (number of trips and miles) by older drivers.

Projections of the Older Population

Current Numbers of Older Persons

According to the Census Bureau (U.S. Bureau of the Census, 1996), in 1995 there were 33,640,000 persons 65 years of age and older who now constitute 12.8% of the total U.S. population of 263,434,000. There are now 14.7 million persons 75 years of age and older; they constitute 5.6% of the population. There are 3.6 million persons 85 years of age and older, which makes them 1.4% of the population.

The Potential Growth

The Number of Elderly Persons. The numbers of older people are projected to grow dramatically. The Census Bureau (U.S. Bureau of the Census, 1996) reports that people 65 years of age and older constitute 12.8% of the total U.S. population of 263,434,000 people in 1995. By the year 2050, they are projected to be 80 million of 392 million people (20.4%). The 14.7 million people 75 and older in 1995 are projected to increase to 45.5 million people in 2050, and the 3.6 million people 85 and older in 1995 are projected to increase to 18.9 million in the year 2050. In 55 years, the numbers of people 65 and over will more than double, the numbers of those 75 and over will triple, and the numbers of those 85 and over will quintuple.

The Percentage of Elderly.   The percentages of these older age groups of the total population will also dramatically increase. The overall aging of our society will be seen in much higher proportions of older people. From 1995 to 2050, the proportion of those 65 and older will increase by 60%, the proportion of those 75 and older will more than double, and the proportion of those 85 and over will triple (American Association of Retired Persons, 1995).

Residential Locations

Elders prefer to live and age in their own community rather than in an institutional setting. The baby boomers (people born between 1946 and 1964), who most frequently inhabit the suburbs, are likely to stay there, placing different demands on transportation and service systems as elders than as young parents with children. Subdivisions built miles from services such as stores, pharmacies, and health facilities will be difficult to access for many older persons.

The elderly population is often now overrepresented in rural areas, and many rural areas have fewer transportation options than their urban counterparts. Only 55% of the rural counties in the United States have some kind of public transit service; in many of these communities, the transit services are infrequent and seldom, if ever, reach the outlying portions of these communities. The combination of the outmigration of younger segments of the population and the aging in place of those people who remain has dramatically increased the average age of the rural population in certain areas (such as central Iowa). "Nationally, the rural elderly constitute more than 15 percent of the population in the areas where they live and there are a number of states and individual counties where they make up more than 35 percent of the rural population. Moreover, the oldest old (more than 85) are more concentrated in rural areas" (Tauber, 1992, in Rosenbloom, 1996). As previously mentioned, by the year 2000, almost three-fourths of those over the age of 65 will live in suburban or rural areas in the United States, where alternatives to the automobile are scarce or nonexistent (Rosenbloom, 1993). Nonmetropolitan elderly persons are significantly more likely to be poor or near-poor than their urban counterparts (Glasgow, 1993).

Projections of the Amount of Driving by Older Drivers

Projecting the amount of driving by elderly persons is fraught with uncertainty. Based on changes to lifestyles, patterns of residential development, and driving behavior, the expectation that older drivers will drive more miles than before is probably valid. From 1983 to 1990, the total annual person miles of travel for people 65 or older increased almost 26%, in contrast to a 14% increase for the population as a whole. This overall increase in travel miles is due to a 6% increase in the number of trips and a 19% increase in the average trip length for older people. The average trip lengths for older people are coming closer and closer to that of the overall population.

Another consideration is that the number of miles driven by women is increasing dramatically. From 1969 to 1990, there was an increase of 76% in the total number of annual miles driven by women, according to the 1990 National Personal Transportation Survey (Hu, Young, & Gray, 1993).

If there is a conclusion to be drawn from these figures, it is that the amount of driving by older drivers is likely to increase significantly in the future. When this conclusion is coupled with the projected increases in the numbers of older drivers, the increase in the total amount of driving by older drivers is compounded to an even greater level.

Summary of Projections

Over the next several decades, the numbers of older drivers—people 65 and older, 75 and older, and 85 and older—can be expected to increase substantially: to at least double. If older women begin to drive in greater proportions than is now the case, the numbers of older drivers could be more than three times the current level in 50 years. The proportion of older drivers on our streets will also increase significantly. For many reasons, the amount of travel that older drivers undertake will also increase.

Our society is not yet prepared for such changes. Additional responses will be necessary to provide for the safe mobility of all of our citizens, including new kinds of vehicles, new designs for roadways, and new forms of public transportation services.

PROBLEMS WITH CURRENT TRAVEL OPTIONS

As previously mentioned, the vast majority of Americans have grown up in a culture that strongly depends on automotive transportation for mobility, and most Americans (including elderly persons) now live in communities that are not served well or frequently by public or private transit services.

Problems with Auto Travel: The Mobility vs. Safety Dilemma

When persons with diminished capabilities continue to drive, an increased safety risk is created for all members of society. But the older driver facing the prospect of reducing or terminating his or her driving (because of declining skills or for other reasons) often expects substantially reduced mobility. Such expectations lead in turn to a reluctance among these older drivers, family members, and government agencies to terminate an older person's driving privileges. Thus, the point at which older persons voluntarily give up or are forced to relinquish their driving privileges is often seen by elders and those around them as a watershed event with large implications regarding independence, self-sufficiency, and social responsibilities.

Some researchers have suggested that there may often be serious consequences for older persons when those persons cease to drive because their overall mobility will decline. Consequences that are mentioned in the literature include a loss of personal independence, social isolation, and a reduction or lack of access to essential services.

While some of these issues have been addressed by prior research efforts, no satisfactory overview has been produced that ties all of the related factors together in a comprehensive explanation of causes and consequences. Many questions remain: If an older person reduces or stops driving, how great is the loss of mobility? What other changes follow from the loss of mobility? Are there viable options to reduce the loss of mobility when a person stops driving? What lessons about personal mobility can we learn from those who have ceased to drive and those who never drove? Some of these issues are addressed in the report entitled *Mobility and Independence: Changes and Challenges for Older Drivers* (Burkhardt, Berger, Creedon, & McGavock, 1998). The sponsors of this project were the U.S. Department of Health and Human Services and the National Highway Traffic Safety Administration.

What Are the Consequences of Reducing or Ceasing Driving?

We used the literature and focus groups to determine the mobility consequences of the reduction or cessation of driving among older persons, including travel patterns and travel modes. Items such as loss of independence, loss of a spouse's independence, increased isolation, depressive symptoms, and increased financial costs have all been named as consequences of stopping driving and also of reducing driving.

We conducted a total of 12 focus groups between the months of August and December of 1996. Eighty-six people between the ages of 70 and 95 participated in these groups, 53 women and 33 men. We conducted focus groups with 33 people who had stopped driving, 45 people who were still driving, and 8 people who had never driven. Four groups each were held in Florida, Maine, and Maryland. Portland, Maine was chosen as a site primarily because of the existence of a viable alternative transportation option, the Independent Transportation Network (ITN). Salisbury, a small urban area on the rural eastern shore of Maryland, was chosen as a fairly rural area with relatively few transportation alternatives. Two sites were chosen in Pinellas County on Florida's west coast, which has a large percentage of elderly residents and contains many retirement communities. One locality contains a large number of long-time area residents, and the other was chosen because it consists mainly of people who had moved to Florida upon retirement.

Travel Patterns.   When older drivers begin to restrict their driving, they limit what they can and cannot do, where they can and cannot go. They do this by limiting the number, length, and destinations of their trips.

We already know that women tend to limit their driving more than men, and that they stop driving earlier than men do. Both men and women gradually begin to reduce the variety of destinations to which they will travel. They narrow trip purposes down to essential errands such as the grocery store, doctor's office, pharmacy, bank, and church. As one man put it, "I don't go out too much. When I do, it's to the doctors or the dentist. . . . And I go grocery shopping maybe once a week (by bus or my brother if it's more than a few things). And other places, church, I can walk to and friends that live close by, I walk."

Because of the narrowing of trip purposes, there are a variety of activities that older adults can no longer do or do only rarely. Examples of this include the library book that never gets picked up, the events that are not seen because they take place in the evening, and the work or volunteer opportunities that are missed because the location is in a difficult place to reach. When older adults stop driving or lose access to a vehicle, the ability to travel to and from a job or volunteer opportunity with any regularity is greatly hindered.

Several participants in the focus groups, particularly the ones that were still driving, practice trip chaining, scheduling their errands in consecutive order in one trip to save gas, time, parking, and energy. As one man in Florida said, "If I have three or four things to do in a week I'll put it all together and do it at one time. I don't go out as frequently. I hate jumping in my car to do something and wasting time." Trip chaining, multipurpose trip making, is a travel behavior that is becoming more common among people of many ages, including working parents.

Travel Modes.   During those years when a person is driving, the primary mode of transportation is driving oneself. When older drivers start reducing and ultimately stop driving, they try to compensate for not driving by utilizing several different modes of transportation. They may employ any or all of the following options: obtaining rides from family members and friends, utilizing public transportation or specialized paratransit, taking taxis, and walking. There are costs, either physical, emotional, or monetary, attached to each of these options. Life after reducing or stopping driving was likened to "having one's independence with quite a few limitations" by one of our focus group members. Eisenhandler (1990) found that women without access to a car were more aware of old age as a prominent feature of their identity because their ability to get around as freely as they wished was restricted.

Public Transit; Taxis; Walking: While many of the focus group participants said that they would use public transit if it were available, more convenient, and more reliable, we found that few older persons who lived in areas with public transit actually did use it or had ever used it. A few participants, on the other hand, had moved (changed homes) to be nearer to public transportation. At least two participants had relationships with a local taxi service and had off-the-record fare arrangements. Many, particularly in Florida, found it difficult to walk, either for health reasons or because it was dangerous to walk certain places due to heavy traffic and a lack of pedestrian walkways, crosswalks, and overpasses. This posed a particular problem even when an older person lived across the street from a supermarket or a mall because many of Florida's urban streets are high speed multilane streets with few crosswalks. Even in areas where a variety of transportation options are available, the number one mode of transportation for older people remains the car, preferably with them as the driver.

Rides with Friends and Families: Exdrivers prefer to control the way they travel. If a man can use the bus, he may feel more independent than if he rode in a car with a friend. By using the bus, the man chooses when and how he would get somewhere. By receiving a ride from a friend, the man goes not by his own schedule but by that of the friend. He thus feels dependent on the driver.

Asking for and accepting rides from family and friends is often difficult for an older person, particularly one raised in the tradition of independence and self-sufficiency. Some persons have thought that women may have an easier time asking for rides than men do because of the ways in which women are socialized in our society. In our focus group with people more than 70 who had stopped driving, we found feelings of a loss of independence and a loss of some control in life among both men and women, with few noticeable distinctions between the genders. Our interviewees reported that it was substantially more palatable to ask for a ride if the driver were already going to the same destination and would accept some form of payment or reciprocity.

The focus group participants discussed the fact that they disliked asking for rides and then making the driver wait while they did their shopping or had their doctor's appointment. Some participants said that they might accept a ride to the doctor's office and then take a taxi home so that no one would have to wait for them. One woman shared the story of the time she finally accepted a ride to the doctor's office from her neighbors who had been offering her rides for quite some time. She was kept waiting in the doctor's office for more than 2 hours. She felt so mortified that she would never again ask these neighbors for another ride. In fact, the neighbors have not offered a ride since that incident.

Alternative Transportation: The people in Portland who had stopped driving did appear to be somewhat more satisfied than people in the other locations with their ability to get around. Few of the participants in any of the groups enjoyed having to rely on family and friends for rides; the Portland participants seemed to feel that they were able to retain more of their independence and mobility through the use of the ITN, an alternative transportation option in Portland.

Changes, Adjustments, and Adaptations

There is a real paucity of research conducted on the effects of driving cessation. Rothe's 1994 study to determine the extent to which losing a license affects older adults concluded that the license to drive is synonymous with self-respect, social membership, independence, and quality of life. The loss of the right to drive creates a crisis in the older adult's life; that it does create a crisis supports the proposition that quality of life and personal transportation are closely related. Other research points to the automobile and driver's license as a sign of youth, power, and masculinity, positing that the loss of a license presents more of a threat to men than to women (Carp, 1971). While this is in line with the theory that women are more internally motivated and men are more externally motivated, both the men and the women in our focus groups discussed the importance of a license with passion; men and women planned to keep their license for as long as possible for identification purposes, even after they stopped driving.

For the most part, the participants in the focus groups, including the people who had never driven, did make trips for medical appointments, grocery shopping, and errands—but it was often difficult. Because it is the most difficult to obtain transportation to recreational activities without driving, most of those who have stopped driving have severely curtailed their recreation. Even for those who use public transportation and are willing to go out at night, it is still difficult to go to recreational activities as the buses stop running before programs would be finished. People who still drive but no longer drive at night experience similar difficulties. Some persons actively miss going to events like shows and going on trips, while others feel quite content staying home.

It requires a great deal of planning on the part of the older person to get somewhere if they do not drive there. A Florida woman stated that: "I live alone and don't like to depend on friends. . . . I walk to the grocery, get rides from the Red Cross to the doctor's office. The logistics are driving me up a wall. If I had to do it over again, I wouldn't give up my car. . . . " Some participants who no longer drove preferred to use taxis when they could afford it so that they could control when and how they got somewhere. One woman explained that to feel independent when she did not drive, she " . . . would have to depend on a cab. Taxi is the only way I could go if I want to be independent from my point of view."

Most of the changes experienced by the participants who had stopped driving were negative changes. For those elders who were reducing their driving, the major changes that were mentioned frequently include having to plan your life around other people's schedules and the reduction or total loss of recreational activities such as going out to eat, movies, socialization—especially at night. Some were experiencing less enjoyment of and pleasure in driving since they started to restrict their driving. It did not seem to matter whether the restrictions were self imposed, imposed by family members, or imposed by officials, such as the Department of Motor Vehicles.

Feelings of Independence

Many of the participants expressed the feeling that they had lost all or some of their independence once they started reducing their driving. They did not like having to depend on other people for rides and therefore not having control over where they went, how they got there, and when they got there. They found it necessary to cope with reduced freedom. Independence means spontaneity, the ability to get up and go where you want to, when you want to—in short, driving. Having stopped driving, they were only independent within very discrete limitations. Having to make a call or plan for the future (either immediate or far off) does not constitute independence for most of the participants.

Having viable alternative transportation options available was seen as useful, even if one does not use them, as they represent the capacity to get up and go without having to be dependent upon family and friends. Research such as that by Frances Carp (1988), and more recently, Mary Ann Thompson (1996), has shown that higher order activities, those activities that center on socialization and the mental health of a person, are important to the quality of life of the former driver. Viable alternative transportation options may be the keys to allowing those who do not drive the ability to retain the degree of socialization and recreation in their lives that they are used to.

Overall Perspectives on the Adaptation Process

The men and women in Portland who stopped driving seemed, for the most part, to be more satisfied with their ability to get around than participants in the other locations. Much of this satisfaction can be attributed to the availability of a viable transportation alternative in their community. But while the presence of a viable, accessible transportation alternative does appear to enable older persons to maintain a satisfactory quality of life once they are no longer driving, it does not appear to make the transition from driving to no longer driving that much easier.

The transition from driver to ex-driver can be seen as a multipart endeavor. First, there is the denial stage. Then there is the actual cessation of driving, the adaptation to a new status, and finally, the acceptance that one is really not going to drive again. The presence of the ITN in Portland most likely did help seniors there to adapt to a new status: ITN provides a way for people to get around without fostering the feelings of dependence that accompany relying on family and friends. Moreover, ITN most likely helps with the acceptance of this new status as well. However, the actual cessation, that act of giving up the car keys, was not made any easier despite the knowledge of a transportation option that would enable them to be mobile with dignity. We conclude that the concept of independence and what it means to an individual in his or her daily life is very important to the psychology of transitioning from being a driver to being an exdriver.

The majority of the focus group participants who were still driving were adapting to functional and environmental circumstances that caused them to limit or change their driving behaviors. Most were familiar with or had availed themselves of public transit or transportation alternatives. There seemed to be a pattern of constant adaption until they had to face the actual moment of driving cessation. Most did not want to plan for that moment, but would deal with it when it occurs. As one man put it: "The day is going to come—have to give up or cut back. Haven't thought about that day. I'll talk to other drivers then. It will be a great shock when I have to give up the car. Giving up independence."

Some elders are able to meet their basic transportation needs for grocery shopping, medical appointments and related errands reasonably well after stopping driving. These are people who live with spouses who drive, live with children or have children in the area, have sufficient financial resources to purchase transportation, are heavily involved in their religious institution, live in areas with viable alternative transportation options, are physically able to use public transportation, and have reduced their activities and their expectations to fit their present circumstances.

Travel Problems with Public Transportation

We see that automotive travel is a hard habit to break because of the nearly unfettered mobility it offers and because of the psychic and symbolic rewards that have been associated with auto travel. Mass transit services are more limited than auto travel in both the spatial dimensions of service (described as routing) and the temporal dimensions of service (described as scheduling). Thus, the first attribute of public transit is that it just is not like driving a car. Persons who are used to the high level of mobility and the psychic rewards offered by driving may find it more difficult to adapt to life without a car than are those persons who have never been drivers.

Public mass transportation—usually conceptualized as big buses—has trouble matching these and other attributes of private automotive transportation. Compared with the private auto, mass transit has these characteristics:

- **It connects fewer origins and destinations.** Many locations outside of central cities are not served at all by public transit or are served so poorly that travel to and from these sites requires multiples of the travel time required by auto.
- **It provides service at more limited times of day and days of the week.** Most mass transit operations are not available late at night, on weekends, or on holidays. Persons who wish to travel at these times will seldom be able to make mass transit connections. As more jobs shift away from the standard 9 to 5, Monday through Friday pattern, fewer and fewer work trips will be able to be accommodated by mass transit.
- **Trips may appear to be more costly on an out-of-pocket basis.** Many auto users do not realize the full extent of the costs they pay to operate an automobile because many of the major relevant costs—such as insurance, maintenance, and depreciation—are not strictly associated with the costs of one specific trip, but are spread out over many trips and are thus hidden from view. Even some specific per-trip costs, such as parking, may be subsidized by businesses and others, so that the driver may say that the trip is free. Of course, for most persons in most communities, owning and operating an auto is actually a good deal more expensive than using public transportation.

- **It requires certain levels of physical and cognitive abilities for its use.** For older persons, some of the attendant requirements of mass transit are difficult indeed or impossible: walking to the bus stop, waiting in various kinds of weather (often without shelter), climbing the stairs of the bus, maintaining balance while the vehicle is in motion, and determining when and where to exit. Many persons whose declining physical and cognitive abilities preclude the operation of a car are also unable to use public transportation.

- **It requires interaction with the pedestrian environment.** In many areas, the public environment is hostile to pedestrians. Discomfort from factors such as exposure to the elements and fear for one's personal safety among strangers are issues of great importance to many older persons. Use of public transit necessitates interacting with the public pedestrian environment and, in many urban areas, the pedestrian environment needs more amenities—and more personal safety—to attract people (especially elders) to it.

Some of the psychic travel costs and benefits may be where mass transit is at its greatest disadvantage. Most mass transit services, particularly those that operate on fixed routes and schedules, do not appear to be responsive to individual needs. Indeed, since the routes and schedules of these systems are, by definition, established on a mass or system basis—rather than on an individual basis—the lack of individual control or influence on factors such as departure or arrival times is a reality.

- **Service quality** is an area where mass transit could conceivably exceed auto travel, but service quality—on-time performance, cleanliness of vehicles, friendliness of drivers and other staff, and comfort—are areas in which numerous transit operations need improvements.

- **Flexibility** is an arena in which auto travel triumphs, both in terms of scheduling and routing.

- **Control of one's environment and activities** is an issue of increased importance. There is not a lot of control in the hands of the consumer of mass transit services. Now that we live in a

world where custom orders for food, clothing, and even computers are becoming the norm, a product that is not particularly
responsive to individual consumer preferences will be at a distinct disadvantage against products that focus more directly on
the individual consumer. Driving provides multiple options for
many components of travel—even to the extent of changing
trip destinations or trip purposes after the trip has begun.

To be sure, public transportation performs critical functions in
our society. It moves large numbers of travelers efficiently, is often
more environmentally friendly, and makes possible a density of land
use development that is highly valued by many persons. But the ways
in which our mass transit systems are currently configured do not
meet many of the travel needs of older persons.

THE POSSIBLE BENEFITS OF ALTERNATIVE
TRANSPORTATION (MOBILITY) OPTIONS

There is an obvious need to consider the benefits of mobility (and
the consequences of losing it) as a separate issue from that of owning
and driving a car. There are indeed other ways of obtaining mobility
than by driving, even though not many communities in this country
have paid much attention to them:

- Not even 20% of those persons 60 years of age and older (Burkhardt, 1994) use these other (nondriving) means as their usual
  mode of travel.
- More than 95% of the trips by elderly persons are taken in their
  own car or in someone else's car.
- For all persons 60 years of age and older, after driving, traveling
  with a relative is next most frequent, then traveling with friends
  and neighbors, then public transit, specialized transportation
  services, taxis, walking, and other means of travel.

But what if there is no someone else? If one is not a passenger
in someone else's car, the options are public transit, taxis, specialized
transportation services (often providing door-to-door services but
only for qualified clients of a specific human service agency), walking,
and miscellaneous modes (such as boats, bicycles, horseback, and

others, none of which could be expected to be satisfactory to many elderly persons).

Another alternative is, of course, to forego the trip. Since many communities lack one or more of these modal options, the choices may be so restricted that the individual simply does not travel. Furthermore, the other modes are generally more expensive on an out-of-pocket per-trip basis and are often not as convenient in terms of times of travel and destinations. It sometimes appears that some specialized transportation services are more concerned with the needs and demands of their drivers and their managers than with the needs of their customers. So the possibility of suffering a loss of mobility from not being able to drive is a very real possibility.

Adding to the difficulty of assessing the impact of alternative transportation options on decisions to reduce or cease driving is the obvious distinction between objective and subjective measures of the availability (and attractiveness) of the alternative modes within a specific locality. We find some communities where nominally transit good services are not well known or patronized by elders. There are other communities with transit services that offer fewer miles and hours of service, but these systems are more well known and highly patronized by seniors. We suspect that the level of promotion of the service (marketing) is as significant as the actual level of service offered.

There are several sites across the country where attempts have been made to interrupt the typical stream of consequences said to occur as older persons reduce or eliminate their driving. Among them are the Driving Decisions for Seniors program in Portland, Oregon, which focuses on counseling seniors, and the Independent Transportation Network in Portland, Maine, which focuses on transporting seniors using a wide range of services and payment plans. This distinction between counseling efforts and actual transportation options is one we expect to find useful. Additional transportation efforts that are probably worthy of investigation include the gypsy cabs in southeast Washington, DC; longstanding public paratransit efforts in Pittsburgh, Pennsylvania; private driver services in Philadelphia and Maine; the Senior Transportation Program in Wichita, Kansas; the new jitney services in Montgomery, Alabama; or the volunteer program in Huntsville, Alabama. Private resources should also be considered. These resources would include: limousine services, driving services, senior home care services, taxi companies, delivery services, and private transit services.

We suspect that successful interventions will be those that provide not only rides, but also provides feelings of security, independence, and dignity. Therefore, successful interventions will provide mobility and will also address the satisfactions that older persons receive from cars in addition to transportation. When older persons see retiring from driving as a positive step forward, more of them will be willing to let go of the keys to the cars. Driving Decisions for Seniors has successfully encouraged former drivers to use public transit. They do this by presenting transit use as "mastery of a complex network, with written and unwritten rules." This positive perspective allows seniors to view their own transit use with a sense of pride and a sense of ownership.

The measures that should be used to evaluate the effectiveness of alternative transportation services should include the following:

- Does it provide quality transportation?
- Does it fulfill values identified in the focus groups (ubiquity, convenience, cost)?
- Does it address basic values (independence, control, responsiveness)?
- Does it work at the macro level? Does it work at the micro level?
- Who pays?
- Who benefits?
- Is it sustainable over time?

The benefits of intelligent interventions need to be fully recorded also. These could include the overall increase in highway safety from getting high-risk drivers off the road, an elder's sense of pride from helping to make driving safer for others by ceasing to drive, the end to worries about the older driver by families and friends, and the end of fears about crashes that might result in injuries or fatalities. Some alternative forms of transportation will also provide seniors with increased opportunities for social interaction.

FUTURE RESEARCH EFFORTS

Much more needs to be known about what mobility means to older persons and what are the best alternatives to get or provide it. For many older persons of today, the reduction or cessation of driving leads to mobility losses. Furthermore, these mobility losses lead in turn to significant declines in the quality of their lives. Future research in this area should focus on at least the following:

1. *A better definition of mobility.* The usual practice of equating the number or frequency of trips with mobility is misleading because it omits considerations of real meaning to those making the trips. It is not just the number of trips that is important, but a whole range of qualitative factors as well:

   • Are the trips destined to the primary desired destinations or are less optimal substitutions being made?
   • Is there a sufficient comfort level with the significant components of the trip, such as the waiting times for pickup on both the outbound and the return trip and the time available at the destination?

2. *Measures to increase the attractiveness of public transit.* Would supportive education at the time of driving reduction/cessation increase senior use of public transport systems? What useful roles could be designed for mediating structures (e.g., schools, churches, and clubs) in transporting senior nondrivers? What incentives would maximize transit use by seniors? Possibilities include free travel, senior discounts, frequent traveler reward programs, travel companion programs (matching a senior wishing to travel with a neighbor or fellow senior so they would not travel alone), and travel information programs. Many of these incentives are already in place in different places around the country. An evaluation needs to be conducted of the relative effectiveness of these incentives and the ability of the incentives to be duplicated.

3. *The opportunities presented by innovative transportation services.* The possibilities shown by services such as the privately operated ITN in Maine or the demand-responsive public transit services offered by the Sweetwater County Transportation Authority in Wyoming indicate that high-quality services can be designed that meet the travel needs of older persons in effective ways. We need to investigate the possibility of other services, and we

also need to determine how to inspire the creation of additional
prototypes that can be widely adopted.
4. *The opportunity costs of the isolation of older citizens.* It is clear
   that some older persons have lost their ability to contribute to
   society because of their loss of mobility. The corollary is that
   our society as a whole has lost the value of their potential
   contributions. A worthy research effort would be the further
   specification of the kinds of contributions possible from our
   elders if certain levels of mobility were assured for them.

Public pressures are increasing on state driver licensing authorities, legislators, and doctors to discourage or prevent risk-prone older
drivers from continuing to drive. Comprehensive information about
the impacts of driving reduction or cessation might influence future
public policy toward license restrictions, provide steps to extend
years of safe driving by older motorists, encourage education to
influence drivers' self-regulation, and generate suitable alternatives
to driving.

CONCLUSION

Our auto-dominated society continues to create barriers to obtaining
the fruits of that society for those individuals with limited or no
access to automobiles. Just as we need mobility for persons with
disabilities, we need mobility for those who have outgrown their
driving skills. The pain of immobility may be even more acute for
those who once possessed mobility than for those who have never
had it.

We need non-auto-driver transportation alternatives. It is manda-
tory that these alternatives provide two features: the physical mobility
to safely afford real connectedness with community opportunities
and the consummately American psychic rewards now associated
with auto ownership—independence, self-reliance, and a sense of
dignity and self-worth.

Mobility can be considered the link to life for persons of any age.
According to our focus group participants, mobility means freedom,
independence, and control over one's own life. We have shown that
the need for mobility poses a dilemma for older people: do they

risk compromising their own safety and that of others to maintain their mobility, however limited it is; or do they stop driving, recognize they will have a lower level of mobility and determine to get around as best they can. We need public policies that address enhanced and appropriate levels of senior mobility.

These public policies should be founded on the maintenance of senior independence to the optimum extent feasible. As Waller (1991) has written,

> Although it is commonplace to complain about older drivers, it is essential that society recognize the value of older drivers' meeting their own transportation need for as long as possible. This value extends well beyond the older drivers themselves. Society benefits in at least two major ways: facilitation of the driving task for all roadway users and reduction of the transportation burden. However, when older persons can no longer drive with reasonable safety, it is essential that their transportation needs be addressed in a coordinated manner.

The public policies need to be comprehensive and integrated. They should be designed to reduce dependency on driving as the sole means of mobility. Other thoughtful and feasible options should be provided through a combination of coordinated transportation and land use policies. They should be designed to help older people monitor their own driving behavior. Policy objectives should: (a) allow older people to maintain their mobility through driving as long as they can do so without posing a safety risk for themselves and others, and (b) offer other mobility options for those whose driving skills are not adequate for driving. To achieve these objectives, we need to maximize transportation options, develop integrated land use planning, and enlist the assistance of related professions.

ACKNOWLEDGMENTS

Some of the concepts in this paper are derived from a research project performed pursuant to a cooperative agreement with the U.S. Department of Health and Human Services (DHHS), under the auspices of the Joint USDHHS/USDOT Coordinating Council on Human Service Transportation, with additional funding provided by the National Highway Traffic Safety Administration (NHTSA). The report resulting from that project is entitled *Mobility and Independence: Changes and Challenges for Older Drivers*. The author wishes to thank persons involved in that project for their insights and assistance, including Dianne McSwain of DHHS and John Eberhard of NHTSA for their significant guidance and assistance in this project. Lois Albarelli of the Administration on Aging and Doug Gurin of NHTSA also provided reviews and assistance. Michael Creedon and Katherine Freund were consultants to this project and provided key inputs into our conceptual design and focus group tasks. At Ecosometrics, Arlene Berger and Karen Burkhardt helped conduct and interpret the focus groups, and Adam McGavock provided statistical analyses. The opinions and conclusions expressed are solely those of the author and should not be construed as representing the opinions or policies of any agency of the federal government or of any other individual.

REFERENCES

American Association of Retired Persons. (1995). *A profile of older Americans*. Washington, DC: Author.

Burkhardt, J. E. (1994). *Transportation needs and problems among the elderly*. Bethesda, MD: Ecosometrics.

Burkhardt, J. E., Berger, A. M., Creedon, M. A., & McGavock, A. T. (1998). *Mobility and independence: Changes and challenges for older drivers*. Bethesda, MD: Ecosometrics, Incorporated.

Carp, F. M. (1971). On becoming an exdriver: Prospect and retrospect. *The Gerontologist, 11,* 101–103.

Carp, F. M. (1998). Significance of mobility for the well-being of the elderly. *Transportation in an Aging Society: Improving Mobility and Safety for Older Persons* (Vol. II: Technical Papers). Washington, DC: Transportation Research Board, National Research Council.

Eisenhandler, S. A. (1990). The asphalt identikit: Old age and the driver's license. *International Journal of Aging and Human Development, 30*(1), 1–14.

Glasgow, N. (1993). Poverty among rural elders: Trends, context, and directions for policy. *The Journal of Applied Gerontology, 12*(3), 302–319.

Hu, P. S., Young, J., & Gray, C. (1993). *1990 NPTS databook: Nationwide personal transportation survey* (Vol. I). Washington, DC: Oak Ridge National Laboratory for the Federal Highway Administration.

Retchin, S. M., Cox, J., Fox, M., & Irwin, L. (1988). Performance-based measurements among elderly drivers and nondrivers. *Journal of the American Geriatrics Society, 36,* 813–819.

Rosenbloom, S. (1993). Transportation needs of the elderly population. *Clinical Geriatric Medicine, 9,* 279–296.

Rothe, P. J. (1994). *Beyond traffic safety.* London: Transaction Publishers.

Tauber, C. (1996). In Rosenbloom, S. (Ed.), *Understanding the influence of older driver disability on mobility and quality of life.* Washington, DC: Government Printing Office.

U.S. Bureau of the Census. (1996). *65+ in the United States.* Washington, DC: Government Printing Office.

Thompson, M. A. (1996). *The older person as a former driver: Quality of life, mobility consequences and mobility adaptation.* Unpublished doctoral dissertation. Columbia University, New York.

Transportation Research Board. (1988). *Transportation in an aging society* (Vol. I: Committee Reports and Recommendations). Washington, DC: National Research Council.

Waller, P. F. (1991). The older driver. *Human Factors, 33*(5), 499–505.

Social Structures and Processes in Public and Private Transportation

Harvey L. Sterns and Ronni Sterns

Older adults, as a result of necessity or preference, want to maintain the independence and convenience of traveling by automobile. Regardless of race, ethnicity, gender, or rural/urban residential location, the vast majority of trips by elderly persons are made in a private vehicle. About 75% of adults aged 65 and above are licensed to drive, and when they are not driving themselves, they often rely on rides from family members and friends (Rosenbloom, 1993; U.S. Department of Transportation, 1993).

Unless there is compelling evidence to the contrary, older adults should be encouraged to maintain their lifestyle and activities, including driving. However, we can expect that if a person lives long enough, at some point physiological changes and risks associated with diseases common in older persons may have an impact. For example, changes in visual capability, loss of cognitive ability or other major changes in health may alter the older adults' performance levels of critical skills needed for driving (Reuben, Silliman, & Traines, 1988; Seo & Takamiya, 1996).

Dr. Burkhart (this volume) presents compelling evidence for the transitions that many older adults will face as they outlive their driving skills. There is no doubt regarding the importance of automobile ownership as a key to mobility and feelings of freedom of movement. A major concern is the transition from driving to nondriving status. Often, this transition is complicated by the lack of transportation alternatives that meet the physical and emotional needs of current and potential older riders. The problem is clearly most acute in rural and suburban areas with limited or no public transportation services. In this chapter we will report on our research and experiences with the role of family and friends in driving cessation, and with the development of new alternative transportation services (Lifespan Associates, Inc, 1996; Nelson & Sterns, 1993; Nelson & Sterns, 1996; Sterns, Nelson, Sterns, Fleming, Brigati, McCleary, & Stahl, 1996; Sterns, Sterns, Aizenberg, & Anapolle, 1997).

Previous transportation research has often focused on finding predictors of unsafe driving behavior among aging drivers and how to keep older drivers on the road in the face of declining capabilities. These research results indicate that older adults who give up driving also give up much independence and participation in activities away from home. Such individuals frequently experience reductions in quality of life and life satisfaction (Burkhart, this volume; Rosenbloom, 1993; Thompson, 1996). A few studies, some discussed in this volume, have addressed developing realistic transportation solutions to meet the travel needs of older drivers when driving is no longer an option, by choice or by necessity.

FAMILY AND FRIENDS CONCERNED ABOUT AN OLDER DRIVER

The National Highway Traffic Safety Administration (NHTSA) funded a series of studies between 1995 and 1997 to assess the feasibility of involving family and friends in assisting unsafe older drivers to modify or stop problem driving behaviors. One project (H. Sterns, et al., 1997) involved completing a series of six focus group discussions to understand issues, problems, and potential solutions among family and friends, as well as professionals. Focus groups with a total of 50 panelists were conducted in 1996 in St. Louis,

Missouri and Akron, Ohio. Three groups were conducted among family members, two among friends and age peers, and one among professionals. Virtually all expressed concern for the safety of a specific older driver. Groups among family and friends were further divided into females and males to gain an understanding of gender differences that may exist.

Intervener's Characteristics

Overall, women were most concerned about the safety of the older drivers and others on the road, while men were more vocal about issues related to the freedom of driving and relinquishing that freedom by giving up driving. Those most likely to intervene to help the problem older driver modify or stop driving expressed the strongest concerns and caring for the older driver—generally the same individuals who were likely to become caregivers or decision-makers for caregiving. Interveners were most likely to be a spouse or an adult child of an older driver.

Awareness and Observation of Functional Limitations

Virtually all family members and friends were able to recognize unsafe driving behavior among the elderly person of their concern. While many family and friends associated unsafe driving with specific medical conditions, many others did not do so. The common denominator for discussing impairments was functional, rather than related to a specific medical condition or diagnosis. Further, relatives seemed to recognize signs of impairments well before a triggering incident or medical diagnosis occurs. Some potential interveners were faced with family members who refused to go to a physician. These findings suggest that family and friends of problem older drivers need information about aging and functional impairments, early signs of medical conditions that would impair driving performance, and recognizing the signs of dangerous situations.

Identification of At-Risk Driving

Family and friends characterized unsafe driving among older adults as forgetfulness, confusion, bad judgment, not following the rules of the road, inability to see where they are going, and aggressive driving. Indicators of unsafe situations were an accident; new dents and dings on the older driver's car; police, neighbors, friends or others calling family members about the driving problem; and the family member's or friend's observing the unsafe driving while a passenger. Although most family and friends reported a change from relatively safer driving to unsafe driving, a few noted unsafe driving over much of the family member's lifetime. Interestingly, family members, friends, and professionals agreed that unsafe older drivers also had noticeable impairments in the performance of other daily activities. Results indicate that family and friends could be encouraged through social marketing to look for signs of unsafe driving, along with other indicators of functional impairments, and to recommend that the elder undergo a driving assessment by qualified personnel. Findings also suggest that geriatric assessment clinics and social service agencies that often deal with caregivers should consider establishing driving assessment clinics to assist older adults and families in making safe driving decisions.

Involvement in Driving Modification and Cessation

Many problem older drivers, on their own, had already limited their driving to daytime, certain kinds of traffic, and driving only in good weather. Some interveners had suggested driving modifications to their unsafe older driver. A few believed their problem older driver paid lip service to their suggestions for modifications. A few others said their problem older driver would not stop driving. Older family members and age peers both reported self-modifications. Some age peers also reported they were anticipating and planning for the time when they would no longer drive.

Ability of Family Members and Friends to Intervene

A number of family members and friends had tried to intervene to get the problem older driver to modify unsafe driving behavior or stop driving. Most who had success in intervening did so on their own, generally by removing the car keys or the car. Only a few had the support of a physician. None had the support of the police or department of motor vehicles, although some had tried, and still others would have liked these authorities to have helped.

Although interveners wanted and expected the support of physicians, the police, department of motor vehicles, and lawmakers in their intervention attempts, this support was often lacking. Physicians did not always agree with family members about the seriousness of the problem. Given the lack of social norms about driving cessation and the strength of cultural norms for independence and mobility, the police and department of motor vehicles often missed opportunities to intervene in the interest of public safety. It appears that physicians, police, and others in a position to protect public safety need to be informed about how to recognize impaired drivers, assist family members in their interventions, support legal efforts to get unsafe drivers off the roads, and advocate for public safety when independence and mobility become a threat to others.

Levels of Family Functioning and Care-Giving: Motivations and Barriers to Intervention

Although intervention is difficult, at best, for those who intervened or potentially will, it appears that interveners are generally able to cope with most family interactions and relationships. This ability to cope, along with a strong concern for safety and feelings of responsibility, seems to provide interveners with the motivations they need to intervene. Only a few would not be able to intervene. In these instances, the family member or friend did not define unsafe driving as serious enough for intervention at this time or was not able to cope with the perceived consequences of intervention and driving cessation. Conflicts over the child guiding the parent and guilt in intervention; dependence on the family member or friend by the older driver for rides; and family members being too busy to provide rides served as barriers to intervention.

These findings suggest that a social marketing campaign to remove unsafe drivers from the roads may help some of those less able to cope with an elder's impairment. Findings also suggest that social service agencies may increase their client base through outreach efforts to assist families and older adults early in the impairment process when the elder is still driving. Additional opportunities exist for transportation providers to target older adults who may be transitioning to driving cessation. Older adults may drive themselves for some trips but use public transportation services for others. There may be times when transportation services are more convenient.

Fear of Meddling

Fear of meddling appeared to be a minor concern among family and friends. Most family members said they want to be told by friends, neighbors, coworkers, or others about an older relative's unsafe driving. Most age peers stated that family members should be responsible for intervening, rather than friends. Most family and friends said they would tell the at-risk driver, the family, or authorities about the elder's unsafe driving. A few mentioned that they did not want to stick their nose in someone else's business. Only one relative, a daughter-in-law, expressed the belief that she was not a close enough relative to intervene and consequently left that task to her husband and his sister. A number of friends discussed their intervention on behalf of others, not all of which resulted in success. A few family members spoke negatively about nonrelatives who could have intervened but chose not to.

Alternative Transportation

Many panelists were aware of alternative transportation, including public fixed-route and demand responsive bus services, the new Metro Link train service in St. Louis, church and organization services, and taxi cabs. Most panelists said they would encourage their older relatives to use these alternatives, especially if the services met their travel needs. Some perceived current services to be inadequate to meet those needs. A few panelists said they or the older family member now use these alternatives. A few others said they would not let their older relatives use public transportation. Most agreed that public policy initiatives should improve transportation alternatives so that older adults now and in the future will be able to give up driving more readily with the knowledge that they will remain independent and mobile. This finding suggests that public transportation may be a viable alternative to driving one's own car when the service is perceived as meeting riders' needs.

Use of Community Supports

Many panelists mentioned going to their physician for help. Because a number of panelists were recruited with the assistance of the Alzheimer's Association using their client base, it is not surprising that the most frequently cited community organization resource in St. Louis was the Alzheimer Association. While this agency provides support for driving cessation for older adults as well as family members, it appeared that unsafe driving may not be the primary reason family members first go to this agency for help. However, family members found a great deal of support at this agency through attending support groups and getting information related to the disease and ideas for intervention. Generally, those affiliated with the Alzheimer Association mentioned contacting the police or department of motor vehicles for help. No one mentioned using another social service agency for help in driving cessation. Only one family member mentioned going to a driving assessment clinic. She and her husband went to a driving clinic 5 years earlier, when her husband, the at-risk older driver, perceived he was experiencing memory loss. He continued to go periodically for testing and passed the driving assessment test for a number of years before it was recommended he stop driving.

No one mentioned being aware of or going to a volunteer organization for assistance in intervention. Further, professionals believed that there are few resources for older drivers and families related to safe driving decisions. Professionals also document their unmet needs for information and education tools for themselves and for distribution to family members and at-risk older drivers. Results suggest that the physician is the most frequent contact for issues related to safe driving. Results also indicate that volunteer groups that support safe driving decisions may be particularly valuable as a resource, provided these are guided and facilitated by qualified personnel. Ideally, community resources should have the ability to refer family and friends to a regional driving assessment clinic.

Willingness to Report

Most discussants in Missouri and Ohio did not appear to have a good knowledge of how to report a problem driver to state authorities. Those who had tried to report a driver for a retest or a license revocation learned there were no procedures for follow-up to correct the problem driving behavior in these two states. Except for those affiliated with the Alzheimer Association, most St. Louis panelists were unaware of pending legislation that would permit reporting in Missouri.

About two thirds of panelists said they would be willing to report a problem older driver to state authorities. Several had tried to report to the department of motor vehicles for retesting or inquire about procedures for getting a license revoked. With no reporting regulations in Missouri or Ohio, these attempts to notify state authorities did not result in positive action. A number had also tried to enlist the help of a physician. While a few had success, others did not. The remaining third of family and friends hesitated to report. Most panelists believed reporting was a last resort, to be used when all else has failed. Those who were reluctant to report even as a last resort were concerned about lack of anonymity and confidentiality for the reporter and worried about possible revenge and retribution. A few others said they believed their elder driving was not yet bad enough. A few others were unsure they would be able to determine when the elder unsafe driving would be really bad. Still others were fearful that reporting would lead directly to license revocation without a hearing or retest. These findings indicate a willingness to report among family members, especially when their own interventions have not succeeded. Results also suggest family members prefer to report under conditions of anonymity and confidentiality.

Readiness to Intervene

Focus group results reflect issues present in the readiness to change literature that indicate people with a problem behavior won't stop the behavior until they are ready to do so. Prochaska, Norcross, and DiClemente (1994) discuss the process of changing problem behaviors for people who behave in undesirable ways. Research results reveal stages in the change process that those with problem behavior must undergo for change to occur. Before change can occur, the problem behavior must be recognized. Precontemplation is the stage prior to problem recognition. This stage represents a denial of unsafe driving behaviors with resistance to modifying or stopping unsafe driving. During the succeeding stage of contemplation, the at-risk driver reevaluates the driving situation. The next stage is one of action in which at-risk driving may be substituted for safe driving practices or driving cessation. During the maintenance stage, problem drivers either practice safe driving or do not drive at all, but return to unsafe driving at some time. In the final stage, termination of unsafe driving results in driving cessation. Panelists indicated through their discussions that they, as well as the problem older driver, must be ready to change for the intervention or driving cessation to occur.

Conditions Conducive to Intervention

Focus group results reveal that the family members and friends who are most likely to intervene display at least one or more of several characteristics. They believe the older driver is in imminent danger to themselves and others on the road. They believe they have a responsibility for and to the older person and will most likely be the primary or secondary caregiver when the elder needs more assistance. They are able to make decisions for the elder good, over the elder's objections. They are able to overcome any feeling of disrespect or guilt. They have the support or at least the tacit approval of other family members. They are willing to provide or secure transportation when the elder stops driving. They perceive alternative transportation exists. They attend support groups dealing with functional disabilities or caregiving. They have the support of the physician, law enforcement personnel, and the department of motor vehicles for reporting and retesting.

Family and friends who are most likely to intervene feel both a social responsibility for public safety was well as a responsibility in caring for the problem older driver. Interveners are themselves able to make decisions and belong to families who are also capable of decision making. Interveners also are willing to engage in increased care giving through providing some or all of the unsafe driver travel needs. The presence of alternative transportation is a factor for some in their willingness to intervene, as is participation in a support group.

PERSPECTIVES ON TRANSPORTATION MODES: A NEW FRAMEWORK FOR ANALYSIS

At every level of capability, older adults desire to maintain independence, decision-making, and choice. Traditionally, transportation choices have been studied in the framework of a transit-centered continuum, which emphasizes the modes of transportation. This bipolar continuum begins with drivers of a private vehicle, considered by transportation planners to be most desirable, hence providing the greatest independence, and ends with riding a public fixed route bus or train, considered by transportation planners to be the least desirable, hence resulting in the greatest degree of dependence (Figure 3.1). By placing private and public transportation modes on the same continuum, the transit-centered approach negates the importance of an individual's independence and decision-making capabilities inherent in choosing public modes. Further, the approach does little to recognize or support those older adults who use more than one mode to travel.

By emphasizing the bipolar anchors of personal independence and dependence instead of discrete points along the continuum, gerontologists offer another way to consider decisions about using transportation modes.

This person-centered approach recognizes the relationship between an individual's capabilities and the environment in which those capabilities must fit and leads to a categoric division in assessing degrees of personal independence in using private versus public modes. The market-centered continuum (Figure 3.2) focuses on the highest levels of personal independence and decision making available in the private modes, such as walking and driving a car, and in public modes, such as using fixed-route transportation services. In the most independent mode, public or private, the individual chooses where, when, and how to travel. In both instances, the person must display high levels of capability and independence in travel ability for system use.

The market-centered continuum emphasizes the individual user's independence of choice and action in modal use and the complexity involved in making modal choices. Research studies indicate that older adults, especially those with limited functional capabilities, do not rely on a single transportation mode for all trips. They tend to

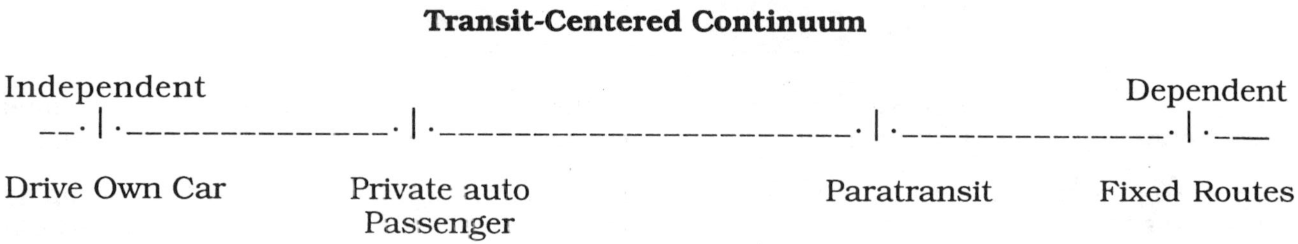

Transit-Centered Continuum

Independent ——|·|————————|·|——————————————|·|——— Dependent

Drive Own Car · · · Private auto · · · Paratransit · · · Fixed Routes
· · · · · · · · · · · Passenger

Figure 3.1 Transit-centered continuum of transportation modes.

135

Market-Centered Continuum

Independent |----------------------.|.-------------.|------------------.|.---- Dependent

	Walking	Driving Own Car	Taxi	Passenger in a Private Car
Private Mode				

	Fixed Routes	Service Routes	Paratransit Service	Ambulance
Public Mode				

Figure 3.2 Market-centered continuum of transportation modes.

choose among a variety of transportation modes for specific trips, depending in their capability for making a particular trip and mode availability. As Burkhart (this volume) points out, older adults prefer the independence afforded by fixed routes and demand-responsive public transportation to the dependence on family or friends for a ride (Nelson & Sterns, 1993; Nelson & Sterns, 1996; R. Sterns, et al., 1996).

MARKET-CENTERED TRANSPORTATION SERVICES

A 1993 Project ACTION study, sponsored by the National Easter Seal Society and the Federal Transit Administration, determined unmet transportation needs among older adults and people with disabilities in Westmoreland County, Pennsylvania and Portage County, Ohio. An additional goal of the research in these two mostly rural counties with urban population centers was to solve the problem of unmet needs by finding public and private solutions to travel problems. A total of 94 people, one third of whom were age 65 or more, kept travel diaries for a 1-week period. Public transportation was available to over half (53%) of those who completed that the travel diary. Fifty-six percent of all respondents reported that they chose both private and public (fixed-route or paratransit) modes for all trips away from home. An additional 18% used public modes only; 10% used only private modes (Lifespan Associates, 1993). It is apparent that many older adults can and do meet their transportation needs through both public and private modes. However, public modes must meet their physical and emotional travel needs and wants.

Between 1993 and 1995 the Administration on Aging funded a demonstration project in Portage County, Ohio to deliver new fixed-route, route-deviation, and demand-responsive public transportation services to low-income elderly persons in urban areas. Additional transportation services were also targeted to the rural elderly population. The new services were designed to improve transportation services to older adults through expansion of services available to the general public. Service delivery grew over the 2-year period from zero rides to completing over 6,000 rides per month.

Results of the Project ACTION study served as baseline information in the development of market-centered and person-focused transportation services. The services were evaluated and improved at regular intervals throughout the project demonstration period. Evaluation methods included focus groups, on-board and telephone surveys with older adults and other community residents, and discussions with social service agency staff and community leaders. Findings were used to increase levels of customer satisfaction and improve service design and delivery. Shared-ride demand-responsive and route-deviation services were most popular, with almost 1,300 registered riders. More than half of registrants were over age 60 (Nelson & Sterns, 1996).

The public transportation services contributed importantly to the mobility and independence of its riders. A telephone survey was completed among 205 registered riders to gauge changes in travel patterns that may have occurred before and after services became available. Riders were asked about the kind of transportation they used most often. By the end of 1995, the average rider traveled more frequently than before registering for services and rode with family and friends less often. Before service availability, 52% of respondents generally traveled with a friend or relative. After the first year of service, about 38% generally traveled with a friend or relative, while 37% of shared-ride and 16% of fixed-route riders most often traveled using new public transportation services.

Individuals who used the new public transportation services were asked how often they use these services. People who said they used the services always or frequently increased from 36% to 47%. People who had registered but never used the new services dropped from 35% at the end of the first year to 19% at the end of year 2. This result indicated that people with other transportation choices were occasionally choosing the new public transportation services instead of other ways to travel. The frequency of use increased significantly among older adults with disabilities—up from 7% after 12 months of service to 15% after 24 months of service.

Survey respondents were also asked whether they felt more independent, about the same, or less independent since registering for public transportation bus services. For all services provided, at all ages and ability levels, survey respondents felt more independent after the services became available. Older adults (aged 60 or more) felt somewhat more independent than those who were under age 60. Overall, two thirds of shared-ride and nearly 80% of fixed-route users said they feel more independent since registering for the new public transportation services. This sense of independence was supported by the 25% of shared riders and 46% of fixed-route riders who indicated they now travel away from home more frequently since public transportation services became available. These results continue to demonstrate that older adults will use public transportation when those services meet their needs.

Service Routes

Transportation research carried out in the analytical framework of the market-centered continuum results in outcomes conducive to developing transportation services that older adults will use and also encourages the development of new transportation services to meet varying levels of functional capabilities, independence, and decision-making. An example of new service development, route deviation, and service routes provide an alternative to fixed routes, which demand high levels of personal independence and functioning, and to demand-responsive, door-to-door services, which are often reserved for those with functional limitations, frailty, and greater dependency.

Providing transportation in neighborhoods, service route vehicles are sometimes accessed in less than 24 hours, through a phone call to the transportation provider, can be boarded closer to the rider than a fixed-route bus stop, and offer drop-offs at specific destinations by request. Service routes work well for those who are unable or choose not to walk more than a block to a bus stop but who want or need more challenges than those provided by door-to-door services.

Service routes were pioneered in Sweden about 15 years ago to increase independence among older adults and people with disabilities. Low-floor buses are often used to enhance independence in getting on and off the bus. While some communities in the United States, such as Madison, Wisconsin experienced disappointing ridership levels with service routes, in Akron, Ohio use of service routes has surpassed use of door-to-door transportation in neighborhoods where both services are available. Low ridership on service routes elsewhere has been attributed to a lack of meeting riders' stated transportation needs (R. Sterns, et al., 1996; Stahl, 1992).

Transportation Coordination

Through the coordination of transportation services, communities have found ways to meet the travel needs of residents, including older adults, people with disabilities, and individuals with low incomes. By coordinating the transportation services provided by transit authorities, social service agencies, and private providers, needs can be met more effectively and efficiently. However, there has been a lack of consensus on a definition. Coordination is typically defined in broad terms. It involves elements such as the sharing of vehicles and other resources; joint use arrangements; and centralized operation, dispatching, and scheduling. It is up to the service providers, community leaders, and key stakeholders of an area to define for what coordination will be.

Project ACTION funded an effort to develop model transportation coordination procedures (Nelson, Sterns, Antenucci, & Goodwin, 1998). These procedures were developed based on the premise that local officials need to be intimately involved in the discussion and debate about how transportation services in their area can be improved. Local officials and key leaders need to work collaboratively to determine the role that coordination of transportation services can play, and the form that transportation coordination should take. The process of local collaboration and decision making is critical for addressing difficult issues, weighing the strength of positive and negative elements, and building a consensus for coordination and change to achieve better outcomes for public transportation systems and the customers that they serve (Nelson et al., 1998).

It is necessary for an individual or group responsible for coordinating transportation services to bring together key leaders and stakeholders to work through the process of collaboration and consensus building. Leaders and stakeholders should assess the responsiveness of current services to public needs; assess the extent and quality of services provided; identify potential markets and opportunities; identify the area's unmet travel needs; examine relationships between public, agency, and private transportation services; assess the level of public and community leader support for current and improved transportation services; identify sources of public leadership support for local public funding of public transportation services; identify sources of funding for improved coordinated public transportation; determine the process to establish coordinated transportation services; identify trends that will impact public ridership in the future; and identify actions that the local area should take to coordinate transportation services (Nelson et al., 1998).

Mobility Training

The use of mobility training for older adults, an adaptation of mobility training for people with disabilities, still in its infancy, is another example of a new transportation service to help maintain independence and transportation choices (Nelson & Sterns, 1996; Nelson et al., 1998). In Mahoning County, Ohio transportation and human service agency providers have been collaborating in efforts to train older adults to use public transportation alternatives.

CONCLUSIONS

The challenge of the present and the future is to give older adults and their families options that facilitate the transition from driving to not driving. Older adults themselves, their spouses, and other family members want support from physicians, law enforcement, and departments of motor vehicles and access to evaluation centers when needed. At the same time, opportunities for evaluation and retraining can make it possible for older adults to drive longer.

Family members are able to identify unsafe driving behavior and take action to stop unsafe older drivers. Often due to a lack of alternative transportation, family members wait to take action. In some families, individuals are not able to deal with the driving cessation issue due to fear of retribution or inability to influence their older family member.

Older adults and families need to recognize that a problem may exist and to receive information to effectively facilitate the transition to nondriving. Family and friends will intervene if they feel a social responsibility and care about the problem older driver.

Alternative modes of transportation need to be considered from a market-centered continuum. Families, health care providers, law enforcement officials, and others will be much more willing to take action when mobility options are available. New transportation approaches such as service routes, coordination of service, travel training, and so forth can make mobility available to all people.

ACKNOWLEDGMENTS

This chapter contains results from several funded projects. We wish to acknowledge support from the following: Project ACTION Local Demonstration Project, 1992–1993, "Portage County, Ohio and Westmoreland County, Pennsylvania: Where Are the People with Disabilities? What Are Their Transportation Needs? What Kinds of Transportation Services Are Responsive to Their Needs?"; American Association of Retired Persons, 1993–1994, "Public Transportation in an Aging Society: The Role of Service Routes"; Administration on Aging, 1993–1995, "Integrated Transportation Services for Older Adults in Portage County, Ohio"; National Highway Traffic Safety Administration, 1995–1997, "Family and Friends Concerned About An Older Driver"; Project ACTION, 1996–1998, "Model Procedures for Coordination Among Transportation Providers." We also wish to acknowledge the contributions of our coworkers, Charles A. Nelson, Anthony A. Sterns, Rhonda Aizenberg, Jackie Anapolle, and Vincent Antenucci. The opinions and conclusions expressed are solely those of the authors and should not be construed as representing the opinions or policies of the American Association of Retired Persons, any agency of the Federal Government, or of any other individual.

REFERENCES

Lifespan Associates. (1996). *Integrated transportation services for older adults in Portage County, Ohio. Final report.* Department of Health and Human Services Administration on Aging demonstration project grant award, 1993–1995, #90-AM-0662.

Nelson, C. A., & Sterns, R. (1993). *Local demonstration project, Portage County, Ohio and Westmoreland County, PA. Where are the people with disabilities?*

What are their transportation needs? What kinds of transportation services are responsive to their needs? Project ACTION of the national Easter Seals Society and the Federal Transit Administration: Washington, DC.

Nelson, C. A., & Sterns, R. (1996). *Integrated transportation services for older adults in Portage County, OH. Final Report on the Senior Transportation Demonstration Project.* U.S. Administration on Aging. September 1993–September 1996.

Nelson, C. A., Sterns, R. S., Antenucci, V. M., & Goodwin, S. K. (1998). *Model procedures for coordination among transportation providers: The key role of local collaboration and decision-making.* Report for Project ACTION, Washington, DC.

Prochaska, J. O., Norcross, J. C., & DiClemente, C. C. (1994). *Changing for good: A revolutionary six-stage program for overcoming bad habits and moving your life positively forward.* New York: Avon.

Reuben, D. B., Silliman, R. A., & Traines, M. (1988). The aging driver: Medicine, policy, and ethics. *Journal of the American Geriatrics Society, 36,* 1135–1142.

Rosenbloom, S. (1993). Issues of concern in aging and transportation. *Elder Transit Facts.* Washington, DC: National Eldercare Institute on Transportation.

Seo, T., & Takamiya, S. (1996). Improving road environments for the aging society. *Journal of the International Association of Traffic and Safety Sciences Research, 20,* 21–28.

Stahl, A. (1992). Mobility and accessibility for elderly and disabled people in Sweden. *Journal of International Association of Traffic and Safety Sciences, 16*(2), 80–97.

Sterns, H., Sterns, R., Aizenberg, R., & Anapolle, J. (1997). *Family and friends concerned about an older driver: Final focus group report.* Washington, DC: U.S. Department of Transportation, National Highway Traffic Safety Administration.

Sterns, R., Nelson, C., Sterns, H., Fleming, J., Brigati, P., McCleary, J., & Stahl, A. (1996). *Public transportation in an aging society: The potential role of service routes.* Washington, DC: American Association of Retired Persons.

Thompson, M. A. (1996). *The older person as a former driver: Quality of life, mobility consequences and mobility adaptation.* Unpublished doctoral dissertation, Columbia University, New York.

U.S. Department of Transportation Federal Highway Administration. (1993). *Highway statistics 1993.* Washington, DC: U.S. Government Printing Office.

Into the Transportation Future

Katherine Freund

J on Burkhardt's essay (this volume), *Limitations of Mass Transportation and Individual Vehicle Systems for Older Persons,* is clearly conceived and clearly argued, well documented and well done. He establishes the demographic and travel trends that are the sources of the senior mobility problem, then explains the dilemma facing diminished capacity older drivers who must choose between safety and mobility, whether they are contemplating limiting their driving or stopping altogether. Burkhardt goes on to enumerate the inadequacies for seniors of existing mass transportation and, best of all, he provides a succinct framework with which to evaluate the effectiveness of proposed transportation alternatives.

This chapter neither restates Burkhardt's essay, nor focuses on minor differences of opinion amidst major areas of agreement. Rather, an attempt is made to move forward, into the transportation future, taking as its points of departure the operational and psychological barriers at which Burkhardt's excellent analysis of the present stops. By restating the problem in its broadest terms, this paper shows how the limitations of mass transit and the symbolic value of automobiles can be used to frame the characteristics of a future transportation solution for seniors. The Independent Transportation Network of Portland, Maine is seen as a forerunner of future transit solutions that create new kinds of mobility through the marriage of technology and consumer needs. Finally, public policy and the incentives it creates for personal and public solutions are seen as the brightest avenue for an economically sustainable transportation future for seniors.

STATING THE PROBLEM

We are a country in love with the automobile, and love, of course, is blind. For many years, planners and policy makers have properly identified many of the unintended consequences of that apparent passion: urban sprawl, air pollution, high death and injury rates, and dependence on foreign oil, to name a few. To this list we now must add the problems of an aging driver population. What happens when a large and rapidly growing segment of the population outlives the functionality of the predominant transportation system? Those who would answer this question fall into two groups: researchers and planners who cannot see past the automobile and think only of road, vehicle, and driver adaptations; and researchers and planners who cannot see past the automobile and cast their eyes longingly backward, toward the mass transportation systems of the past century, toward trains, buses, and streetcars.

Restating the Problem

What if the reason we cannot get past this love of the automobile and the problems that it causes is something even bigger than our love of the automobile? What if the private auto, which we think is the cause of our problems, is really the effect?

Perhaps we love automobiles for the same reason we love telephones, computers, and the Internet. Automobiles are another manifestation of our modern sensibility, the part of us that craves speed, immediate gratification, and above all, endless free choice of limitless options. In this construct, automobiles do not define the way we are. Rather, the way we are causes our desire for automobiles.

Now the problem may be restated. The problem is not, How do we keep people in automobiles because automobiles meet their transportation needs? The restated problem is, How do we design a transportation system that meets the needs of twenty-first century seniors? It is no surprise that this conceptualization, as Burkhardt recommends, "consider(s) the benefits of mobility (and the consequences of losing it) as a separate issue from that of owning and driving a car" (p. 116).

Turning Barriers into Opportunities

Burkhardt's essay is a well-organized discussion of everything that is wrong with mass transportation from the point of view of an older person. Public mass transportation, says Burkhardt:

- Connects fewer origins and destinations
- Provides service at more limited times of day and days of the week
- Appears to be more costly on an out-of-pocket basis
- Requires certain levels of physical and cognitive abilities for its use
- Requires interaction with the pedestrian environment
- Does not respond to the needs of individuals, in terms of service quality, flexibility, and control of one's environment and activities.

If we look at these characteristics through the lens of the restated problem, we see the characteristics of the transportation system that meets the needs of twenty-first century seniors. We also see how barriers become elements of the solution.

To meet the mobility needs of the aging population, transportation in the twenty-first century will use small, flexible vehicles, available on-demand, just like a car. No cash will change hands in the vehicle, so comparisons of out-of-pocket costs will not be apparent. The vehicle will come to the door, and it will be available evenings and weekends, as well as during daylight hours. It will go everywhere, and it will offer a high level of customer service. Seat belts will be buckled for arthritic fingers, doors will be opened for people with canes, and packages will be carried for weakened arms.

Customer service will be so exemplary, many seniors who struggle with driving in bad weather, at night, or in unfamiliar locations will choose the alternative transportation service rather than risk their safety and comfort by driving themselves. When the day comes for a senior to stop driving, the alternative transportation service will help make that transition a possibility. It isn't likely the transition will be easy, but it will be easier than it would have been without the availability of an alternative designed to suit the modern sensibility and lifestyle.

Symbolic Value of Automobiles

Burkhardt writes about more than the problems of mass transit and mobility compromises of seniors who limit or stop driving. He writes about transportation dependence—asking for rides as favors from family and friends—and about transportation independence in the form of free choice, personal control, and financial responsibility. These qualities, so readily apparent in automobile ownership, are missing entirely from mass transit, as we know it today. In these qualities—choice, control, responsibility—lives the powerful symbolic value of automobile ownership and the accompanying psychic rewards.

In literature, writers create symbols as powerful devices around which characters and actions orbit, often without awareness or understanding. The reader, however, may have insights the characters lack, and the writer knows all. The writer creates the symbol by attaching abstract, intangible feelings to concrete objects. Once attached, symbolic objects take on the power of the emotions they represent.

Cars work as symbols of independence in exactly the same way. When they are most effective as a transportation mode, automobiles provide freedom to come and go, independently, without planning, anytime of the day or night. The cars become symbols of the independence they provide. As a driver ages, however, the transportation value of the vehicle wanes. Older drivers cannot, in fact, travel any time of the day or night, because many of them cannot see at night. Nor can they travel on interstate highways, because they cannot merge with oncoming traffic. They may not be able to travel at rush hour or through busy intersections, construction zones, or unfamiliar neighborhoods. But the symbolic value of the car remains, long after the transportation it provides has become limited, disproportionately expensive, and unsafe.

Burkhardt writes about marketing and transportation. It will take far more than this simplistic marketing approach of telling consumers they should use public transit, however, to penetrate the psychology of cars as symbols and to separate seniors who can no longer drive safely from the automobiles in which they feel free. Marketing for the senior transportation services of the future must begin with a consumer product that meets seniors' mobility needs by affording them choice, control, and responsibility; from these fundamental qualities will flow such higher order associations as pride of ownership and belonging.

The Model T of the Twenty-First Century

Several times in his essay, Burkhardt writes about the Independent Transportation Network (ITN) in Portland, Maine. The ITN may be a forerunner of future transportation systems, a Model T service of the twenty-first century. Although it is still in a developmental stage, the ITN is important because it concretely demonstrates that the many service qualities and psychic characteristics previously described as essential for a future senior transportation service can be incorporated into a real-life service.

The ITN delivered its first ride in June 1995 and developed many payment and service components through the Transportation Research Board's IDEA Program (Ideas Deserving Exploratory Analysis). It did not take off, however, until August 1997, when it received a Federal Transit Administration (FTA) Deployment Grant to use the research results to develop an economically sustainable model of community-based, nonprofit transportation for seniors.

The Portland ITN uses cars and both volunteer and paid drivers to provide demand responsive, door-to-door service, 24 hours a day, 7 days a week. ITN drivers and volunteers escort seniors from the doorway of their home or ride origination to the vehicle. They buckle seatbelts, open doors, and carry packages. At the destination, they repeat the customer service process, taking care to offer the level of attention and help that will afford maximum independence for a senior customer. Seniors pay for their rides by the mile, but no cash changes hands in the vehicle. ITN customers open prepaid transportation accounts and receive a statement, once a month, debiting their prepaid account for the rides they have taken the previous month, and suggesting the amount they should advance for the next month. Prepaid accounts are a voluntary form of community support.

The benefits of mass transit are incorporated into the ITN by offering seniors a fare discount for advance scheduling and ride-share. All ride and scheduling decisions, however, remain with the senior customer, so all service quality tradeoffs with price are free consumer choices. Eighty percent of rides, for example, are voluntarily scheduled in advance, and 79% of seniors have indicated a willingness to share rides with others. The strongest indication, however, that a transportation service such as the ITN is on the right track, is the growth in rides and revenue. (See Table 3.4 and Figures 3.3 and 3.4.)

Seniors, their families, and interested members of the business and private community may become members of the ITN, just as they may join any other membership-based nonprofit organization, such as the American Automobile Association, the Nature Conservancy, or the Smithsonian. Members receive a bimonthly newsletter, birthday ride certificates, incentives for referrals, and special discounts for gift certificate purchases. The ITN has approximately 450 dues-paying members in 25 states, and over 600 seniors in the Greater Portland area registered to use the service.

Many of the day-to-day service characteristics described above are easily recognizable from the previous discussion, Turning Barriers into Opportunities. Not as easily apparent are the reasons behind such organizational features as ITN membership and the use of transportation accounts. These characteristics are designed to provide feelings of ownership and belonging. They are one attempt to capture, in a form other than automobile ownership, some of the psychic rewards that Burkhardt tells us must be addressed when we develop alternative transportation for seniors. Joining an organization that cares about your transportation needs may not be as much fun as 50 years of Madison Avenue messages about automobile owner-

TABLE 3.4 ITN ride & revenue growth, Portland service area, August 1997 to December 1998

Month	Number of Rides	Revenue
Aug 97	663	$3328
Sept 97	763	$3869
Oct 97	873	$4446
Nov 97	852	$4189
Dec 97	1038	$5223
Jan 98	960	$4647
Feb 98	1038	$4955
Mar 98	1159	$5662
Apr 98	1211	$5982
May 98	1120	$5710
June 98	1232	$6498
July 98	1201	$6246
Aug 98	1145	$5823
Sept 98	1304	$6668
Oct 98	1475	$7244
Nov 98	1373	$7011
Dec 98	1543	$7718
Total	18950	$95219

Source: Independent Transportation Network.

ship would have us believe, but it is a good first step beyond the next apparent alternative, accepting favors from family and friends.

Technology

One of the subjects Burkhardt does not address is technology. Even though that subject will be included in other chapters in this book, it is worth saying a word or two here, in the context of this discussion of the transportation future. There are countless ways to apply technology to our transportation systems. Some of the most obvious are applications to improve the safety and navigation of automobiles and applications to improve the efficiency of mass transit through electronic fare collection. Time will tell, but it is likely that such

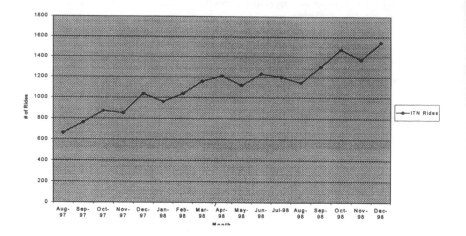

Figure 3.3   ITN ride growth, August 1997 to December 1998.

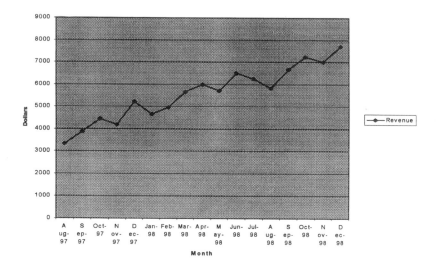

Figure 3.4   ITN revenue growth, August 1997 to December 1998.

efforts are only the first learning steps in the process of exploring the potential of computers and the information age in transportation. The best applications will occur when we synthesize new technology with what consumer needs, rather than when we impose new technology onto an existing older system with which consumers are already struggling.

At the ITN, for example, a Geographic Information System (GIS) is being used to develop a human-assisted, computerized routing and scheduling system that dispatches both paid and volunteer drivers and that calculates senior rideshare fares among customers who schedule their rides at different times and who enter and exit the vehicle at different destinations. The ITN uses GIS technology to integrate what we know about senior transportation needs into a solution that captures the senior rideshare market in a virtual community within the database. We know 79% of seniors wish to share rides. We also know that 80% of women are living alone. The technology allows them to share rides, based on common travel time, common destination, or common travel direction. They have a safe environment in which to meet other ITN customers in their community; at the same time, they are saving money for themselves, while painlessly conserving fuel and mitigating traffic congestion for society. The ITN software creates a shared ride for seniors that cannot occur without the GIS technology.

Leading with Public Policy and Planning

The greatest opportunity for leadership in alternative transportation is in public policy and planning. Policy makers can lay an invisible hand on our collective shoulder, and turn us, gently, in the direction of sustainable solutions.

The characteristics of future transportation solutions are that they must provide sufficient mobility for older people to live full lives, satisfying both physically and psychologically. The components of these future solutions are: (a) the mechanism or mode of transport; (b) the resources to pay for that mode; and (c) a plan to bring it all together. This essay has been entirely devoted to the first of these components. The second and third components are addressed through public policy.

To do nothing is always an option for policy makers, and until fairly recently, that has been the course most have taken. It is now apparent that this course will lead to an increasingly unacceptable toll of senior driver fatalities. By 2030, there will be between 24,000 and 29,000 elderly driver fatality involvements annually. Compare this to 7078 elderly driver fatality involvements and 17,126 alcohol-related driving fatalities in 1996 (Burkhardt & McGavock, 1999).

Another alternative is to publicly fund the solution. That is the justification for funding public transit; there are those who would argue that more funding for public transit will solve the transportation problem for older Americans. Burkhardt's essay makes a convincing argument that public transit, by virtue of its system and design, does not meet the transportation needs of older people. More of the same, therefore, would not be a wise use of public resources.

A third policy alternative is to regulate undesirable consequences. This is the path chosen by those who seek to test and restrict diminished capacity older drivers. Setting aside the difficulty safety activists and legislators experience trying to pass such legislation, licensing restrictions define the senior mobility problem, without necessarily solving it. The best way to understand this is to ask whether the problem will be solved if the desired policy, the testing of older drivers, is enacted and implemented. Imagine that every state has a law testing older drivers, and every bureau of motor vehicles restricts or revokes the license of every impaired older driver. Is the problem solved? The answer is, no. The diving safety problem may be solved, but the mobility problem is bigger than ever.

The fourth and final policy alternative is to provide incentives for private solutions. This alternative has never been applied to transportation for seniors, and it holds the most promise. The opportunities are almost limitless. With most Americans accustomed to spending 14 to 17% of their income on transportation, policy makers need to create economic instruments that encourage people to continue to pay for their own transportation beyond the driving years. When the day arrives and a senior can no longer drive, an incentive should be available to encourage that person to liquidate his or her vehicle and invest the proceeds in a special transportation account, instead of giving the car to a waiting grandchild or parking the vehicle in the garage and visiting it. Perhaps casualty insurance companies can be induced to provide some of a senior's last year of premium as an incentive to invest the proceeds from the sale of that last vehicle in a transportation account.

Why don't we have policy for macro-level planning for senior transportation at the societal level, just as we have social security? At the micro-level we can have policy for planning by individuals, just as we now have policies that create incentives for individual retirement accounts? In the area of employee benefits, policy makers have the power to redefine transportation dependence to allow adult children to pay for their nondriving parent's transportation with pretax dollars. These are only a few ideas. For a policy maker who wants to make a mark on the national scene, there is work here, especially if we are to create a plan that takes into account the needs of taxpayers who will be supporting Social Security and Medicare for the largest senior population in history.

Looking Forward

Developing sustainable transportation for seniors is neither mysterious nor impossible. We know it is about rides and resources, and we know we need to listen carefully to senior consumers to build a dignified and satisfying solution they will be willing to buy. We have the best technology in history at our fingertips, and we have an extraordinary array of untouched policy opportunities to explore. This is actually a great adventure. Why look back, when we can look forward!

REFERENCES

Burkhardt, J. E., & McGavock, A. (in press). *Tomorrow's Older Drivers: Who? How many? What impacts?* Washington, DC: Transportation Research Board.

CHAPTER 4

Characteristics of Motor Vehicle Crashes Related to Aging

Thomas Bryer

O ver the last several years, increased attention has been given to older drivers and safety concerns. This effort is directed toward a better understanding of crash characteristics associated with driver's age. Data used to define characteristics are primarily based on Pennsylvania Accident Record Systems and only reflect Pennsylvania relationships.

The proportion of the population over age 65 has grown significantly over the last few decades and is growing larger every day. This national trend toward an aging population is especially pronounced in Pennsylvania. In the past 40 years, the states's older population has more than doubled to the 1.8 million reported in the 1990 census. Of these, 760,000 were age 75 or older. Pennsylvania is the fourth largest state in terms of population age 65 and over, but ranks second only to Florida in the percent of its population that is 65 and over. In 1990, 15.4% of Pennsylvanians were 65 or older. Projections for the year 2010 place this proportion at 16.1%.

While the percentage of the over-65 population continues to grow, changing demographic trends also have resulted in changing transportation needs within this group. Mobility is essential to the quality of life of older people, and all trends indicate that the majority of their transportation needs into the next century will be met by the private automobile. Many of the individuals who moved to the suburbs after World War II are retiring there as well. Most people live in the same house from middle age through their older years and, increasingly, these homes are located in the suburbs. In addition, most of the trips by older persons are not into or out of a city, but between two suburban locations where population density is often too low to support transit systems. Today, more than 80% of the trips by individuals age 65 and older are made by automobile. We can expect this to increase in the future. The safety of these trips is a prime concern.

The following components will be discussed:

- General characteristics of highway crashes in Pennsylvania by age.
- More specific information on older driver crash characteristics in terms of the traditional who, what, when, where, and why question process.
- Summary of important, defined characteristics.
- Potential opportunities to impact the important characteristics.

GENERAL CHARACTERISTICS OF AGE-RELATED CRASHES

In Pennsylvania, we are fortunate that the total number of highway deaths has declined significantly in the 1990s from 1646 in 1990 to 1470 in 1996. In fact, in 1994, Pennsylvania had the lowest number of highway deaths (1,440) since World War II (Figure 4.1). However, deaths of people over the age of 65 (Figure 4.2) have remained virtually unchanged over the same time period and remained slightly above 300 annually. One of the reasons this may be occurring is that the older driving population is increasing, and older drivers are driving more miles per year. Unfortunately, we do not have any

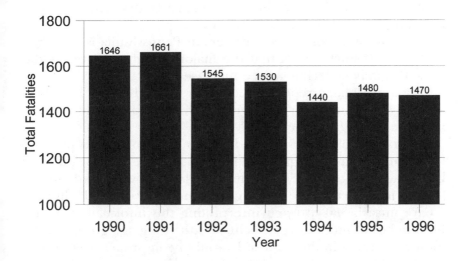

Figure 4.1   1990–1996 fatalities vs. year (includes all age groups).

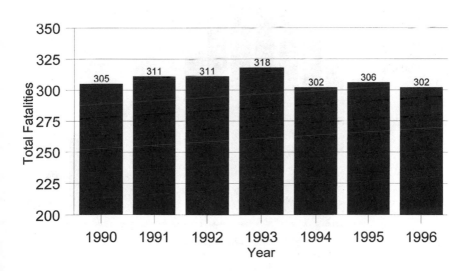

Figure 4.2   1990–1996 fatalities vs. year (includes ages 65 and greater).

reliable data to define exposure (i.e., vehicle miles driven per year by driver age) and couple it to crash data.

The distribution of licensed drivers in Pennsylvania is similar to most states (Figure 4.3) in that the majority of drivers are middle-age and numbers decline as age increases.

In Pennsylvania, a reportable crash is defined by law to involve either a death, injury, or damage to a vehicle to an extent that it has to be towed from the scene.

The crash involvement role of drivers in terms of crashes per 1000 drivers of a certain age group (Figure 4.4) is the highest for entry drivers ages 16 to 19 (80 crashes per 1000 drivers) and steadily declines to about the 70 to 74 age group and then very gradually rises.

Care must be taken when interpreting this information in that the number of miles driven declines with rising age groups and is not incorporated in these rates. It would be improper to infer that age 70 to 74 drivers (13.05 crash rate) are about twice as safe as age 35 to 39 drivers (25.52 crash rate) because each group drives at different exposure levels.

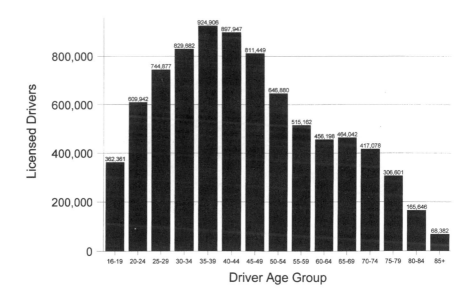

Figure 4.3   1996 licensed drivers vs. age group.

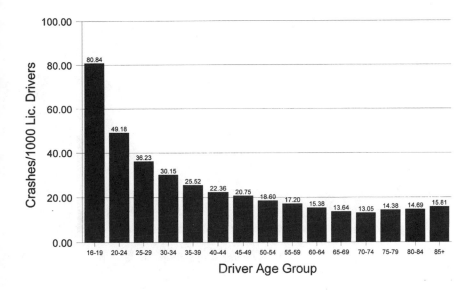

Figure 4.4 1996 driver crash involvement vs. age group (crashes per 1000 licensed drivers by age group).

The potential for drivers dying in these crashes can be expressed in terms of driver deaths per 1000 reportable crashes (Figure 4.5) by age group. Approximately four drivers die per 1000 drivers in crashes for ages 20 through 69. The potential for a driver dying then increases substantially for older groups with an approximate fivefold increase in the age 85 and above group.

The information in Figures 4.3, 4.4, and 4.5 can also be expressed in the familiar U-shaped curve (Figure 4.6), which illustrates driver fatalities per 100,000 drivers of the same age group.

SPECIFIC CHARACTERISTICS—WHO

Highway deaths can occur in three basic categories: drivers, occupants, and pedestrians (Figure 4.7). For all age groups, driver deaths is the major category but as groups age, deaths as occupants and pedestrians became almost as important.

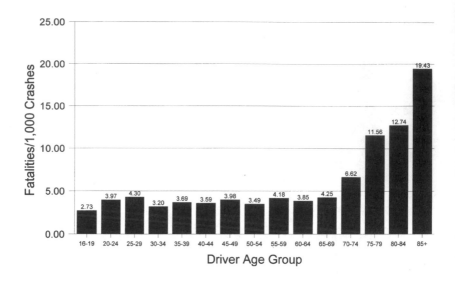

Figure 4.5   1996 driver fatalities vs. age group (per 1,000 crashes).

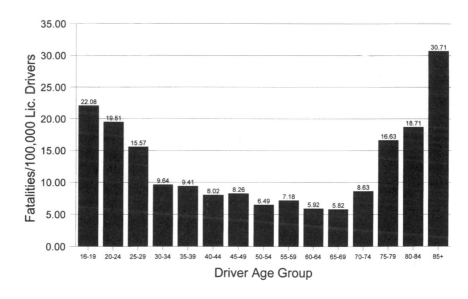

Figure 4.6   1996 driver fatalities vs. age group (per 100,000 licensed drivers).

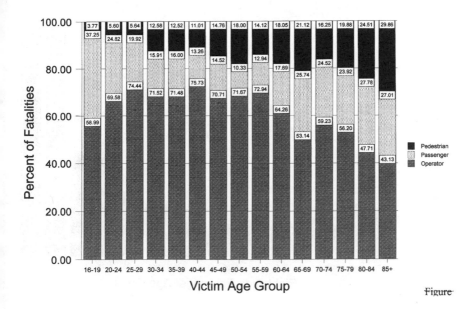

Victim Age Group

Figure

Figure 4.7 Type of fatality vs. age group (percent distribution of pedestrian, driver, and passenger fatalities).

Deaths as right-side occupants per 1000 crashes also increase with age as indicated in Figure 4.8. While there are fewer deaths as rear seat occupants and the relationships less reliable (Figure 4.9), the survivability of crashes as a rear seat passenger per 1000 crashes is better than as a right seat passenger, even though the probability of death increases as groups age.

Deaths as pedestrians per 1000 pedestrians struck also increases as groups age (Figure 4.10). Approximately one in six pedestrians over the age 80 who are struck die in crashes.

There is a tendency for a higher proportion of male drivers in crashes for both younger and older driver groups (Figure 4.11).

Out-of-state drivers comprise, on the whole, approximately 9% of all drivers in Pennsylvania crashes, but as age increases the percentage of out-of-state drivers involved in crashes decreases by age group (Figure 4.12).

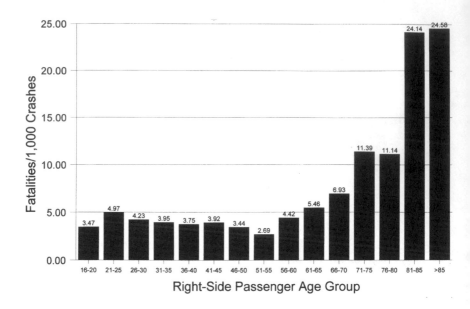

Figure 4.8 1992–1996 passenger car right-side passenger fatalities vs. age group (per 1,000 crashes).

SPECIFIC CHARACTERISTICS—WHAT

Crashes can be classified as single and multiple vehicle crashes. Approximately 95% of all multiple vehicle crashes are two-vehicle crashes. The primary types of two-vehicle crashes are rear-end, head-on, angle, and sideswipe.

Tables 4.1, 4.2, and 4.3 provide information on drivers involved in all single, two-vehicle crashes, and three or more vehicle crashes by age group. It is clear that as groups age, their proportion of all crashes diminish. Note that the proportion of two-vehicle angle crashes increases with age as head-on and rear-end decline.

Tables 4.4, 4.5, and 4.6 provide the same information as Tables 4.1–4.3 except that they contain only fatal crashes. While the proportion of fatal crashes diminish with age, it is not at the same reduction as all crashes. As an example, drivers above age 85 comprise 0.2% of all single-vehicle crashes but 1% of all single-vehicle fatal crashes.

TABLE 4.1 Single Vehicle Crashes by Driver Age

	Age groups															
	16–20	21–25	26–30	31–35	36–40	41–45	46–50	51–55	56–60	61–65	66–70	71–75	76–80	81–85	85>	Total
	1992–1996 Single-vehicle crashes/not hitting pedestrian															
Frequency	54,817	43,793	31,489	27,058	21,536	16,492	11,734	7949	5656	4410	3932	3251	2168	1213	509	236,007
Percent	22.3	17.8	12.8	11.0	8.8	6.7	4.8	3.3	2.3	1.8	1.6	1.3	.9	.5	.2	96.1
	1992–1996 Single-vehicle crashes/hitting pedestrian															
Frequency	2628	3064	2897	2630	2378	2005	1602	1233	1024	953	819	627	426	225	97	22,608
Percent	9.1	10.7	10.1	9.2	8.3	7.0	5.6	4.3	3.6	3.3	2.9	2.2	1.5	.8	.3	78.9

Note: Percentages do not add up to 100% because of small number of unknown age drivers.

TABLE 4.2 1992–1996 Two-Vehicle Crashes by Age Group

	Age groups															Total
	16–20	21–25	26–30	31–35	36–40	41–45	46–50	51–55	56–60	61–65	66–70	71–75	76–80	81–85	85>	
						Angle										
Frequency	53,783	49,355	42,530	39,712	34,945	29,345	23,320	17,559	14,209	13,689	13,048	12,053	8857	4829	1850	359,084
Row percent	14.4	13.2	11.4	10.6	9.3	7.8	6.2	4.7	3.8	3.7	3.5	3.2	2.4	1.3	0.5	96.0
Column percent	55.9	53.4	51.9	50.9	50.5	50.6	51.4	52.2	53.5	58.0	60.5	65.0	67.2	70.6	71.8	—
						Backing up										
Frequency	595	701	717	723	643	567	421	306	251	191	164	126	79	47	9	5540
Row percent	10.0	11.8	12.1	12.2	10.8	9.6	7.1	5.2	4.2	3.2	2.8	2.1	1.3	0.8	0.2	93.4
Column percent	0.6	0.8	0.9	0.9	0.9	0.9	0.9	0.9	1.0	0.8	0.8	0.7	0.6	0.7	0.4	—

(continued)

TABLE 4.2 *(continued)*

							Age groups									
	16–20	21–25	26–30	31–35	36–40	41–45	46–50	51–55	56–60	61–65	66–70	71–75	76–80	81–85	85>	Total
							Head-on									
Frequency	7799	7557	6777	6456	5748	4751	3565	2661	2032	1580	1408	1066	689	351	109	52,549
Row percent	14.4	14.0	12.5	11.9	10.6	8.8	6.6	4.9	3.8	2.9	2.6	2.0	1.3	0.7	0.2	97.2
Column percent	8.1	8.2	8.3	8.3	8.3	8.2	7.9	7.9	7.7	6.7	6.5	5.8	5.2	5.1	4.2	—
							Rear-end									
Frequency	26,558	26,576	24,525	24,036	21,578	18,176	14,043	10,135	7828	6390	5461	4223	2801	1289	464	194,083
Row percent	13.1	13.1	12.1	11.9	10.6	9.0	6.9	5.0	3.9	3.2	2.7	2.1	1.4	0.6	0.2	95.8
Column percent	27.6	28.8	30.0	30.8	31.2	31.3	31.0	30.1	29.5	27.1	25.3	22.8	21.2	18.9	18.0	—

(continued)

TABLE 4.2 *(continued)*

	Age groups															Total
	16–20	21–25	26–30	31–35	36–40	41–45	46–50	51–55	56–60	61–65	66–70	71–75	76–80	81–85	85>	
							Sideswipe									
Frequency	7455	8171	7330	7133	6300	5156	4014	2965	2231	1737	1471	1064	763	323	144	56,257
Row percent	12.4	13.6	12.2	11.8	10.5	8.6	6.7	4.9	3.7	2.9	2.4	1.8	1.3	0.5	0.2	93.7
Column percent	7.8	8.6	9.0	9.1	9.1	8.9	8.9	8.8	8.4	7.4	6.8	5.7	5.8	4.7	6.0	—
Total frequency	96,190	92,360	81,879	78,060	69,214	57,995	45,363	33,626	26,551	23,587	21,552	18,532	13,189	6839	2576	667,513
Total row percent	64.3	65.7	60.3	58.4	51.8	43.8	33.5	24.7	19.4	15.9	14.0	11.2	7.7	3.9	1.3	—
Total column percent	100.0	99.8	100.1	100.0	100.0	99.9	100.1	99.9	100.1	100.0	99.9	100.0	100.0	100.01	100.4	—

Note: Percentages do not add up to 100% because of small number of unknown age drivers.

TABLE 4.3 1992–1996 Three-Vehicle or More Crashes by Age Group

Age groups

	16–20	21–25	26–30	31–35	36–40	41–45	46–50	51–55	56–60	61–65	66–70	71–75	76–80	81–85	85>	Total
Frequency	18,026	20,292	19,220	19,024	17,512	15,044	11,800	8737	6560	5302	4724	3606	2126	979	366	153,318
Percent	11.4	12.8	12.1	12.0	11.1	9.5	7.4	5.5	4.1	3.3	3.0	2.3	1.3	0.6	0.2	96.6

Note: Percentages do not add up to 100% because of small number of unknown age drivers.

TABLE 4.4 Single Vehicle Fatal Crashes by Driver Age

| | \| Age groups | | | | | | | | | | | | | | | |
	16–20	21–25	26–30	31–35	36–40	41–45	46–50	51–55	56–60	61–65	66–70	71–75	76–80	81–85	85>	Total
	1992–1996 Fatal single-vehicle crashes/not hitting pedestrian															
Frequency	464	528	400	283	224	182	119	90	71	77	69	100	51	47	28	2733
Percent	16.9	19.2	14.5	10.3	8.1	6.6	4.3	3.3	2.6	2.8	2.5	3.6	1.9	1.7	1.0	99.3
	1992–1996 Fatal single-vehicle crashes/hitting pedestrian															
Frequency	98	119	115	91	91	78	68	38	34	32	27	15	17	4	2	829
Percent	10.9	13.2	12.8	10.1	10.1	8.7	7.5	4.2	3.8	3.6	3.0	1.7	1.9	0.4	0.2	92.1

Note: Percentages do not add up to 100% because of small number of unknown age drivers.

TABLE 4.5   1992–1996 Fatal Two-Vehicle Crashes by Age Group

	Age groups															
	16–20	21–25	26–30	31–35	36–40	41–45	46–50	51–55	56–60	61–65	66–70	71–75	76–80	81–85	85>	Total
								Angle								
Frequency	190	204	172	174	146	131	110	81	64	54	65	97	84	70	28	1670
Row percent	11.0	11.8	10.0	10.1	8.5	7.6	6.4	4.7	3.7	3.1	3.8	5.6	4.9	4.1	1.6	96.9
Column percent	36.4	32.6	32.3	32.0	28.9	34.6	30.5	30.1	30.5	30.3	35.1	47.6	52.2	57.4	57.1	—
								Backing up								
Frequency	1	0	1	1	1	1	1	1	0	1	0	1	0	0	0	9
Row percent	10.0	0	10.0	10.0	10.0	10.0	10.0	10.0	0	10.0	0	10.0	0	0	0	90.0
Column percent	0.2	0.0	0.2	0.2	0.2	0.3	0.3	0.4	0.0	0.6	0.0	0.5	0.0	0.0	0.0	—
								Head-on								
Frequency	289	338	284	296	294	19 9	206	154	119	100	99	88	63	44	12	2585
Row percent	11.2	13.0	11.0	11.4	11.3	7.7	7.9	5.9	4.6	3.9	3.8	3.4	2.4	1.7	0.5	99.7
Column percent	55.4	54.1	53.4	54.5	58.1	52.5	57.1	57.3	56.7	56.2	53.5	43.1	39.1	36.1	24.5	—

(continued)

TABLE 4.5 (continued)

| | | | | | | | | | Age groups | | | | | | | |
	16–20	21–25	26–30	31–35	36–40	41–45	46–50	51–55	56–60	61–65	66–70	71–75	76–80	81–85	85>	Total
								Rear-on								
Frequency	21	51	47	36	45	34	29	21	17	16	12	11	8	2	7	324
Row percent	5.7	13.8	12.7	9.8	12.2	9.2	7.9	5.7	4.6	4.3	3.3	3.0	2.2	0.5	1.9	96.8
Column percent	4.0	8.2	8.8	6.6	8.9	9.0	8.0	7.8	8.1	9.0	6.5	5.4	5.0	1.6	14.3	—
								Sideswipe								
Frequency	21	32	28	36	20	14	15	12	10	7	9	7	6	6	2	225
Row percent	9.0	13.7	12.0	15.4	8.6	6.0	6.4	5.1	4.3	3.0	4.0	3.0	2.6	2.6	0.9	96.6
Column percent	4.0	5.1	5.3	6.6	4.0	3.7	4.2	4.5	4.8	4.0	4.9	3.4	3.7	5.0	4.1	—
Total frequency	522	625	532	543	506	379	361	269	210	178	185	204	161	122	49	4813
Total row percent	46.9	52.3	55.7	56.7	50.6	40.5	38.6	31.4	17.2	24.3	14.9	2.5	12.1	8.9	4.9	—
Total column percent	100.0	100.0	100.0	99.9	100.1	100.1	100.1	100.1	100.1	100.1	100.0	100.0	100.0	100.1	100.0	—

Note: Percentages do not add up to 100% because of small number of unknown age drivers.

TABLE 4.6 1992–1996 Fatal Three-Vehicle or More Crashes by Age Group

								Age groups									
	16–20	21–25	26–30	31–35	36–40	41–45	46–50	51–55	56–60	61–65	66–70	71–75	76–80	81–85	85>	Total
Frequency	121	163	185	176	172	147	126	82	82	58	49	43	33	16	5	1458
Percent	8.2	11.0	12.5	12.0	11.6	10.0	8.5	5.5	5.5	3.9	3.3	2.9	2.2	1.1	0.3	98.5

Note: Percentages do not add up to 100% because of small number of unknown age drivers.

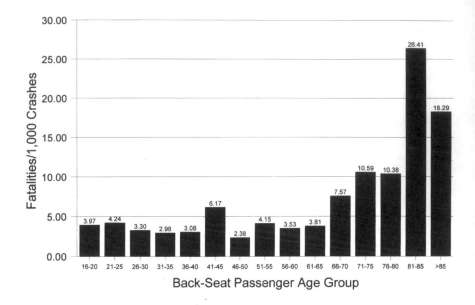

Figure 4.9 1992–1996 passenger car back-seat passenger fatalities vs. age group (per 1,000 crashes).

Another way of looking at the data is shown in Table 4.7, which provides crash data by midblock, signalized, and stop-controlled intersections by age group. Note that the intersection data sets have higher distributions in the older age groups.

Fatal crashes can be classified as single, multivehicle midblock and multivehicle intersection crashes. Figure 4.13 shows the proportion of these crashes by age. Note that as groups age, the proportion of single vehicle and multivehicle midblock crashes decrease while multivehicle intersection crashes increase.

Two-vehicle crashes can be classified as rear-end, backing, head-on, angle, and sideswipe. Within the crash record system, it is possible to ascertain the striking at-fault driver for many collision types. In rear-end crashes, the striking vehicle is the following vehicle that runs into the back of a forward moving or stopped front vehicle. In head-on crashes, it is the vehicle that crosses the center line and enters an opposing lane. Angle crashes are more difficult because

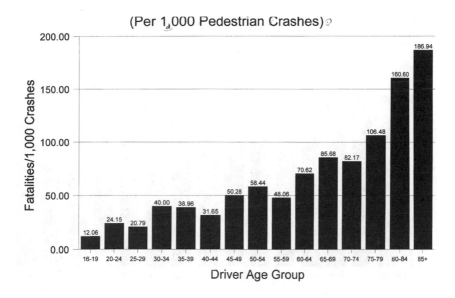

Figure 4.10   1992–1996 pedestrian fatalities vs. age group (per 1,000 pedestrian crashes).

a driver pulling out from a stop sign could either strike or be struck by a mainline vehicle. As such, certain collision types and movements can be identified that likely define at-fault drivers. Examples include left-turn drivers from the mainline into a driveway or side street colliding with opposing flow mainline drivers, drivers pulling out from a stop-controlled intersection colliding with a mainline vehicle, and drivers turning left at signalized intersections colliding with an opposing mainline driver.

In rear-end crashes, the distribution of striking and struck drivers (Figure 4.14) indicates that both young and older drivers are disproportionately striking other vehicles rather than being struck. Note also the large differences in crashes by group with young drivers having over a fivefold number of rear-end crashes than older drivers.

Similarly, in head-on and sideswipe crashes, a driver's encroachment into opposing lanes and crashing with oncoming vehicles are proportionally greater than drivers of oncoming vehicles involved in head-on crashes of the same age group as groups age (Figures 4.15 and 4.16).

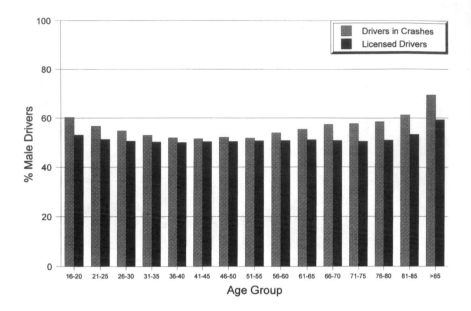

Figure 4.11 1992–1996 percentage of male drivers vs. all drivers (drivers in crashes vs. licensed drivers).

The distribution of mainline drivers to driveway drivers in crashes by age group in crashes where the driveway driver pulled out is shown in Figure 4.17. Again there are higher proportions of young and older driveway drivers.

At stop-controlled intersections, where the left-turn movement from the mainline has a crash with opposing flow (Figure 4.18), young and older drivers have disproportionately more crashes when turning left than mainline flow.

At signalized intersections, similar to stop-controlled intersections, the left-turn movement from one direction has a crash with opposing flow, Figure 4.19 again shows that the 16 to 20 age group and the over 61 age group drivers have disproportionately more crashes when turning left than opposing "thru" drivers. Note that the disproportion becomes significantly greater in the 71 to 75 age group.

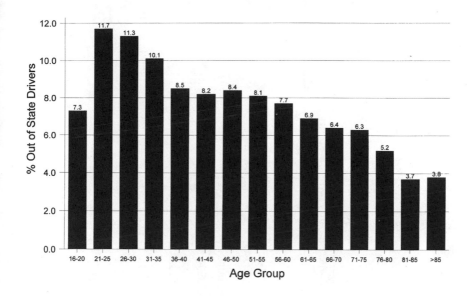

Figure 4.12 1992–1996 percentage of out-of-state drivers in crashes by age group.

SPECIFIC CHARACTERISTICS—WHERE

Highways can be categorized using a federal classification system that first separates highways into urban and rural categories and then by type of highway ranging from interstate to local road. Crashes by age group by the classification system is shown in Table 4.8. As drivers age, there is a tendency for older driver groups to have a lower proportion of crashes on the interstate system but a higher proportion of crashes occur on the urban principal and minor arterials.

Similar to functional highway type, crashes by age group by speed limit can also be compiled (Table 4.9). Again, there is a reduction in crashes on 65 and 55 miles per hour (MPH) speed limit highways and a slight tendency for a higher proportion of crashes to occur on lower speed limits as groups age. For example, in age group 26

TABLE 4.7 1992–1996 Crashes by Age Group

	16–20	21–25	26–30	31–35	36–40	41–45	46–50	51–55	56–60	61–65	66–70	71–75	76–80	81–85	85>	Total
									Age groups							
							Signalized intersection									
Frequency	23,885	27,621	24,953	23,146	20,677	17,218	13,609	10,153	8111	7260	6617	5644	3821	1919	710	195,344
Percent	11.6	13.4	12.1	11.2	10.0	8.3	6.6	5.0	4.0	3.5	3.2	2.7	2.0	1.0	0.3	94.9
							Stop sign-controlled intersection									
Frequency	41,078	33,628	28,988	27,290	24,846	20,799	16,280	12,137	9568	8996	8561	7687	5658	3059	1216	249,791
Percent	16.0	13.0	11.1	10.7	9.5	8.0	6.3	4.7	3.7	3.5	3.3	3.0	2.2	1.2	0.5	96.7
							Midblock									
Frequency	97,770	89,713	74,394	68,954	59,183	48,667	37,023	26,662	20,056	16,140	14,217	11,337	7480	3768	1429	4,215,770
Percent	16.2	15.0	12.4	11.5	9.8	8.1	6.1	4.4	3.3	2.7	2.4	2.0	1.2	0.6	0.2	96.0

Note: Percentages do not add up to 100% because of small number of unknown age drivers.

TABLE 4.8 1992–1996 Crashes by Federal Functional Classification System by Age

								Age groups								
	16–20	21–25	26–30	31–35	36–40	41–45	46–50	51–55	56–60	61–65	66–70	71–75	76–80	81–85	85>	Total
								Rural								
								Interstate								
Frequency	1874	2891	2284	2224	2043	1792	1550	1098	818	590	461	286	148	65	16	18,140
Row percent	10.1	15.5	12.3	11.9	11.0	9.6	8.3	5.9	4.4	3.2	2.5	1.5	0.8	0.4	0.1	97.5
Column percent	2.0	3.2	3.0	3.1	3.3	3.5	3.9	3.8	3.7	3.2	2.8	2.1	1.6	1.4	0.9	—
								Principal arterial								
Frequency	6349	6983	5721	5468	4876	4320	3423	2406	1893	1515	1285	1088	748	416	105	46,596
Row percent	13.4	14.8	12.1	11.6	10.3	9.1	7.2	5.1	4.0	3.2	2.7	2.3	1.6	0.9	0.2	98.5
Column percent	6.8	7.7	7.5	7.6	7.8	8.4	8.6	8.3	8.6	8.1	7.9	8.0	8.0	8.8	5.9	—
								Minor arterial								
Frequency	11,395	10,314	8468	7884	6873	5637	4428	3366	2473	2069	1814	1566	1033	563	192	68,075
Row percent	16.5	14.9	12.2	11.4	9.9	8.2	6.4	4.9	3.6	3.0	2.6	2.7	1.5	0.8	0.3	98.9
Column percent	12.2	11.3	11.1	11.0	11.1	11.0	11.2	11.7	11.2	11.1	11.1	11.6	11.0	12.0	10.9	—

(continued)

TABLE 4.8 (continued)

	16–20	21–25	26–30	31–35	36–40	41–45	46–50	51–55	56–60	61–65	66–70	71–75	76–80	81–85	85>	Total
							Age groups									
							Major collector									
Frequency	10,879	8457	6883	6414	5471	4380	3248	2358	1759	1466	1222	1023	726	359	145	54,790
Row percent	19.5	15.2	12.3	11.5	9.8	7.9	5.8	4.2	3.2	2.6	2.2	1.8	1.3	0.6	0.3	98.2
Column percent	11.6	9.3	9.0	9.0	8.8	8.5	8.2	8.2	8.0	7.8	7.5	7.6	7.8	7.6	8.2	—
							Minor collector									
Frequency	7115	4460	3473	3338	2813	2122	1588	1148	823	659	589	438	331	164	67	29,128
Row percent	23.9	15.0	11.7	11.2	9.4	7.1	5.3	3.9	2.8	2.2	2.0	1.5	1.1	0.6	0.2	97.9
Column percent	7.6	4.9	4.5	4.7	4.5	4.1	4.0	4.0	3.7	3.5	3.6	3.2	3.5	3.5	3.8	—
							Local									
Frequency	4004	2473	1822	1674	1426	1108	752	562	420	340	314	232	186	97	44	15,454
Row percent	25.2	15.6	11.5	10.5	9.0	7.0	4.7	3.5	2.6	2.1	2.0	1.5	1.2	0.6	0.3	97.3
Column percent	4.3	2.7	2.4	2.3	2.3	2.2	1.9	2.0	1.9	1.8	1.9	1.7	2.0	2.1	2.5	—

(continued)

TABLE 4.8 (continued)

| | Age groups | | | | | | | | | | | | | | | |
	16–20	21–25	26–30	31–35	36–40	41–45	46–50	51–55	56–60	61–65	66–70	71–75	76–80	81–85	85>	Total
Urban																
Interstate																
Frequency	2645	3568	3038	2679	2337	1952	1561	1054	789	551	426	353	181	81	33	21,248
Row percent	12.0	16.2	13.8	12.2	10.6	8.9	7.1	4.8	3.6	2.5	2.0	1.6	0.8	0.4	0.2	96.7
Column percent	2.8	4.0	4.0	3.7	3.8	3.8	3.9	3.7	3.6	3.0	2.6	2.6	1.9	1.7	1.9	—
Principal arterial																
Frequency	23,118	26,254	23,038	21,335	18,268	15,367	11,749	8725	6842	6026	5421	4536	3271	1608	627	176,185
Row column	12.6	14.3	12.5	11.6	10.0	8.4	6.4	4.8	3.7	3.3	3.0	2.5	1.8	0.9	0.3	96.1
Column percent	24.7	28.9	30.1	29.8	29.4	30.0	29.6	30.2	31.0	32.2	33.1	33.5	35.0	34.1	35.5	—
Minor arterial																
Frequency	15,782	15,145	13,006	12,454	10,916	8801	6828	4951	3973	3478	3217	2767	1926	974	385	104,603
Row percent	14.6	14.0	12.0	11.5	10.1	8.1	6.3	4.6	3.7	3.2	3.0	2.6	1.8	0.9	0.4	96.8
Column percent	16.9	16.7	17.0	17.4	17.6	17.1	17.2	17.2	18.0	18.6	19.7	20.4	20.6	20.7	21.8	—

(continued)

181

TABLE 4.8 (*continued*)

| | Age groups | | | | | | | | | | | | | | | |
	16–20	21–25	26–30	31–35	36–40	41–45	46–50	51–55	56–60	61–65	66–70	71–75	76–80	81–85	85>	Total
Collector																
Frequency	6758	5324	4416	4088	3692	3071	2325	1623	1243	1182	981	815	540	286	104	36,448
Row percent	17.9	14.1	11.7	10.8	9.8	8.1	6.2	4.3	3.3	3.1	2.6	2.2	1.4	0.8	0.3	96.6
Column percent	7.2	5.9	5.8	5.7	5.9	6.0	5.9	5.6	5.6	6.3	6.0	6.0	5.8	6.1	5.9	—
Local																
Frequency	1216	888	700	725	636	454	350	245	198	183	151	133	86	41	19	6025
Row percent	19.1	14.0	11.0	11.4	10.0	7.1	5.5	3.9	3.1	2.9	2.4	2.1	1.4	0.6	0.3	94.8
Column percent	1.3	1.0	0.9	1.0	1.0	0.9	0.9	0.9	1.0	1.0	0.9	1.0	0.9	0.9	1.1	—

Note: Percentages do not add up to 100% because of small number of unknown age drivers.

TABLE 4.9 1992–1996 Crashes by Speed Limit by Age

	Age groups															
	16–20	21–25	26–30	31–35	36–40	41–45	46–50	51–55	56–60	61–65	66–70	71–75	76–80	81–85	85>	Total
	25–30 MPH															
Frequency	35,904	33,873	29,039	26,522	23,068	18,930	14,192	10,646	8371	7528	7277	6191	4288	2228	873	20,817
Row percent	14.6	13.8	11.8	10.8	9.4	7.7	5.8	4.3	3.4	3.1	3.0	2.5	1.7	0.9	0.4	93.2
Column percent	21.3	21.5	21.7	21.1	21.0	20.9	20.3	20.8	21.3	22.4	24.2	24.8	25.2	25.7	26.4	—
	35 MPH															
Frequency	45,642	40,412	34,547	32,743	28,891	23,645	18,089	13,312	10,478	9346	8540	7208	4986	2515	986	28,134
Row percent	15.6	13.8	11.8	11.2	9.9	8.1	6.2	4.6	3.6	3.2	2.9	2.5	1.7	0.9	0.3	96.3
Column percent	27.1	25.7	25.8	26.1	26.3	26.0	25.9	26.0	26.7	27.8	28.4	28.9	29.3	29.0	29.8	—
	40–50 MPH															
Frequency	44,114	39,240	33,782	32,345	28,220	23,760	18,071	13,407	10,091	8417	7360	6053	4181	2092	806	271,939
Row percent	15.9	14.1	12.2	11.6	10.2	8.6	6.5	4.8	3.6	3.0	2.7	2.2	1.5	0.8	0.3	98.0
Column percent	26.2	24.9	25.2	25.7	25.7	26.2	25.9	26.2	25.7	25.0	24.4	24.2	24.5	24.1	24.4	—

(continued)

TABLE 4.9 (continued)

	Age groups															
	16–20	21–25	26–30	31–35	36–40	41–45	46–50	51–55	56–60	61–65	66–70	71–75	76–80	81–85	85>	Total
55 MPH																
Frequency	31,626	33,034	27,111	25,353	22,019	18,279	14,570	10,253	7536	5957	4876	3777	2413	1258	433	209,095
Row percent	14.5	15.1	12.7	11.6	10.1	8.4	6.7	4.7	3.5	2.7	2.2	1.7	1.1	0.6	0.2	95.8
Column percent	18.8	21.0	20.7	20.2	20.1	20.1	20.8	20.1	19.2	17.8	16.2	15.1	14.2	14.5	13.1	—
65 MPH																
Frequency	908	1311	1025	1106	968	914	784	531	411	260	192	129	71	29	10	8649
Row percent	10.3	14.8	11.6	12.5	11.0	10.3	8.9	6.0	4.7	3.0	2.2	1.5	0.8	0.3	0.1	98.0
Column percent	0.5	0.8	0.8	0.9	0.9	1.0	1.1	1.0	1.1	0.8	0.6	0.5	0.4	0.3	0.3	—
Total frequency	158,194	14,787	126,104	118,069	103,166	85,528	65,706	48,149	36,887	31,508	28,245	23,358	15,939	8122	3,108	538,634
Total column percent	93.9	93.9	94.2	94.0	94.0	70.2	94.0	94.1	94.0	93.8	93.8	93.5	93.6	93.6	95.3	—

Note: Percentages do not add up to 100% because of small number of unknown age drivers and speed limits.

to 30, 20.7% occur on 55 MPH highways but only 15.1% in the 71 to 75 age group. In contrast, for 35 MPH highways, 25.8% occur in age group 26 to 30 and 29.0% for age group 71 to 75.

SPECIFIC CHARACTERISTICS—WHEN

We know that, in general, the aging process results in a cumulative degradation in vision, however, an examination of the proportion of night to total crashes by age group (Figure 4.20) indicates a reduction as groups age. The phenomenon can be largely attributed to changes in life style or self regulation where a great majority of older drivers minimize night driving to compensate for reduced night vision capabilities.

An examination of when at-night crashes occur (Figure 4.21) indicates that as drivers age, the proportion of night crashes that occur in the 5:00 to 9:00 PM evening hours increases whereas the midnight to 4:00 AM hours decreases.

The time of day that crashes occur varies significantly as drivers age. The percent of each age group that occurs during the morning hours of 6:00 to 9:00 AM (Figure 4.22) is flat from ages 26 to 60 but drops substantially because many people retire and do not have to commute to work. The 9:00 AM to 4:00 PM midday period (Figure 4.23) shows a continued growth in the proportion of crashes by age group as age increases. Note that about two thirds of all drivers age 71 and older experience crashes during this time frame but only one third of young drivers under the age of 30.

The 4:00 to 7:00 PM time frame (Figure 4.24) is slightly convex, with a gentle peak occurring in the 40 to 55 age group.

The 7:00 PM to midnight time frame (Figure 4.25) shows a steady decline in the proportion of crashes during this time frame as groups age.

The midnight to 6:00 AM distribution (Figure 4.26) is similar to the 7:00 PM to midnight period except the decline is more pronounced, and it does not peak until the age 21 to 25 age group. The legal age of 21 to consume alcohol may account for the shift to peak to the 21 to 25 age group.

In addition to time of day, the proportion of crashes by weather conditions (dry, raining, snow/sleet) by age group (Figure 4.27)

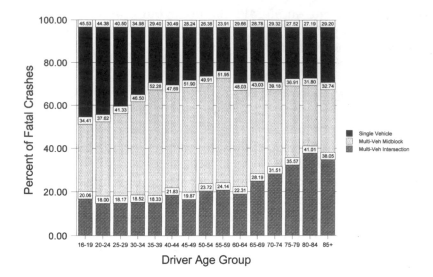

Figure 4.13   1992–1996 fatal crash category vs. age group (% drivers in multivehicle intersection, multivehicle midblock, and single-vehicle crashes).

indicates that proportionately fewer crashes occur during inclement weather as groups age. Perhaps the opportunity to take more discretionary trips as conditions improve is a factor in reducing the number of trips during adverse weather.

SPECIFIC CHARACTERISTICS—WHY

The major factor in fatal crashes is impaired driving. The percent use of alcohol for all drivers in all fatal crashes by age group (Figure 4.28) indicates that the 21 to 25 age group has the highest percentage (40.53) and the proportion drops as groups age. Note that it is less than 10% for age 65 and up.

Safety belt usage does not vary significantly by age (Figure 4.29) but does slightly increase after age 35 and remains relatively constant for older ages.

Frontal crashes (11:00 p.m. to 1:00 a.m. strike direction) are not only the most frequent points of collisions but also can be the most

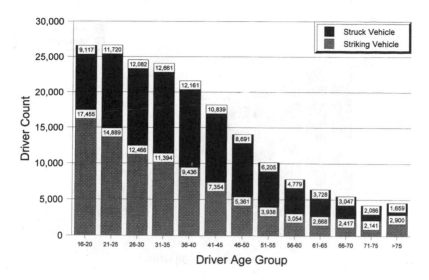

Figure 4.14   1992–1996 rear-end crashes vs. age group (distribution of striking vehicle vs. struck vehicle).

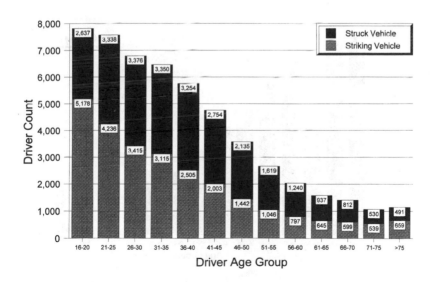

Figure 4.15   1992–1996 head-on crashes vs. age group (distribution of striking vehicle vs. struck vehicle).

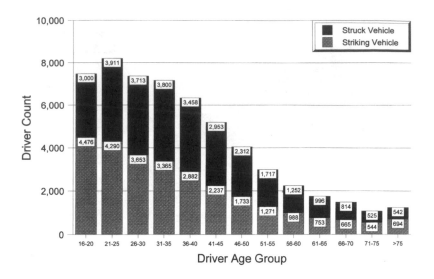

Figure 4.16   1992–1996 sideswipe crashes vs. age group (distribution of striking vehicle vs. struck vehicle).

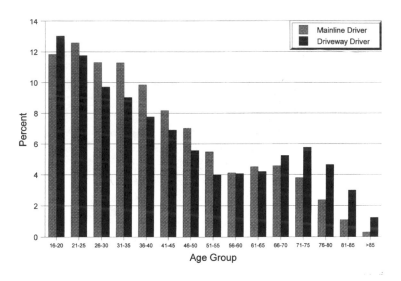

Figure 4.17   1992–1996 age group vs. percent of drivers in crashes during 9 a.m.–4 p.m. time period (mainline driver vs. driveway driver).

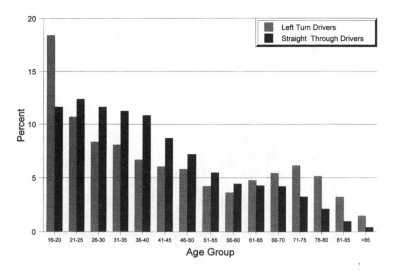

Figure 4.18   1992–1996 age group vs. percent of drivers in crashes during 9 a.m.–4 p.m. time period (stopped control intersection—left-turn drivers vs. straight-through drivers).

severe types of crashes that occur. An assessment of injury severity to drivers of older passenger cars, 1980–1986 models, not air bag-equipped, is illustrated in Table 4.10. The data comparing deaths per 1000 crashes when seat belt is used or not used should be considered with caution because of the probable inaccuracy of belt use reporting at the lower injury levels. What is important are the disproportionate number of deaths in each unbelted age group. Safety belt usage in Pennsylvania has ranged from 65 to 70% belted during the crash year periods. In frontal crashes of newer air bag-equipped cars, air bag deployment has to be incorporated into the mix. Table 4.11 provides information on driver injuries in frontal crashes (11:00 p.m. to 1:00 a.m. strike direction) of 1993 and newer passenger cars when air bags deployed. It is obvious from the data that severity of crashes is significantly related to safety belt usage in air bag-deployed crashes. Of significance is the fact that a majority of the deaths occurred with unbelted drivers. In addition, the higher rate of deaths of older drivers may infer a problem similar to children

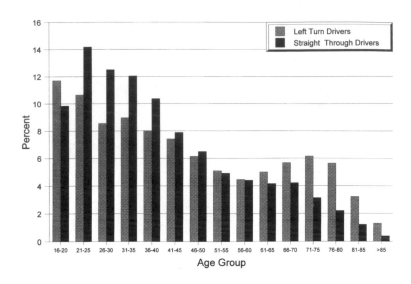

Figure 4.19 1992–1996 age group vs. percent of drivers in crashes during 9 a.m.–4 p.m. time period (signalized intersection—left-turn drivers vs. straight-through drivers).

under age 12 and the inability of the older body to withstand the energy of the air bag deployment.

Crash data does have information on causation factors in crashes. The accuracy of the data is somewhat suspect because the police officer provides a narrative description of the crash occurrence based on interviews and personal observations. The police crash report is then reviewed by a data analyst who makes a further interpretation of the narrative report to define probable causation factors from a computerized listing of causation factors.

Causation factor data has been identified by striking driver in single-vehicle, rear-end, head-on, mainline and driveway, and left turn and straight through at signalized intersections by age.

Table 4.12 provides data on causation factors for drivers in single-vehicle crashes by age group. Driver lost control is the predominant factor identified for all age groups except for driver drinking in the 21 to 50 age categories. Of significance is failure to heed pedestrian as groups age.

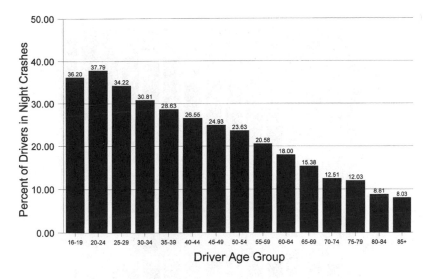

Figure 4.20 1992–1996 percent of drivers in night crashes vs. age group (dawn, dusk, and unknown illuminations omitted).

Table 4.13 provides data on causation factors by striking driver by age in rear-end collisions. Note that failure to heed a stopped vehicle initially is high in the 16 to 20 age group, then drops and again rises above age 71. Tailgating is a relatively constant percentage regardless of age but too fast for conditions associated with traffic or pedestrians has a slight increase in the older age groups. Some factors such as driver drinking, over speed limit, slippery pavement, and too fast for conditions (associated with weather) essentially disappear as age groups increase, but another factor illegal stop on roadway appears.

Table 4.14 provides data on causation factors by striking driver by age in head-on crashes. The striking driver is always the driver who enters the opposing traffic lane. The leading causation factor driving on the wrong side is relatively constant by age and does not give any insight on why the driver ended up on the wrong side. A number of factors such as slippery pavement, over speed limit, too fast for conditions, and driver drinking tend to diminish as age increases. Other factors including improper/careless turning; im-

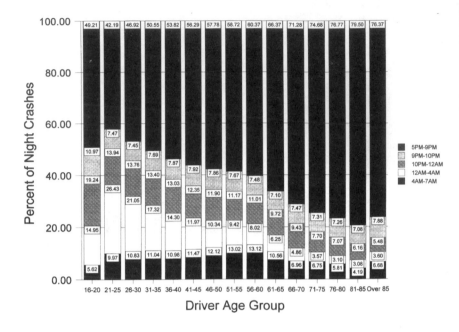

Figure 4.21   1992–1996 night crash distribution—time vs. age group.

proper exit from highway; and drowsiness, fatigue, asleep increase as groups age.

Table 4.15 provides data on causation factors by striking driver by age in mainline and driveway crashes. The striking driver may be the mainline or driveway driver. The leading causation factor making improper entrance is relatively constant over all age groups, and accounts for approximately 60% of all crashes in this category. As groups age, over speed limit and driver drinking causation factors decrease, however, proportionately, ran red light increases.

Table 4.16 provides data on causation factor by age group for left turn and straight through crashes at signalized intersections by age group. The major causation factor improper/careless turning remains relatively constant through all age groups at approximately 60%. Causation factors involving driver drinking, hitting a stopped vehicle, and over the posted speed limit, decrease as groups age. In addition, running red lights and glare become an increased problem for the older groups.

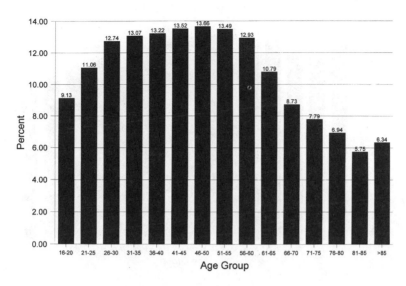

Figure 4.22   1992–1996 age group vs. percent of grouped drivers in crashes during 6 a.m.–9 a.m. time period.

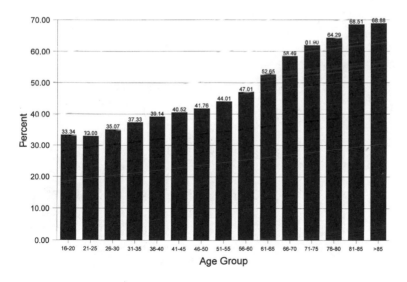

Figure 4.23   1992–1996 age group vs. percent of grouped drivers in crashes during 9 a.m.–4 p.m. time period.

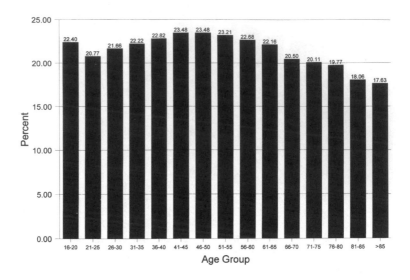

Figure 4.24   1992–1996 age group vs. percent of grouped drivers in crashes during 4 p.m.–7 p.m. time period.

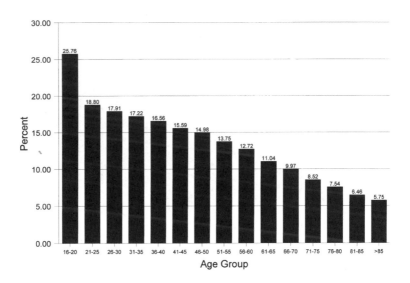

Figure 4.25   1992–1996 age group vs. percent of grouped drivers in crashes during 7 p.m.–12 a.m. time period.

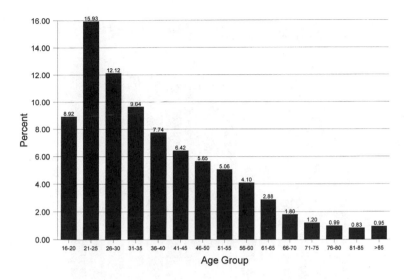

Figure 4.26   1992–1996 age group vs. percent of grouped drivers in crashes during 12 a.m.–6 a.m. time period.

SUMMARY

Major conclusions drawn from the crash data are as follows:

- The data cannot be used to infer that any one age group is safer than another age group because reliable exposure data by age group is not available
- Older drivers have fewer crashes per 1000 drivers of their age group, however, the survivability of those crashes decreases substantially as age increases for drivers and passengers.
- The survivability of pedestrian crashes decreases as age increases.
- When addressing the total transportation safety problem of older people, we must not only consider drivers, but passengers and pedestrians, who comprise nearly equal shares of highway deaths in older populations.
- Older drivers, like younger drivers, are more disproportionally the striking or at-fault driver in rear-end, head-on, sideswipe,

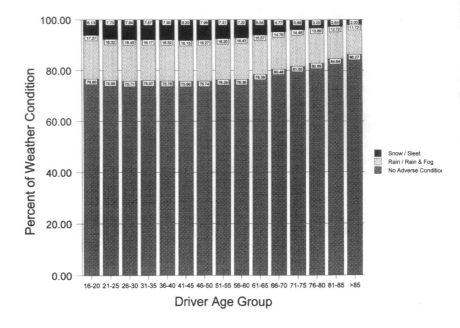

Figure 4.27 1992–1996 drivers by weather condition in crashes.

pulling out from a driveway, and turning left at a traffic signal crashes.

- Older drivers have fewer crashes on high speed limit and interstate highways.
- The night to total crash rate decreases as age increases. A significant number of older driver night crashes occur in the 5:00 to 9:00 PM time period.
- Crashes that occur during the midday hours, 9:00 AM to 4:00 PM increases as age increases, with older drivers experiencing approximately two thirds of their crashes in this time frame.
- The proportion of impaired drivers substantially decreases as age increases. It is not a significant factor for older drivers.
- A significant loss of life occurs at all age groups because people do not buckle-up.
- Safety belts have a significant impact on the survivability of crashes regardless of age.

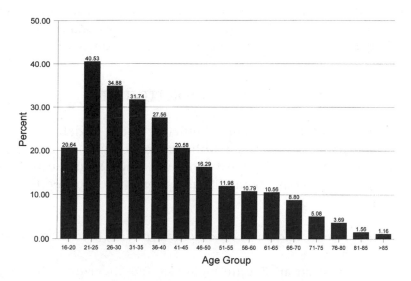

Figure 4.28   1992–1996 percent of drivers who were drinking by age group (fatal crashes).

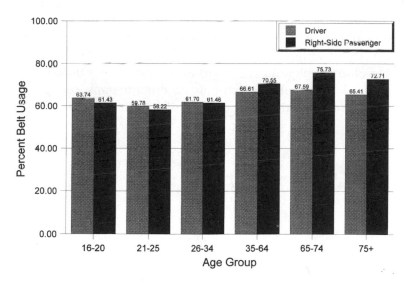

Figure 4.29   1992–1996 belt usage of drivers and right-side passengers in crashes vs. age group (percent usage within age group).

- Hitting pedestrians, drowsiness, sleep, fatigue, blackout, hitting parked cars, and improper turning proportionately become larger factors in single vehicle crashes as groups age.

POTENTIAL OPPORTUNITIES

While crash data do not contain sufficient detail to define specific failure mechanisms associated with crashes, certain opportunities related to crash data may have a positive impact on future crash occurrence or outcome. Some of the opportunities related to crash data findings are as follows:

- Enhance education and enforcement initiatives to increase seat belt usage.
- Target pedestrian countermeasures (engineering, education, and enforcement) to improve safety of older pedestrians.
- Develop alternate transportation modes for night social activities in the 5:00 to 9:00 PM time frame.
- Provide targeted education and training for older drivers to better recognize stopped vehicles and pedestrians in roadway.
- Provide targeted education and training to better estimate acceptable gaps, speed, and distances to more safely pull into or through traffic.
- Develop Intelligent Transportation System technologies to improve drivers ability to estimate acceptable gaps, recognize traffic signals, and define the onset of fatigue or drowsiness.

TABLE 4.10 Drivers in 1980–1986 Vehicles

| | | | Injuries | | | | Death rate |
	Deaths	Major	Moderate	Minor	Property damage only	Total	per 1000
			Age 16–20				
Seat belt used	25	156	836	5279	16,718	23,014	1.08
Seat belt not used	68	287	1055	2820	3182	7412	9.17
Total	93	443	1891	8099	119,900	30,426	3.05
			Age 21–25				
Seat belt used	8	126	561	3181	10,018	13,894	0.58
Seat belt not used	76	305	920	1938	2179	5418	14.03
Total	84	431	1481	5119	12,197	19,312	4.35
			Age 26–34				
Seat belt used	20	159	701	3986	11,679	16,545	1.21
Seat belt not used	75	312	994	2090	2402	5873	12.77
Total	95	471	1695	6076	14,081	22,418	4.24

(continued)

TABLE 4.10 (continued)

	Deaths	Injuries				Property damage only	Total	Death rate per 1000
		Major	Moderate	Minor				
Age 35–64								
Seat belt used	46	255	1220	6857		19,358	27,736	1.65
Seat belt not used	158	377	1072	2438		2916	6961	22.70
Total	204	632	2292	9295		22,274	34,697	5.88
Age 65–74								
Seat belt used	13	48	243	1245		3685	5234	2.48
Seat belt not used	38	59	171	361		528	1157	32.85
Total	51	107	414	1606		4213	6391	8.98
Age 75 >								
Seat belt used	29	41	206	995		2778	4049	2.16
Seat belt not used	42	54	133	327		437	993	42.30
Total	71	95	339	1322		3215	5042	14.08
Grand total	598	2179	8112	31,517		17,588	118,286	—

TABLE 4.11 Frontal Impacts

1993–1996 Passenger Cars—Driver Airbag-Equipped Injury Distribution of Drivers

Age groups	Deaths	Major	Moderate	Minor	Property damage only	Total	Death rate per 1000
			Injuries				
			Safety belt used airbag deployed				
16–20	5	22	773	115	972	1887	2.6
21–25	4	26	918	151	1235	2335	1.7
26–34	6	37	1309	225	1548	3125	1.9
35–64	16	84	2401	401	2697	5599	2.9
64–74	2	24	376	70	372	844	2.4
≥75	6	8	221	54	199	488	12.3
			Safety belt not used airbag deployed				
16–20	10	16	146	39	105	316	31.6
21–25	11	18	164	52	125	370	29.7
26–34	9	22	152	63	118	364	24.7
35–64	18	40	216	87	136	497	36.2
64–74	9	5	24	14	28	80	112.5
≥75	6	5	26	11	16	64	93.7

Note: Accuracy of belt usage in many of the less severe crashes is not considered reliable because the police officer has no verification process available to question driver's response.

201

TABLE 4.12 Single-Vehicle Crashes

Causation factors	16–20	21–25	36–40	46–50	56–60	71–75	76–80	81–85	>85
Driver lost control	11.5†	10.5	10.9	12.0	12.1	11.4	13.1	11.1	12.1
Driving wrong side	11.2	9.7	9.3	7.9	7.4	8.8	9.6	8.5	6.4
Over speed limit	9.2	7.7	5.0	4.2	*	*	*	*	*
Over/under compensation of curve	9.2	6.9	6.3	5.9	5.6	6.4	7.3	5.0	6.4
Too fast for conditions—weather	8.0	8.3	8.9	10.1	9.3	6.4	4.2	4.0	*
Driver drinking	5.3	14.4	16.4	11.9	6.8	4.3	*	*	*
Forced movement	5.0	4.5	4.8	5.7	4.9	4.0	*	3.5	*
Too fast for conditions—combination	3.9	3.4	4.0	4.5	3.5	*	3.2	*	*
Too fast for conditions—roadside design	3.6	2.6	*	*	*	*	*	*	*
Drowsiness/sleep/fatigue	3.4	4.5	3.3	3.5	4.6	4.7	5.9	4.4	5.7
Engine failure	*	*	2.2	3.0	3.6	*	*	*	4.2
Failure to heed pedestrian	*	*	*	*	5.6	4.9	4.2	5.5	5.7
Blackout	*	*	*	*	*	3.3	4.4	*	*
Hit parked car—unknown reason	*	*	*	*	*	2.6	*	7.0	3.6
Improper/careless turning	*	*	*	*	*	*	3.6	5.0	3.6

*Not in 10 top factors for a particular age group.
†Percent of an age group crashes attributed to a causation factor.

TABLE 4.13   Rear-End Collisions

Causation factors	Age groups								
	16–20	21–25	36–40	46–50	56–60	71–75	76–80	81–85	>85
Failure to heed stopped vehicle	31.7†	27.8	28.4	29.4	31.4	37.9	38.8	42.7	40.9
Tailgating	30.4	31.5	31.1	31.2	30.6	29.5	28.9	27.5	30.3
Sudden slow or stopping	2.9	3.5	3.7	3.4	3.6	2.3	2.4	1.4	1.7
Too fast for conditions—traffic or pedestrians	2.8	2.3	2.4	2.2	2.3	2.4	2.7	2.4	3.1
Driver drinking	*	2.8	4.6	3.5	2.7	1.2	*	*	*
Over posted speed limit	2.7	2.3	*	*	*	*	*	*	*
Other distraction—day dreaming	2.4	2.1	2.0		2.0	2.4	1.2	2.5	2.6
Slippery pavement	2.2	2.8	2.5	2.5	2.0	1.2	*	*	*
Too fast for conditions—weather	2.0	1.9	2.0	2.1	2.0	*	*	*	*
Illegal stop on roadway	*	*	*	*	*	*	1.2	1.3	1.1

*Not in 10 top factors for a particular age group.

†Number is the percentage of all rear-end crashes by age group attributed to the raw causation factor.

TABLE 4.14 **Head-On Collisions**

	Age groups								
Causation factors	16–20	21–25	36–40	46–50	56–60	71–75	76–80	81–85	>85
Driving on wrong side	41.2	38.8	39.0	38.3	38.1	39.8	40.8	42.1	41.3
Slippery pavement	6.5	7.6	7.2	7.3	6.9	4.45	3.2	4.2	*
Improper careless turning	6.2	6.7	7.0	8.8	9.1	17.1	17.5	18.8	22.9
Over posted speed limit	4.1	3.1	2.3	2.0	*	*	*	*	*
Over/under compensating for curves	3.5	2.4	2.7	2.3	*	2.6	*	*	4.6
Too fast for conditions—combination	3.8	3.6	3.2	3.1	2.6			*	*
Too fast for conditions—weather	3.5	3.3	3.2	4.3	3.7	2.6	2.5	1.8	*
Driver lost control	3.3	2.9	3.0	3.7	3.5	1.8	1.4	2.1	1.8
Driver drinking	2.0	7.0	8.8	5.7	4.8	2.3	*	*	*
Tailgating	1.3	*	*	*	1.7	*	*	*	*
Careless passing	*	1.5	*	*	*	*	*	*	*
Improper exit from highway			1.3	*	2.4	3.0	4.1	4.5	5.5
Drowsiness/fatigue/asleep	*	*	*	*	*	1.4	1.6	1.2	*

*Not in 10 top factors for a particular age group.

TABLE 4.15 Mainline and Striking Driver Crashes: Driveway

	Age groups										
Causation factors	16–20	21–25	36–40	46–50	56–60	71–75	76–80	81–85	>85
Making improper entrance	60.5	59.0	59.4	60.8	62.4	63.8	65.5	62.0	62.8
Stopped vehicle	4.4	5.4	5.3	6.1	6.0	4.1	3.5	2.1	1.6
Over posted speed limit	3.0	2.4	1.7	1.0	*	*	*	*	*
Careless or illegal backing on roadway	2.8	2.4	2.7	3.3	3.1	2.6	2.4	2.1	2.1
Making improper exit from highway	2.5	3.2	3.8	3.3	3.2	2.7	2.8	5.2	5.3
Proceeding without clearance	2.1	1.8	2.6	2.0	1.6	2.6	2.1	2.5	2.1
Ran red light	2.1	1.9	2.1	2.4	3.5	3.8	3.8	6.2	6.4
Driving on wrong side of roadway	1.7	1.6	2.3	1.4	1.0	*	0.9	1.1	1.1
Improper/careless turning	1.5	1.4	1.3	1.3	*	1.4	1.1	2.0	3.7
Parked vehicle	1.1	*	*	*	1.7	*	*	*	*
Driver drinking	*	2.8	2.5	2.3	1.9	1.1	*	*	*

*Not in 10 top factors for a particular age group.

205

TABLE 4.16 Left Turn and Straight Through at Signal Striking Driver Causation Factor

	Age groups								
Causation factors	16–20	21–25	36–40	46–50	56–60	71–75	76–80	81–85	>85
Improper/careless turning	60.0	58.3	59.8	60.6	59.9	57.7	55.5	60.1	61.6
Ran red light—unknown reasons	14.3	15.4	14.9	15.5	15.9	20.8	22.8	19.3	21.2
Ran red light—trying to beat yellow	2.0	2.0	1.9	1.3	1.6	1.2	1.9	2.4	2.0
Ran red light—other reasons	1.8	1.3	1.4	1.4	1.6	1.3	1.5	1.9	1.9
Stopped vehicle	1.8	2.7	2.3	2.3	2.6	2.7	*	*	*
Turning from wrong lane or position	1.7	1.7	*	1.5	2.0	.9	1.8	1.6	*
Driver drinking	1.7	3.6	4.2	4.1	2.1	.9	*	*	*
Proceeding without clearance	1.4	1.7	1.5	1.3	1.5	1.3	1.8	1.1	*
Over posted speed limit	1.2	1.2	*	*	*	*	*	*	*
Ran red light—did not see signal	1.1	*	.9	1.3	1.1	1.2	1.2	1.3	2.0
Ran red light—did not see change to red	*	1.0	1.0	1.3	1.2	1.7	2.4	1.0	2.0
Glare condition	*	*	*	*	*	*	*	1.3	2.0

*Not in 10 top factors for a particular age group.

What Do Driving Accident Patterns Reveal About Age-related Changes in Visual Information Processing?

Frank Schieber

Bryer's (this volume) analysis of automobile crash data in the State of Pennsylvania is consistent with previous epidemiological studies of the relationship between advancing adult age and driving safety (e.g., Cerrelli, 1989). Most noteworthy among his conclusions are that: (a) older drivers are more likely to die in automobile accidents due to their increasing physical frailty; and (b) the lack of reliable risk exposure data greatly limits our ability to interpret age-related trends in the accident data base. Bryer's does an excellent job presenting the case for these conclusions. Especially interesting is his statistical manipulation of risk exposure by limiting some of his analyses to accidents occurring between 9 a.m. and 4 p.m.—the time of day when most middle-aged persons are at work and when older drivers tend to be over-represented as vehicular occupant and drivers. However, there is another major conclusion one can draw from Bryer's analysis that is somewhat understated in his report. Namely, there is evidence in his data that the causes of accidents among older drivers are shifting away from reckless behaviors such as speeding and alcohol consumption to a new set of causes characterized by limitations in drivers' visual information processing efficiency.

Based on the percentage of total accidents experienced by an age group, Bryer's older drivers are less likely to be involved in freeway, single-vehicle, or nighttime crashes (all classes of accidents heavily influenced by reckless behaviors on the part of the driver). On the other hand, these same older drivers are more likely to be involved in multivehicle or intersection accidents (classes of accidents heavily influenced by failures of visual information processing). The trivial interpretation of this trend is that older drivers are not really suffering from the effects of limited visual information processing efficiency. Instead, the percentage of their accidents that involve multivehicle or intersection collisions has become artificially inflated due to the fact that they are under involved in single-vehicle and midblock accidents. However, there is important new evidence in Bryer's report that argues for the information processing deficit interpretation of this shift in the types of accidents experienced by older drivers.

The data in Figure 4.30 are taken from Table 4.7 in Bryer's report. This figure depicts age-related trends for percent accident involvement at intersections (stop sign and signalized) versus nonintersections (midblock). As already noted, there is an obvious shift in relative accident frequency from nonintersection to intersection accidents. More interesting, however, is the difference in the age-trends for the stop-sign controlled versus the traffic-light controlled (signalized) intersections. As the driving population ages from 51 to 85, there is no apparent change in the relative number of accidents occurring at intersections controlled by traffic lights. However, there is a sharp age-related increase in the relative number of accidents occurring at intersections controlled by stop signs. This pattern of results appears to be highly diagnostic. The visual information processing demands required of the driver to safely negotiate an intersection are greatly reduced when external decision-making aids such as traffic lights are present. However, intersections controlled with stop signs (especially two-way stop signs) place great demands on the visual information processing capacity of the driver. This selective shift in the relative frequency of accidents from midblock to stop-sign

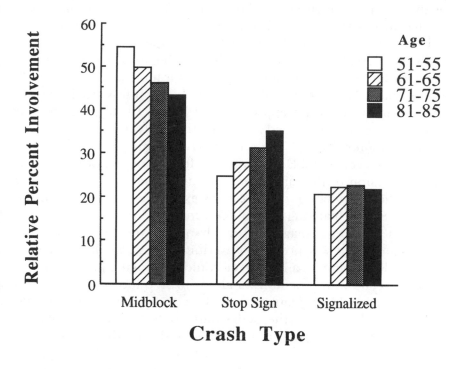

Figure 4.30 Relative percentage of accident involvement as a function of age and accident category.

controlled intersections strongly suggests that age-related declines in visual information processing efficiency may mediate a large number of accidents among older drivers.

What type of age-related information processing deficit might account for the increased likelihood of an accident at an intersection controlled by a stop sign? In an analysis of drivers age 65 and older, Hakamies-Blomqvist (1993) reported that "Older drivers typically collided in an intersection with a crossing vehicle, which they did not notice at all, or saw so late that they did not have enough time to try an avoiding maneuver" (p. 19). These older drivers apparently looked, but didn't see the opposing vehicle(s). Evidence from studies conducted by Karlene Ball and her colleagues (e.g., Ball & Owsley, 1991) suggests that deficits involving low-level visual processes—such as the failure of preattentive (i.e., automatic) acquisition of targets in the near peripheral field of vision—may predispose many older drivers toward such looked but didn't see type accidents.

Recent results reported by Rensink, O'Regan, and Clark (1997) serve to underscore the significance of low-level preattentive (i.e., perceptual) processes in real-world visual search tasks such as scanning an intersection for approaching vehicles. Participants in their experiments were presented with a picture of a typical outdoor scene on a computer display. The scene was presented for 240 ms and then the screen was blanked to gray for 80 ms before a slightly altered version of the same scene was presented again for 240 ms. This cyclic presentation of the 240 ms exposure of the scene image and the 80 ms blanking interval continued while the participants searched the scene image for any changes. Every other time that the scene image was presented a critical object in the scene was deleted. For example, an observer could be looking at a picture of a traffic scene with a pedestrian about to step into the street then the screen would be blanked and then the original scene would reappear only this time the pedestrian would be missing from the scene. Next, the screen would go blank and then the image would reappear with the pedestrian in its original position. The disappearance and reappearance of the pedestrian—separated by the 80 ms blanking interval—continues repeatedly while the participant searches the screen looking for any noticeable changes. Rensink and his colleagues found that observers had to search such displays for prolonged periods of time (i.e., many object appearances and disappearances) before they noticed the change in the images separated by the blanking interval. It was as if the blanking interval had induced a state of change blindness. When the cyclic presentation of the same scenes with and without the critical object was presented without the separating blanking interval, observers immediately noticed and accurately reported the change at the very first transition of the images.

The Rensink change blindness paradigm described above demonstrates the importance that bottom-up preattentive perceptual processes may play in our real-time search of complex visual environments such as a roadway intersection. There is evidence that the low-level visual mechanisms that may mediate preattentive popout phenomena in peripheral vision decline differentially with advancing adult age (see Kline & Schieber, 1981). That is, older adults may not need to be exposed to Rensink, et al.'s blanking interval to experience occasional failures of the bottom-up perceptual mechanisms that redirect attention to transient events in the visual array. The potential significance of the failure of such bottom-up processes in visual search has been ignored for too long by modern cognitive psychology in favor of hierarchical top-down mechanisms such as selective or divided attention. The fascinating results obtained using Rensink, et al.'s change blindness paradigm may provide the impetus as well as the means to reexamine the potential role of low-level perceptual mechanisms in our pursuit of understanding age-related changes in driving capacity and safety.

REFERENCES

Ball, K., & Owsley, C. (1991). Identifying correlates of accident involvement for the older driver. *Human Factors, 33,* 583–595.

Cerrelli, E. C. (1989). *Older drivers: The age factor in traffic safety.* Washington, DC: U.S. Department of Transportation.

Hakamies-Blomqvist, L. E. (1993). Fatal accidents of older drivers. *Accident Analysis and Prevention, 25,* 19–27.

Kline, D. W., & Schieber, F. (1981). Visual aging: A transient-sustained shift? *Perception and Psychophysics, 29,* 181–182.

Rensink, R. A., O'Regan, J. K., & Clark, J. J. (1997). To see or not to see: The need for attention to perceive changes in scenes. *Psychological Science, 8,* 368–373.

CHAPTER 5

Increasing Mobility and Reducing Accidents of Older Drivers

Karlene Ball and Cynthia Owsley

M obility is a component of daily living that most adults take for granted. In general, it can be defined as a person's purposeful movement through the environment from one place to another (Owsley, Allman, Gossman, Kell, & Sims, 1999). Mobility is extremely important to one's quality of life and personal autonomy, and therefore it is important that it be preserved as long into the lifespan as possible. Loss of mobility increases in prevalence with age, and causes include declining function in physical, cognitive, and sensory systems (Barberger & Fabrigoule, 1997; Guralnik & LaCroix, 1992; Salive, et al., 1994). Therefore, any treatment that can be used to enhance or maintain these functions is significant in that it may also have a positive impact on mobility outcomes.

In an unpublished manuscript from our laboratories, we have discussed the different ways in which mobility can be assessed in older populations. For example, performance of specific maneuvers can be evaluated (e.g., walking, climbing stairs, etc.) in terms of speed, success, and the quality of the movements (Ettinger, 1994; Tinetti, 1986). Alternatively, mobility may be assessed simply by evaluating an individual's ability to carry out either activities of daily living (ADLs) or instrumental activities of daily living (IADLs) that involve movement (Clark, Czaja, & Weber, 1990; Kovar & Lawton, 1994). Another way of evaluating mobility is to assess negative mobility outcomes. These adverse events include falls (Tinetti, Speechley, & Ginter, 1988), motor vehicle crashes (Ball, Owsley, Sloane, Roenker, & Bruni, 1993; Marottoli, Cooney, Wagner, Doucette, & Tinetti, 1994; Owsley et al., 1998), or injuries resulting from these events (e.g., hip fractures) (Cummings et al., 1995; Owsley, McGwin, & Ball, 1998). Finally, a fourth approach is to evaluate the magnitude or extent of travel or the area within which a person typically moves (May, Nayak, & Isaacs, 1985; Stalvey, Owsley, Sloane, & Ball, in press). This life space measure is useful in terms of understanding changes in mobility over time with community-dwelling older adults.

The purpose of this paper is to focus on studies evaluating mobility and mobility outcomes among older individuals who are still living in their communities and who are still driving. Studies relating various risk factors for a variety of mobility outcomes (driving avoidance/cessation, automobile crashes, injuries, and life space/driving space) will be summarized, as well as research evaluating whether interventions in these areas show promise for improving safety and mobility.

WHAT ROLE DO VISUAL AND COGNITIVE IMPAIRMENTS PLAY IN MOBILITY LOSS?

Older adults rely heavily on the automobile for independence, mobility, and an active lifestyle. One survey has suggested that individuals aged 65 years and older use the automobile for 80% of their errands and trips (Kosnik, Winslow, Kline, Rasinski, & Sekuler, 1988). Thus, changes in driving habits, and particularly reductions in the amount driven, have clear implications for maintaining mobility.

Driving Avoidance

There is evidence that at least some older drivers reduce their driving in certain driving situations. For example, older drivers are less likely as a group to drive at night or in heavy traffic (Planek, et al., 1968), to make left turns, drive in the rain and fog, drive at sunrise and sunset, drive in heavy traffic, and drive alone (Hennessy, 1995). There are several potential reasons why older adults might modify their driving habits in later life. They may have more flexible daily schedules that permit greater freedom to choose driving routes and time of travel, they may have less need to drive on a daily basis, or they may recognize that they have functional impairments that prompt safety concerns. There may be individual differences as to the underlying rationale for changes in driving habits, but several studies imply that as a group, elderly persons tend to limit their driving to those times and places where they feel the safety risk is lower (Hennessy, 1995; Janke, 1994; Planek, et al., 1968). While this practice may help to prevent some adverse events, such as crashes, it may also signal the onset of reduced mobility in this population. To examine the implications for mobility restriction, we examined self-reported driving avoidance in a sample of 257 older drivers with objectively established visual and cognitive functional capabilities to determine which types of driving modifications older drivers are most likely to make, as well as whether declining cognitive or sensory function is predictive of changes in driving habits (Ball, et al., 1998).

Study participants were recruited from the population of licensed drivers aged 55 years or older residing within Jefferson County, Alabama ($N = 118,553$). A detailed description of the recruitment and study population is provided elsewhere (Ball, et al., 1998). The mean age of the sample was 70 years (range 56–90 years) and included 137 males and 120 females. The mean age for males was 70 ($SD = 9$), and for females it was 71 years ($SD = 9$).

Several functional measures of visual and cognitive function were obtained for each participant. Visual acuity was measured with the Early Treatment of Diabetic Retinopathy Study chart (Ferris, Kassoff, Bresnick, & Bailey, 1982). Contrast sensitivity was measured with the Pelli-Robson Contrast Sensitivity Chart (Pelli, Robson, & Wilkins, 1988). Visual field sensitivity was measured with the Humphrey Field Analyzer screening program for the central 60 degrees (Haley, 1987). All participants received an eye health examination by an ophthalmologist and were rated on a 3-point scale for deficits in central vision, peripheral vision, and ocular media, as well as overall eye health (see Owsley, Ball, Sloane, Roenker, & Bruni, 1991). Each participant was also assigned to a primary diagnostic category (e.g., normal, cataract, age-related macular degeneration (AMD)).

Cognitive function was assessed with the Mattis Organic Mental Status Syndrome Examination, (MOMSSE), which was specifically designed to assess cognitive status in the elderly (Mattis, 1976). The MOMSSE provides a composite score of cognitive function covering several domains including abstraction, digit span, verbal and visual memory, and block design.

Useful field of view, a measure of visual attention and processing speed, was assessed using the UFOV Visual Attention Analyzer, Model 2000 (Visual Resources, Inc., Chicago, IL). This microprocessor-based instrument uses three subtests that provide a reliable measure of the size of the useful field of view, expressed in terms of the percentage of reduction (0 to 90%) of a maximum 35° radius field (Ball, Roenker, & Bruni, 1990). Subtests were presented on a 20-inch (diagonal) video monitor at a viewing distance of 23.5 cm. Targets were presented at high contrast (99%), and subtended 5.1 horizontal × 3.2 vertical degrees of visual angle. In the first subtest, designed to assess speed of visual processing under minimal cognitive demand, the participant was required to identify a target of varying duration, presented in the fixation box. The target was the silhouette of a car or a truck. The second subtest, designed to assess the ability to divide attention, required the localization of a simultaneously presented peripheral target (a silhouette of a car) in addition to the identification of the central target. The peripheral target appeared unpredictably at any one of 24 different peripheral locations along eight radial spokes (four cardinal and four oblique) at three eccentricities (10°, 20°, and 30°). The duration of the display was varied to measure speed of processing for this divided attention task. The third subtest, designed to assess selective attention abilities, was the same as the second task with the exception that the peripheral target was embedded in distractors (triangles). Performance on the UFOV test is then expressed as a function of three variables: the minimum target duration required to perform the central discrimination task (subtest 1), the ability to divide attention between central and peripheral tasks successfully (subtest 2), and the ability to filter out distracting stimuli (subtest 3). For subtest 1, the minimum duration that subjects can perform the task with 75% correct is noted. For subtests 2 and 3, the best fitting line reflecting the relationship between eccentricity and localization errors is computed for each test duration, and useful field of view size is defined as the eccentricity at which a subject can localize the peripheral target correctly 50% of the time. Performance on the subtests is combined to arrive at three scores representing the extent of difficulty with regard to speed of processing, divided attention, and selective attention. These scores range from 0 (no problem) to 30 (great difficulty). Deficits in each of these abilities have been shown to be additive in their effect on UFOV test size (Ball, Roenker, & Bruni, 1990). Therefore, to summarize performance, the three scores are combined to yield a score between 0 and 90 that represents the percentage reduction of a maximum 35° radius field.

A driving habits questionnaire (DHQ) asked about driving exposure and the avoidance of potentially challenging driving situations. The question on driving exposure asked how many days/week the subject typically drove. The DHQ items on avoidance were as follows: (a) do you avoid driving at night, (b) do you avoid high-traffic roads, (c) do you avoid rush-hour traffic, (d) do you avoid high speed interstates/expressways, (e) do you avoid driving alone, (f) do you avoid left-hand turns across oncoming traffic, and (g) do you avoid driving in the rain. The response options covered a range of 1 to 5 (1 = never, 2 = rarely, 3 = sometimes, 4 = often, and 5 = always).

Table 5.1 lists the Spearman correlation coefficients among visual and cognitive function, eye health, driving exposure (days/week), and the seven DHQ avoidance items. Scores on the avoidance items were expressed in their original form in this analysis, that is, as scores ranging from 1 to 5. As shown in Table 5.1, subjects reporting more avoidance were more likely to have visual or cognitive impairments and eye health problems. Specifically, frequent avoidance of driving in heavy traffic, high speed, and rain were significantly associated with all types of functional assessments, as was reduced driving exposure (days/week).

In general, associations between the reported avoidance of night driving and the functional measures were weak, which may reflect the relatively high level of night driving avoidance displayed by almost all individuals in the cohort. Relationships between mental status and the avoidance items were generally weaker than those between visual function and avoidance. One exception is the relationship between mental status and driving alone, in which case mental

TABLE 5.1 Correlations Among Visual and Cognitive Measures, Eye Health, and Items on Driving Habits Questionnaire

	Contrast sensitivity	Central	Peripheral	Eye health	Mental status	UFOV	Exposure	Night	Traffic	Rush hour	High speed	Alone	Left turns	Rain
Acuity	−0.66	0.44	0.37	0.62	0.14	0.36	−0.27	0.17	0.33	0.25	0.24	0.11	0.11	0.24
Contrast sensitivity	1.00	−0.5	−0.46	−0.7	−0.2	−0.45	−0.3	−0.23	−0.34	−0.26	−0.28	−0.13	−0.10	−0.33
Central		1.00	0.83	0.49	0.3	−0.47	−0.22	0.13	0.34	0.33	0.33	0.20	0.17	0.36
Peripheral			1.00	0.39	0.36	0.46	−0.2	0.08	0.31	0.24	0.29	0.16	0.11	0.29
Eye health				1.00	0.2	0.38	−0.28	0.18	0.32	0.20	0.26	0.19	0.06	0.30
Mental status					1.00	0.44	−0.19	−0.10	0.22	0.02	0.14	0.26	0.10	0.20
UFOV						1.00	−0.27	0.14	0.28	0.25	0.21	0.18	0.15	0.37
Exposure							1.00	−0.26	−0.23	−0.24	−0.22	−0.20	−0.03	−0.23
Night								1.00	0.04	0.07	0.20	−0.01	0.04	0.21
Traffic									1.00	0.53	0.58	0.12	0.14	0.22
Rush hour										1.00	0.50	0.07	0.03	0.18
High speed											1.00	0.18	0.05	0.25
Alone												1.00	0.37	0.39
Left turns													1.00	0.24
Rain														1.00

UFOV, Useful Field of View Visual Attention Analyzer.

status showed the strongest relationship with driving alone, compared to all other functional measures.

In the next stage of data analysis, cutpoints for impairment were established for each visual and cognitive variable. These cutpoints are listed in Table 5.2. The visual cutpoints were based on the minimum level of vision required to adequately perform a suprathreshold visual discrimination task, as determined in our prior work (see Owsley, Ball, & Keeton, 1995). For mental status, the cutpoint for the MOMSSE test was based on clinical convention and our prior work on crash-involved older drivers (Ball, et al., 1993). For the useful field of view, the cutpoint was based on that used in our prior work on older drivers. Before pursuing further analyses on impaired versus unimpaired drivers, we noticed that according to our definition of acuity impairment (worse than 20/40, the legal limit for driving in many states in the United States), there were scarcely any subjects with impaired acuity (only 5%). Thus, acuity impairment was dropped from further analysis. Furthermore, because 90% of subjects with impaired mental status also had impaired useful field of view, and useful field of view reduction was the more prevalent cognitive impairment, mental status was not considered as a separate

TABLE 5.2 Criteria Used to Determine Cutpoints for Visual and Cognitive Abilities

Functional variable	Unimpaired	% of Sample	Impaired	% of Sample
Acuity	< 0.48 logMAR	(95%)	≥ 0.48 logMAR	(5%)
Contrast sensitivity	> 1.35dB	(90%)	≤ 1.35dB	(10%)
Humphrey central 30	< 10dB	(86%)	≥ 10dB	(14%)
Humphrey peripheral 30	< 15dB	(73%)	≥ 15db	(27%)
Eye health	0	(46%)	> 0	(54%)
Mental status	< 9	(82%)	≥ 9	(18%)
UFOV	< 40% reduction	(45%)	≥ 40% reduction	(55%)

UFOV, Useful Field of View.

variable to eliminate redundancy in later analyses. As our earlier work has demonstrated (Ball, et al., 1993), useful field of view is a sensitive indicator of poor mental status, and the two share a reliance on some common cognitive domains (e.g., processing speed, attention, decision-making).

Participants were initially placed in one of six groups based on whether they had 0, 1, or more than one of the impairments listed in Table 5.2. Membership in each group was defined in terms of the number of vision impairments types (0–4) and poor (impaired) versus good (unimpaired) useful field of view. These six groups were defined as listed in Table 5.3. Since group 3 (3–4 vision problems and good useful field of view) contained only three subjects, it was dropped from any further analysis. Low membership in this group was not surprising because individuals with extremely poor vision typically fail ($\geq 40\%$ reduction) the useful field of view test (Owsley, et al., 1995).

Mean responses on the remaining five functionally defined groups across the seven DHQ avoidance items are plotted in Figure 5.1. Note that the overall level of reported avoidance differs across the various driving situations evaluated. Specifically, some activities, such as night driving or rush hour traffic, are at least sometimes avoided by most of the older drivers, regardless of functional status, while

TABLE 5.3 Criteria Used to Determine the Six Functional Groups Based on Number of Vision Problems and UFOV Score

Group 1	$N = 59$	0 Vision problems and unimpaired UFOV	(< 40)
Group 2	$N = 55$	1–2 Vision problems and unimpaired UFOV	(< 40)
Group 3	$N = 3$	3–4 Vision problems and unimpaired UFOV	(< 40)
Group 4	$N = 40$	0 Vision problems and impaired UFOV	(> 40)
Group 5	$N = 67$	1–2 Vision problems and impaired UFOV	(> 40)
Group 6	$N = 33$	3–4 Vision problems and impaired UFOV	(> 40)

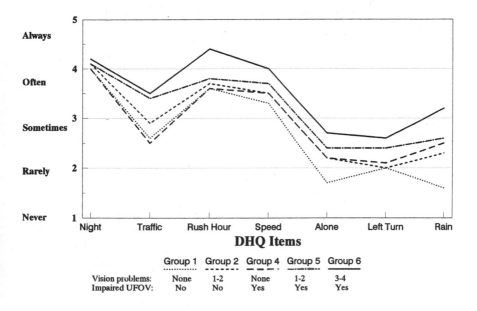

Figure 5.1   Mean responses to Driving Habits Questionnaire items.

driving alone or making left turns are reportedly avoided much less frequently.

A multivariate analysis of variance (MANOVA) was conducted on the five groups to determine whether the pattern of reported avoidance (responses on each of the seven DHQ avoidance items) was significantly different across functional groups. This analysis confirmed significant differences across the five groups ($F(24,988) = 2.37$, $p < 0.0005$), as well as a significant interaction between group and avoidance items ($F(28,984) = 3.34$, $p < .0005$), indicating that the pattern of responses to the avoidance items differed across functional impairment group. Subsequently, a separate univariate analysis of variance was conducted on each item to determine differential responses across groups.

The results of these analyses and their associated post hoc comparisons (Tukey HSD tests, $p < 0.05$) are listed in Table 5.4. Responses on all avoidance items across functional groups differed significantly, except for avoiding night driving, in which all groups reported a

TABLE 5.4   Results of Univariate Analysis on Each Avoidance Item as a Function of Group

Item	F ratio	df	p	Significant post-hoc comparisons
Night	0.71	4249	0.59	None
Traffic	9.47	4249	< 0.0001	1 versus 5, 6; 4 versus 5, 6
Rush hour	5.22	4249	< 0.0005	6 versus 1, 2, 4, 5
High speed highways	4.28	4249	0.0023	1 versus 5, 6
Alone	4.84	4249	0.0009	1 versus 5, 6
Left turns	2.67	4249	0.0327	None
Rain	14.39	4249	< 0.0001	1 versus 2,4,5,6; 2 versus 4; 4 versus 6

similar level of avoidance. For the remaining items, there were differing patterns of responses depending on the driving activity addressed. For the avoidance of heavy traffic, group 1 (the group with good functional ability) reported significantly less avoidance than did groups 5 or 6 (the two groups with the most severe visual/cognitive impairment). In addition, group 4, which had a moderate level of impairment, reported significantly less avoidance of traffic than groups 5 or 6. For avoiding rush hour traffic, group 6 (the most impaired group) reporting significantly more avoidance than each of the other four groups. Avoidance of high speed highways was reported significantly more often in the two most impaired groups relative to the least impaired group, as was avoidance of driving alone. Avoidance of making left turns across traffic differed significantly among the five groups, however, post hoc analysis did not demonstrate significant differences between any two groups in particular. Finally, avoidance of driving in the rain differed significantly between group 1 and each of the other four impaired groups, as well as between groups 2 and 6, and between groups 4 and 6. In summary, results indicated that self-reported driving avoidance varies with functional impairment, with more severely impaired drivers reporting more avoidance. In addition, the level of avoidance differs depending on the type of driving situation evaluated.

This study is consistent with a growing body of work (e.g., Planek, et al., 1968; Hennessy, 1995) demonstrating that many older individuals self-regulate their driving and avoid driving in situations that are more challenging. Evidence indicates that most older drivers minimize their night driving, driving during rush hour traffic and on high traffic roads, and driving in situations where rapid and unexpected events occur in a visually cluttered environment, often under conditions of reduced visibility. Since our results indicate that most drivers, impaired and unimpaired alike, avoid these situations at least sometimes, this modification of driving habits may reflect a safety strategy typical of the older driver population in general. Because many older adults have increased flexibility in the scheduling of car trips, minimizing their exposure to these more challenging driving scenarios is a simple option they can exercise to enhance safety. Avoidance of night driving by most older adults may stem from the fact that vision under low illumination is impaired even in older adults in good eye health, relative to younger adults (Sloane, Owsley, & Alvarez, 1988).

On the other hand, older drivers with multiple impairments (i.e., having both visual and attentional processing difficulties) restricted their driving to a larger extent and in more situations than those with visual impairments alone or those who were functionally normal; the multiply impaired reported that they avoided at least sometimes or often all seven driving situations asked about on the questionnaire. This pattern of extensive avoidance underscores the importance of both visual and attentional skills for controlling a vehicle (Ball et al., 1993; Johnson & Keltner, 1986). Our data also indicate that visual and attentional processing impairments are associated with fewer days of driving/week, suggesting that self-regulation is not only expressed as avoidance of certain driving situations, but also reduction in other aspects of driving exposure.

Studies on driving habits such as this one suggest that some older drivers are aware that their functional declines in visual and cognitive processing capabilities can make driving more difficult, even posing a safety threat, and as a result, they modify when and where they drive. Of course the present cross sectional study does not prove that avoidance is the result of insight into one's visual/attentional impairments and thus signifies self-regulation. However, such an interpretation has a great deal of face validity and garners support from anecdotal reports and focus groups of older adults (Persson, 1993). While this study and others present evidence that older drivers self-regulate through avoidance, the present results do not indicate if avoidance is effective in reducing risk for future crashes. It could be that self-regulation as a safety measure may have its strongest impact within certain types of older drivers. For older drivers with no functional impairments, driving avoidance may simply reflect a common sense approach to avoid aversive driving situations such as heavy traffic or rush hour driving, especially because one's schedule permits it. For these drivers, avoidance would likely be unrelated to crash risk due to the fact that most older drivers free of visual and cognitive impairments have low crash risk; so in essence there is a floor effect. On the other hand, for those drivers with moderate impairment, self-regulation may provide some advantage, keeping them away from those on-road situations that are exceedingly difficult for them. The result could be a reduction in crash risk. The present study did not permit an adequate evaluation of this issue because many of the impaired drivers in the cohort stopped driving or died during the 3-year follow-up of crash data. Driving cessation is the most extreme level of driving avoidance and is interesting as an outcome from this standpoint. However, one cannot utilize safety records as an outcome if the cohort is not on the road.

The promotion of self-regulation as a method for improving safety among older drivers with visual/cognitive impairments is intriguing and deserves further examination. There are many key issues to be addressed as alluded to earlier, such as whether it improves safety, which subpopulations would benefit the most from such an intervention, and how would such an intervention program be implemented, even if shown to be successful. For those drivers with the most severe functional impairments, self-regulation may not sufficiently reduce crash risk, and driving cessation may be the only safe option. Studies on crash risk will be reviewed later in this chapter.

Role of Cataracts in Driving and Mobility Impairment

Many older adults must cope for an extended period with vision impairment induced by cataracts until the time when surgical removal of the cataract is indicated, usually when best-corrected acuity reaches 20/40 or worse (National Safety Council, 1993). In a second study we will now describe, the role of cataracts in driving and mobility impairment was examined (Owsley, Stalvey, Wells, & Sloane, 1999). Earlier work has linked vision impairment and eye disease in elderly persons to changes in driving habits (Evans, 1991; McCoy, Johnson, & Duthie, 1989) and even driving cessation (Koepsell, et al., 1994). This study addressed the following questions: How do the driving habits of older adults with cataracts differ from those without cataracts? Do older drivers with cataracts experience driving difficulties? Are driving habits related to self-perceived driving difficulties, suggesting self-regulation? Finally, do older drivers with cataracts have an elevated crash risk?

Two groups of subjects were evaluated, older drivers with cataracts and those without cataracts (see Owsley, et al., 1999, for detailed visual inclusion criteria). Persons in both groups were required to be between the ages of 55 and 85 years old, living independently in the community, and legally licensed to drive. Participants were recruited from 10 ophthalmology practices and two optometry clinics in Birmingham, Alabama through medical record review of patients seen during the previous 12 months.

The protocol was divided into two parts, interview and assessment. The DHQ, as described above, was expanded for the purposes of this study and addressed six domains.

1. Current driving status and miscellaneous issues. Items 1 through 10 established current driving status, general driving practices (e.g., spectacle and seatbelt use, driving speed), and self-assessed quality of driving.
2. Driving exposure. Items 11 through 14 asked about the average number of days driven per week and where the respondent drove in a typical week. The latter generates an estimate of the number of places traveled to, number of trips made, and number of miles driven in a typical week.
3. Dependence on other drivers. Items 15 and 16 provided a detailed assessment of who the respondent traveled with in a car on a regular basis and who usually drove with that person. From this interview, an estimate of dependency on other drivers was generated, which ranged from 1 to 3 with higher scores meaning greater levels of dependency on others to drive.

4. Driving difficulty. Items 17 through 24 asked respondents to rate the degree of visual difficulty experienced in specific driving situations. Ratings are made on a 5-point scale (5 = no difficulty, 4 = a little difficulty, 3 = moderate difficulty, 2 = extreme difficulty, 1 = so difficult I no longer drive in that situation). A composite score of driving difficulty was computed based on the responses to all eight items and scaled on a 100-point scale [(mean score − 1) × 25]. Lower composite scores indicated a greater degree of difficulty.

5. Driving space. Items 29 through 34 addressed the distance respondents typically drove into their environment away from their home base over the past year (e.g., within the neighborhood, outside the state). Subjects answered yes = 1 or no = 0 as to whether they had driven to the designated region in the past year. A summary score of driving space is computed by summing scores across all items (0–6) where lower scores indicate a smaller driving space.

6. Self-reported crashes and citations. Items 25 through 28 asked respondents to report the number of crashes incurred and the number of citations received during the past year. General health, mental status, and depression were also assessed.

Cataract is an eye condition that can vary in its impact on visual function. Visual functional status of all participants was measured with respect to acuity, contrast sensitivity, and visual field sensitivity as described earlier. The demographic characteristics of the cataract ($N = 279$) and no-cataract groups ($N = 105$) were compared. Those with cataracts were slightly older on average by about 4 years ($t(382) = -6.21$, $p < 0.001$). Both groups were split about evenly between males and females and had similar racial composition, with the majority White and approximately 15% African American.

All drivers free from cataracts and nearly all (96%) drivers with cataracts were current drivers. Four percent of subjects with cataracts ($n = 10$) had stopped driving during the last 3 years because of vision problems, but all these individuals intended to start driving again after they had cataract surgery during the next year. Nearly all subjects in both groups reported wearing glasses and a seatbelt when driving. Compared to drivers without cataracts, proportionally more drivers with cataracts preferred to have someone else drive when they travelled in a car, drove slower than the general traffic flow, and received advice that they limit or stop their driving. Logistic regression analysis evaluated these associations, examining the role of potential confounders (advanced age, impaired health, mental status deficit, depression). Results are presented in terms of relative risk, which indicates that those in the cataract group are more likely (e.g., $RR = 2$; twice as likely) than those in the noncataract group to experience a particular outcome. Confidence intervals, which do not include 1.0, indicate significance at the $p < .05$ level. A cataract was associated with driving slower than the general traffic flow, $RR = 1.79$ (95% CI 1.01 – 3.16, adjusted for impaired health), and receiving advice that the person should limit/stop driving, $RR = 5.00$ (95% CI 1.15 – 21.33, no adjustments necessary). The self-rated quality of driving was about the same in both groups, although there was a tendency for those with cataracts to rate the quality of their driving more poorly than those without cataracts.

Table 5.5 presents information about driving exposure and dependency on other drivers. There were no group differences in the reported number of trips made, miles driven per week, or the number of people with whom the respondent traveled. However, drivers with cataracts reportedly drove fewer days and places per week and were less likely to be the driver when traveling in a car with another person (driving dependency) compared to those free of cataract. Logistic regression analysis was used to examine associations between cataracts and each of these variables, adjusting for potential confounders (advanced age, poor health, impaired mental status, and depression). Cataracts were associated with reduced days of driving, $RR = 1.89$ (95% CI 1.06 – 3.34, no adjustments necessary), and reduced destinations, $RR = 1.75$ (95% CI 1.08 – 2.82, no adjustments necessary), but cataracts were unrelated to driving dependency, $RR = 1.43$ (95% CI 0.90 – 2.27).

With respect to driving, subjects were categorized on each item as having either no difficulty or any difficulty. Cataracts were significantly associated with driving difficulty in the rain, driving alone, making left-turns across oncoming traffic, driving on interstates, driving in high-traffic, driving in rush-hour traffic, and driving at night. There were no differences in the two groups with regard to difficulty in parallel parking, with almost 30% of subjects in both groups reporting difficulty in this driving maneuver. We were inter-

TABLE 5.5　Comparison of Means for Cataract and Control Group on Driving Exposure and Driving Dependency Measures

DHQ Item	Cataract mean	(*SD*)	No cata- ract mean	(*SD*)	*p* value*
Number of days per week	5	(2)	6	(2)	0.020
Number of places per week	5	(2)	6	(2)	0.002
Number of trips per week	11	(7)	12	(6)	0.150
Number of miles per week	174	(233)	201	(218)	0.300
Number of people travel with	4	(3)	4	(3)	0.520
Driving dependency	2.0	(.7)	1.7	(.7)	0.001

*t test.
DHQ, Driving Habits Questionnaire.

ested in the association between cataracts and driving difficulty after adjustments for comorbid conditions and functional impairments believed to impact driving ability (advanced age, impaired health, mental status deficit, depression). For the purposes of this analysis, we used the composite difficulty score that ranged from 0 (extreme difficulty) to 100 (no difficulty). This composite measure of difficulty was then expressed as a categoric variable; driving difficulty was defined as scores < 90; scores ≥ 90 signified those with no difficulty. Cataracts were significantly related to driving difficulty, $RR = 4.50$ (95% CI 2.63 – 7.68 adjusted for depression).

With respect to driving space, there were no differences in the groups with respect to driving in the immediate neighborhood, beyond the immediate neighborhood, and in neighboring towns. However, those with cataracts were less likely to drive to more distant towns and beyond. The composite driving space score was used to generate a categoric variable of driving space. A restricted driving space was defined as driving only as far as neighboring towns, and a large driving space was defined as anything larger. Logistic regression analysis evaluated the association between a restricted driving space (dependent variable) and cataracts adjusting for the potential confounders of advanced age, impaired health, mental status deficit, and depression. Cataract and restricted driving space were significantly associated, RR 1.84 (95% CI 1.00 − 3.53, adjusted for age and mental status).

The results of this study demonstrate that older adults with cataracts are more likely to experience mobility restrictions, as compared to older drivers without cataracts. Those with cataracts reported that they drove fewer days/week and to fewer destinations, limited their driving to areas closer to their home base, and drove slower than the general traffic flow. Comorbid medical conditions and functional impairments, although present in our cohort, did not account for this association between cataracts and restricted driving mobility. Reduced mobility is one of the most commonly reported problems of older adults (Brenton & Phelps, 1986), especially among those who are visually impaired (Ball, et al., 1990; Mattis, 1976). Our demonstration that restriction in driving mobility is related to an eye condition which is reversible suggests that interventions to improve vision in older adults may also improve mobility.

Older drivers with cataracts were much more likely to express difficulty in challenging driving situations (a fourfold increase) than were those who were cataract-free, which agrees with the first study reported above (Monestam & Wachtmeister, 1997). All situations addressed in the interview, except for parallel parking, were more difficult for drivers with cataracts, including driving in the rain, alone, on interstates, on high-traffic roads, in rush hour, and at night, and in making left-turns across oncoming traffic. It is important to point out that these are not rare driving scenarios, but situations commonly encountered on the road in a nonrural population.

With respect to driving safety, this study indicated that older drivers with cataracts have an elevated crash risk compared to those without this condition. Cataract is a common medical condition in older adults, and thus its association with a reduction in driver safety is a critical point. Highly effective treatments for cataract are available, namely surgical removal of the cataract followed by intraocular lens implantation. Like many medical and surgical procedures, cataract surgery is closely scrutinized in terms of its cost versus benefit to quality of life and the patient's well-being (Owsley et al., 1995). As this study continues and subjects are followed postsurgically, we will be able to determine whether cataract surgery indeed lowers crash risk and enhances driving mobility in the elderly. This approach contributes toward evaluating surgical and medical procedures in the elderly using outcomes defined in terms of the performance of activities of daily living and enhanced quality of life.

Life Space: A Measure of the Range of Mobility

A third study we will describe examined the associations between a measure of life space, as assessed by the life space questionnaire (LSQ), and various forms of functional impairment in a sample of 384 older adults who were recruited through eye care clinics. The items of the LSQ (Stalvey et al., in press) are listed in Table 5.6. Mean age for the sample was 70 years old (SD 6.4, range 55–85)

TABLE 5.6　The Life Space Questionnaire Items

1. During the past 3 days, have you been to other rooms of your home besides the room where you sleep?
2. During the past 3 days, have you been to an area immediately outside your home such as your porch, deck or patios, hallway of an apartment building, garage?
3. During the past 3 days, have you been to an area outside your home such as a yard, courtyard, driveway, or parking lot?
4. During the past 3 days, have you been to places in your immediate neighborhood, but beyond your own property or apartment building?
5. During the past 3 days, have you been to places outside your immediate neighborhood, but within your town or community?
6. During the past 3 days, have you been to places outside your immediate town or community?
7. During the past 3 days, have you been to places outside your county?
8. During the past 3 days, have you been to places outside the state?
9. During the past 3 days, have you been to places outside this region of the United States?

Response options are yes/no.
Introduction to subject: "Please think about the places you have been during the past 3 days."

with 199 (52%) men and 185 (48%) women. Fifteen percent were African Americans, and the remainder were White. Self-reported health status in the sample indicated that most were in good to excellent health—12% in excellent health, 31% in very good health, 32% in good health, 21% in fair health, and 4% in poor health.

Visual processing ability and mental status were assessed as described in the previous two studies. General health was measured by asking subjects if they have problems in 17 areas (e.g., heart, cancer, diabetes, stroke), and if so, to what extent they are bothered by the condition on a 3-point scale (1 = not bothered at all, 2 = bothered a little, 3 = bothered a great deal). The questionnaire was derived from an earlier study on eye conditions and quality of life (Steinberg et al., 1994). The questionnaire allows subjects to add conditions not specifically asked about if they so choose. To generate a comorbidity index, each medical condition present is weighted by the bothersome score above, and then all are summed. Scores theoretically range from 0 (no health conditions present) to infinity (because subjects can add conditions to the query list).

LSQ scores for this sample ranged from 3 to 9 (mean = 6; SD = 1.3). Associations between the LSQ score and the functional impairment measures were evaluated by Pearson correlations. Preliminary analysis indicated that the life space score was modestly associated with age (Spearman's rho = −0.1, p = 0.059), as were all the other functional impairment measures assessed in this study. Thus all correlations between life space and functional impairment were adjusted for age.

Results are listed in Table 5.7. Reductions in contrast sensitivity and the useful field of view, impaired cognitive function, and de-

TABLE 5.7 Age-Adjusted Correlation Coefficients for the Life Space Questionnaire Score and Functional and Health Measures

	r^b	p value
Visual acuity	−0.06	0.23
Contrast sensitivity	0.11	0.04
Useful field of view	−0.27	0.0001
Mental status	−0.22	0.0001
Depressive symptoms	−0.12	0.02
Comorbidity index	−0.03	0.56

pressive symptoms were associated with a more restricted life space, even after adjustment for age. The strongest predictors of the LSQ score were useful field of view size and mental status. Interestingly, visual acuity was not associated with life space. This is consistent with the results of earlier studies suggesting that the ability to resolve fine detail plays less of a role in mobility than do contrast sensitivity or visual field characteristics (Ball, et al., 1993; Marron & Bailey, 1982; Rubin, Roche, Prasada-Rao, & Fried, 1994). Impaired health, as represented by the comorbidity index, was not associated with a reduced life space. It is interesting that while the functional manifestations of disease (vision impairment, cognitive deficits) were associated with life space magnitude, the presence of multiple health problems per se was not. This underscores the significance of relying on functional assessment, rather than mere disease presence, in assessing older adults' problems in everyday tasks.

The results of this study indicate that those older adults with functional impairments in skills critical to mobility (vision or cognitive impairment or depression) have a more restricted life space. Our finding is consistent with the large body of research indicating that vision and cognitive problems are associated with mobility and postural stability problems (Marron & Bailey, 1982; Salive et al., 1994; Selikson, Damus, & Hamerman, 1988; Tinetti, et al., 1988), as well as transportation difficulties (Ball, et al., 1993; Tuokko, Tallman, Beattie, Cooper, & Weir, 1995). In addition, a recent study found that driving cessation in elderly persons was associated with the development of depressive symptoms (Marottoli, et al., 1997). Those older adults who drive fewer miles per week, travel to fewer destinations, and make fewer trips in their car also have a more narrow life space. It is important to note that although life space is related to driving habits, the concepts are not identical. For example, there are other ways to travel extensively in the community and not be a driver (e.g., ride with someone else, use public transportation). Thus, information about driving habits and life space are not redundant. In essence, the concept of life space estimates the magnitude or extent of travel into the environment, regardless of how one gets there. As such it takes into account compensatory and coping strategies that individuals implement to get where they want to go.

While the research just summarized converges on evidence that older drivers with visual and cognitive impairments experience reductions in mobility (primarily thought to be due to self-regulation), it may also be the case that these same impairments increase the risk of adverse mobility outcomes. The focus in the next section will be on predicting automobile crashes and injurious crashes using the same variables predictive of mobility loss.

WHAT ROLE DO VISUAL AND COGNITIVE IMPAIRMENTS PLAY IN ADVERSE MOBILITY OUTCOMES (I.E., CRASHES AND INJURIOUS CRASHES)?

Older drivers as a group have more traffic convictions and crashes and incur more fatalities per mile driven than any other adult age group (National Highway Traffic Safety Administration, 1989). However, it is also the case that a significant number of older adults have excellent driving skills. Older adults exhibit marked individual differences in many skills, and driving is no exception. Given that the personal automobile is the preferred mode of travel in most industrialized societies, and given that elderly persons rely on the automobile to maintain mobility, there continues to be a pressing need for research to identify the factors that place certain older drivers at risk for crash involvement (Waller, 1991).

Driving is obviously a highly visual task, and thus it has typically been thought that the higher incidence of visual problems and eye disease in the elderly (Leibowitz, Krueger, & Maunder, 1980) is a primary cause of their increased crash involvement. This expectation is reflected by the practice of assessing vision at driver licensing sites in each state. However, earlier studies have found only weak correlations between visual deficits and vehicle crashes (Henderson & Burg, 1974; Hills & Burg, 1977; Shinar, 1977). Visual deficits were of no practical significance in identifying which older drivers are at risk for crash involvement.

The failure to find a strong link between visual deficits and driving in previous work may have been due to several factors (National Highway Traffic Safety Administration, 1989; Shinar & Schieber, 1991). In samples from earlier studies, there was a preponderance of drivers with zero crashes on record, making it difficult to evaluate a model designed to predict crash frequency. Fortunately, crashes are rare occurrences, but this presents a challenge in trying to predict an improbable event. Another reason for weak links in earlier work is that poor vision may lead drivers to modify their behavior, as described earlier in this chapter, and thus reduce their crash risk. Such self-imposed changes in driving behavior would mitigate against a correlation between poor vision and crash involvement. Finally, previous studies relied almost exclusively on visual sensory tests as the independent (predictor) variables, ignoring higher-order perceptual and cognitive components (Henderson & Burg, 1974; Hills & Burg, 1977; Johnson & Keltner, 1986; Shinar, 1977) or vice versa (Friedland, et al., 1988; Lucas-Blaustein, Filipp, Dungan, & Tune, 1988; Waller, 1965). Sensory tests, although quite appropriate for the clinical diagnosis and assessment of ocular disease and vision loss, do not by themselves reflect the visual complexity of the driving task, and therefore would not be expected to reveal a strong relationship between vision and driving.

Visual/Perceptual Correlates of Vehicle Crashes

We developed a regression model for predicting crash frequency in elderly drivers on the basis of a preliminary study that assessed visual and cognitive skills in a small sample of older adults (Owsley et al., 1991). Figure 5.2 portrays this model. The most prominent feature

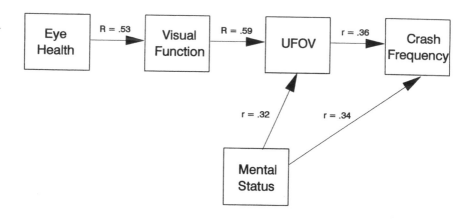

Figure 5.2 Multiple regression model for predicting crash frequency.

of the model is that visual attention and mental status are the only variables that significantly predict crash frequency. Although the model acknowledges that eye health is related to visual sensory function, and visual sensory function is related to visual attention, neither eye health nor visual sensory function is related to crashes. This initial study was critical in developing the model, however, it was far from conclusive because most of our independent variables were restricted in range and our analysis was limited to a total of only 25 crashes. Thus, the large sample study described here was deemed crucial to test the model.

A subsequent study evaluated a large sample of older drivers to test the model in Figure 5.2 by assessing various aspects of visual information processing including health status of the visual system, visual sensory function, visual attentional skills, and cognitive skills. The recruitment population consisted of all licensed drivers aged 55 years and older living in Jefferson County, Alabama (N=118,553). The crash data were obtained from the Alabama Department of Public Safety. A sampling strategy was utilized to produce a stratified sample balanced with respect to age and crash frequency over the previous 5 years. The total population was divided by age group (55–59, 60–64, 65–69, 70–74, 75–79, 80–84, 85+) and crash frequency (0, 1–3, 4 or more). Next, 75 drivers were randomly selected from each of the 21 cells, and contact letters were sent to all those listed in the local phone directory (1342 persons). Recruiting continued until approximately 300 older adults were enrolled in the study and the final sample had 294 participants. The mean age of the entire sample was 71 years (range 56–90 years); 136 were male and 158 were female. All participants lived independently in the community.

There were five parts to the protocol, which were completed in a single visit to the laboratory: visual sensory function, mental status, useful field of view, driving habits questionnaire, and eye health. The visual sensory function tests consisted of visual acuity, contrast sensitivity, disability glare, stereopsis, color discrimination, and visual field sensitivity. Mental status was assessed by the MOMSSE.

All subjects received a detailed eye health examination by an ophthalmologist. A 3-point rating scale was used to determine to what extent clinical changes in the eye would be expected to cause a functional problem in each of three broad categories—central vision problem, peripheral vision problem, and ocular media problem. In addition, each subject was assigned to a primary diagnostic category (e.g., normal, cataract, macular disease). The DHQ described earlier was also administered.

Crash frequency during the previous 5-year period was obtained for each subject from the Alabama Department of Public Safety. Following completion of data collection, the written accident reports (filed by the officer at the scene) which detailed the circumstances surrounding each crash, for all subjects were obtained from the state. Three raters, blind with respect to other data in the study, as well as the identity of the research participant, independently reviewed each accident report to determine whether the research participant was at fault. Our sample of 294 participants were involved in 364 at-fault crashes.

The goal of this study was to test a model designed to predict crash frequency in older drivers on the basis of visual and cognitive measures (Owsley, et al., 1991). We tested our original model using the LISREL VII structural modeling program (Byrne, 1989; Jöreskog & Sörbom, 1989). As shown in Figure 5.3, our model as formulated postulated that eye health, central vision, and peripheral vision have only indirect effects on crash frequency but direct effects on visual attention (useful field of view). It further asserted that mental status has a direct effect on crash frequency, as well as an indirect effect on crash frequency mediated through useful field of view. While the overall model accounted for 74% of the variance in the sample data, it was also of interest to determine the R^2 associated with crash prediction alone. Only two variables, useful field of view and mental status, had direct effects on crash frequency, jointly accounting for 28% of its variance. Even when the LISREL model was respecified so that central and peripheral vision were forced to have direct effects on crash frequency (in addition to their indirect effect through useful field of view), there was still no increase in the amount of crash variance accounted for. The main role of central and peripheral vision in the model is the significant direct effect on the size of the useful field of view; together central and peripheral vision accounted for 30% of the useful field of view variance. Not surprisingly, visual attentional skills crucially depend on the integrity of information entering through the visual sensory channel. With respect to eye health, while eye health by itself did not significantly impact useful field of view, it may have exerted an indirect effect on

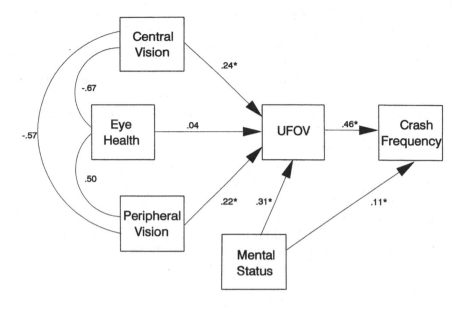

Figure 5.3   LISREL model for predicting crash frequency.

useful field of view through its association with central and peripheral visual function (indicated by the curved lines on the left side of Figure 5.3).

   In summary, eye health and visual function do not contribute any unique variance to crash frequency in addition to their indirect effect through useful field of view. Mental status also had a significant, direct effect on useful field of view, and a small, but statistically significant, direct effect on crash frequency as well. However, the effect of mental status on crash frequency was primarily indirect because removal of its direct effect in the LISREL model only slightly reduced the amount of crash frequency variance accounted for (from 28% to 27%). These results thus supported the hypothesis that useful field of view is a mediating variable between crash frequency on the one hand, and eye health, visual function, and mental status on the other. If the LISREL model is respecified so that useful field of view is entirely removed from the model, the remaining visual variables (eye health, central and peripheral vision) jointly account for only 5% of the crash frequency variance, and with the further introduction of the mental status variable to the model, R^2 only increases to 16%. Therefore the model presented in Figure 5.3, which includes useful field of view and accounts for 28% of the crash variance, clearly maximizes the prediction of crash frequency.

Figure 5.4 illustrates that the average number of crashes increases with increasing severity of useful field of view reduction. We also examined the utility of useful field of view using varying cutpoint criteria. The cutpoint of 40% reduction appeared to provide the best discrimination with both high sensitivity (89%) and high specificity of (81%) with respect to driver classification (crashers vs. non-crashers). Furthermore, odds ratio were calculated indicating that individuals with UFOV reduction greater than 40% were six times more likely to be at least partially responsible for a crash than are those with minimal or no UFOV reduction.

Correlates of Injurious Vehicle Crashes

While the results of this study were initially focused on all at fault crashes, a subsequent analysis evaluated the risk factors for injurious

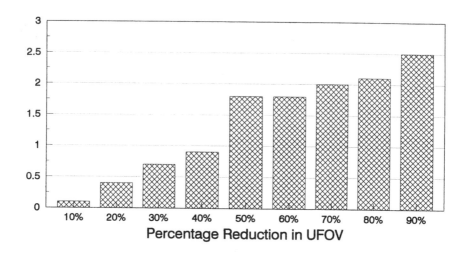

Figure 5.4   Mean crash frequency as a function of Useful Field of View reduction.

crashes (Owsley, McGwin, & Ball, 1998). Injurious crashes are the most catastrophic from a public health standpoint, and a person's risk of being fatally injured increases with age (Barancik et al., 1986; Evans, 1991; McCoy, Johnson, & Duthie, 1989). Odds ratios (ORs) and 95% confidence intervals (CIs) for the association between injurious and noninjurious motor vehicle crash involvement and the visual and cognitive measures described earlier were computed using logistic regression. Variables demonstrating significant univariate associations were selected as candidate predictor variables in multivariable analyses. For injurious cases, these included age, gender, race, chronic diseases, cognitive test score, acuity, stereoacuity, central and peripheral visual field sensitivity, useful field of view, and glaucoma.

For injurious cases, only useful field of view impairment and self-reported glaucoma remained statistically significant in the multivariable logistic regression model (see Table 5.8). Useful field of view reductions of 22.5 to 40%, 41 to 60%, and > 60% were associated with a 5.2-, 16.5-, and 21.5-fold increased risk of an injurious crash (p for trend < .01), compared to those with reductions of < 22.5%. Injurious crashers were 3.6 times more likely to report glaucoma compared to controls. The only variable retained in the noninjurious

TABLE 5.8 Odds Ratios and 95% Confidence Intervals for Significant Variables from Multiple Logistic Regression Models for Injurious Crashes and Noninjurious Crashes

Variables	Injurious crashes ($N = 78$) OR (95% CI)	Noninjurious crashes ($N = 101$) OR (95% CI)
Useful Field of View[+][1]		
< 22.5	1.0 (Referent)	1.0 (Referent)
23.0 to 40.0	5.2 (1.8,12.6)	2.3 (1.1,4.5)
41.0 to 60.0	16.5 (5.8,47.3)	4.6 (2.1,10.1)
> 60.0	21.5 (6.8,68.4)	7.1 (2.9,17.5)
p for trend	< 0.001	< 0.001
Glaucoma	3.6 (1.0,12.6)	—

[+] Higher values represent greater impairment.
[1] Percent reduction score in useful field of view.

crash logistic regression model was useful field of view impairment. Participants involved in noninjurious crashes were 2.3, 4.6, and 7.1 times more likely to have useful field of view impairments of 22.5 to 40%, 41 to 60%, and over 60%, respectively, compared to controls (p for trend < .001). These results illustrate that visual processing impairment, a major cause of disability in older adults (Verbrugge & Patrick, 1995; West et al., 1997) and glaucoma, projected to affect approximately 1.6 million older persons in the United States by the year 2000 (Quigley & Vitale, 1997) increase older drivers risk for involvement in an injurious crash. Since both of these risk factors are potentially modifiable, interventions to reverse vision or visual processing impairments may ultimately assist in reducing motor vehicle crashes and mortality in elderly persons.

While the previous studies demonstrated a relationship between measures of visual and cognitive processing ability and crash frequency, these relationships were retrospective in nature. A follow-up prospective cohort study was recently completed to evaluate whether these previously identified risk factors would adequately identify unsafe older drivers. In this study (Owsley, et al., 1998) the occurrence of a motor vehicle crash during the 3 years following the clinic assessment was considered the primary outcome measure. Participants who died or reported stopping driving during this period were considered censored. For each participant, person-years were accrued from the date of enrollment to the date of first crash, date of censoring, or the end of the 3-year period, whichever came first. To calculate person-miles of travel, the number of person-years was multiplied by the annual miles driven, as self-reported by each participant.

Data were analyzed using Cox proportional hazards modeling to calculate the relative risks (RRs) and confidence intervals for exposure adjusted crash risk. The 294 drivers in the sample accumulated 760.8 person-years of driving and 7,909,240 person-miles of travel. Fifty-six participants incurred at least one crash in the 3-year prospective period, while 11 had two or more crashes. In multivariable analyses, two measures were found to have independent associations with crash risk. Older drivers with 40% or greater reduction in their useful field of view were 2.2 times more likely to have incurred a crash, and older drivers who reported driving fewer than 7 days per week had a 45% decreased crash risk compared to those driving daily.

This study has confirmed that a measure of visual processing impairment, the useful field of view, which had been identified in multiple retrospective studies as a risk factor for unsafe driving, is a risk factor for future vehicle crashes by older drivers. The next question is, therefore, to what extent can this risk be reduced, thus permitting older drivers with such impairments to remain on the road safely? Obviously there are older adults whose visual and cognitive impairments are severe and irreversible. However, many older drivers may have deficits that are remediable through treatment. As our earlier work has shown (Owsley et al., 1991), some older adults fail the useful field of view test due to severe vision impairment because adequate sensory function is needed to detect and discriminate the visual test stimuli. Interventions to improve visual function, such as cataract surgery, intraocular lens implantation, and correction of refractive error, could potentially improve visual function and reduce crash risk. With respect to improving visual processing speed and attentional skills, training studies have demonstrated significant and enduring improvement of these skills in some older adults (Ball, Beard, Roenker, Miller, & Griggs, 1988). This leads to the question of whether such a cognitive intervention would also improving driving skills. The last section of this chapter will address the research results to date bearing on this question.

Interventions to Improve Driving Performance

Prior research on training designed to expand the size of the useful field of view demonstrated that the training generalized to novel targets and faster speeds of information processing (Ball, et al., 1988; Ball, et al., 1988; Ball, et al., 1991; Sekuler & Ball, 1986). In another as yet unpublished follow-up study, the transfer of training to behaviors related to crash involvement and actual driving performance was evaluated.

Four hundred fifty-six licensed drivers from 48 to 94 years of age were screened for participation in this study. The goal of recruitment into the training study was to include a minimum of 50 individuals exhibiting useful field of view reduction in the high risk speed of processing training group, 25 individuals exhibiting equivalent useful field of view reduction in a high risk simulator training social contact control group, and 25 individuals not exhibiting useful field of view reduction in a low risk no contact control group against which the performance of the two high risk groups could be compared. Inclusion in a high risk group required 30% or greater reduction in the useful field of view. Everyone else was eligible for the low risk control group. One hundred four participants ranging in age from 55 to 86 years participated in the training study.

Speed of processing training was conducted on a UFOV Visual Attention Analyzer and was customized for each training participant. In the simplest practice trials, participants trained on identifying a centrally presented target at shorter and shorter stimulus durations until they could perform the task successfully 75% of the time at an exposure duration of 17 ms. Once this criterion was attained, participants practiced a divided attention condition, in which they were required to both identify a centrally presented target and concurrently localize a peripheral target located either 10, 20, or 30 degrees from fixation at shorter and shorter stimulus durations. This continued until 75% accuracy was achieved at a stimulus duration of 40 ms for targets presented 30 degrees from fixation. Once this criterion was attained, participants practiced a selective attention condition, which differed only from the divided attention training in that peripheral targets were embedded in distractors. Thus the training involved improvement in the speed at which participants would perform increasingly more difficult cognitive tasks. The average number of training trials completed was 1040 (average training time was 4.5 hours).

For the simulator training, a certified driving instructor conducted two educational sessions with three to four participants per session. The first 2-hour session consisted of a review of the general rules of the road, instruction about specific driving behaviors for safe driving and crash prevention, and simulated practice of these driving behaviors. The Doron driving simulator was used with films demonstrating techniques for crash avoidance, managing intersections, and scanning. The second 2-hour session continued with the simulation instruction and ended with a 1-hour in-car demonstration of many of the described skills by the driving instructor.

Prior to and following training, all participants were assessed on measures of simple and choice reaction time in a Doron (Model L-225) driving simulator and were given an on-the-road driving evaluation. The datum for the simple reaction time was the distance (in feet) the vehicle would have traveled (at 55 mph) between the onset of brake lights in front of the driver and the release of the accelerator pedal. These data were converted to elapsed time in seconds. For the choice reaction time task the stimuli were international road signs with and without a red slash through them projected on a large screen. Participants were instructed to ignore signs containing a red slash and to react to signs without a red slash. One of three reactions was required. Participants were told to brake as quickly as possible to pedestrian and bicycle signs and turn the steering wheel in the appropriate direction for the right or left turn arrows. Data were again converted to elapsed time in seconds. For the driving evaluation, each participant drove two loops of a 7-mile urban/ suburban course with a driving instructor. Two back seat evaluators used a 455-item behavioral checklist to evaluate driving performance. Three different evaluators were used in sets of two. By comparing the responses of each pair of evaluators it was possible to guard against any potential bias during the driving evaluation. An analysis of interrater reliability among all possible pairs of raters showed that there was no significant change in the interrater reliability when one of the raters was blind to the treatment condition (all $r > .92$).

Results indicated that the speed of processing training group averaged a significant 24.44-point improvement on the UFOV test (Tukeys, $p < .05$) from pre- to posttesting, while the simulator training group and low risk control group did not change significantly from pre- to posttesting. With respect to simple reaction time scores, no overall difference in simple RT was found across testing sessions, nor was there any interaction. An analysis of the choice reaction time scores, however, revealed that only the speed of processing training group significantly improved their time across testing sessions. This group improved significantly by an average of .287 seconds, while the simulator and low-risk control groups did not change significantly. Finally, with respect to the driving evaluation, significant changes in driving behaviors were observed on five measures of driving performance (turning, stop position, signals, changing lanes, and dangerous maneuvers). The simulator training group demonstrated significant improvement in turning, stop positioning, and signals. The low risk control group significantly declined from pre- to posttesting on the changing lanes composite. Finally, on the dangerous maneuvers composite there was a significant reduction in the number of dangerous maneuvers from pre- to posttraining only for the speed of processing trained group. Collectively, the data presented a picture of driving improvements specific to the type of training received. Simulator training resulted in an improvement in the behaviors expressly practiced during training (turning, stop position, and signals). Alternatively, the speed of processing training resulted in fewer risky behaviors during the drive and a decrease in reaction time in complex visual tasks.

The data from this study demonstrated that both speed of processing training and driving simulator training can enhance the driving performance of older adults. The simulator group improved on a few of the specific driving maneuver skills on which they were trained (e.g., turning into the correct lane, positioning the vehicle at stops to see clearly but not obstructing the flow of traffic, and signaling 100–150 feet in advance of a turn), while the speed of processing training and no-contact control groups did not. The speed training group improved on untrained tasks that relied on visual attention. For example, this group improved on the choice reaction time task, which involved scanning a visual scene, detecting changes in stimuli, and reacting to those changes. For a vehicle moving at 55 mph this improvement translates into a 23-foot shorter stopping distance. This group also made fewer dangerous maneuvers in the posttraining drive than in the pretraining drive. The dangerous maneuvers composite consisted of items that primarily measured critical search and judgment abilities in visually cluttered and cognitively demanding situations (e.g., scanning intersections for traffic control devices and making gap selections to make turns across oncoming traffic), the same behaviors (or lack of) that are often cited as causes of crashes (Campbell, 1966; Kline, 1988; Moore, Sedgely, & Sabey, 1982). These latter findings from the speed of processing training, while not surprising to us, would be surprising to the participants in that they did not have an expectation of improvement. Many participants in the training group questioned the link between the training they received and actual driving. Taken together, these data indicate that the benefits of training were localized to logically compatible behaviors, and these effects were present over and above any general training effects.

SUMMARY AND CONCLUSIONS

Mobility is extremely important to personal autonomy, and thus it is an ability that older adults are quite motivated to maintain. The studies summarized in this chapter all converge on the finding that loss of mobility, measured either in terms of ability to carry out activities of daily living such as walking and driving, negative mobility outcomes such as automobile crashes, falls, or resulting injuries, or the extent of one's life space is a consequence of declining sensory and cognitive function. Poorer functional abilities, particularly in visual processing, attention, and mental status, are associated with a smaller life space, lowered exposure to driving in general, and to particularly risky driving times and situations, and overall reduced mobility options. In spite of these mobility restrictions, however, studies also indicate that the same types of functional declines are also related to an increase in negative mobility outcomes such as crash frequency. Thus clearly mobility restriction or self-regulation of exposure to potential negative outcomes does not compensate adequately for declining abilities.

On the other hand, there is also evidence that declining visual and cognitive function are at times reversible, thus suggesting that interventions to improve these abilities may have a positive impact on mobility. For example, highly effective treatments for cataracts are available, and these treatments can be evaluated relative to mobility outcomes as well as visual ones. Similarly, evidence has been presented that cognitive interventions, such as speed of processing training, can result in improved driving performance and potentially expanded mobility. The impact of both medical and behavioral interventions on mobility outcomes is a relatively new area of research, and thus studies are ongoing to evaluate the long-term effects of such programs on both safety and improved mobility. The implications for the development of successful interventions in this area are significant, both with respect to improved quality of life for older persons, as well as for reductions in the cost of health care to society.

ACKNOWLEDGMENTS

Preparation of this chapter and work in our laboratory reported here was supported by the Edward R. Roybal Center for Research in Applied Gerontology at the University of Alabama at Birmingham, funded by the National Institute on Aging/NIH (AG11684), with additional support from NIH grants AG04212 and AG05739, Research to Prevent Blindness, Inc., and the Rich Retinal Research Foundation. We are grateful to the Alabama Department of Public Safety for providing crash data.

REFERENCES

Ball, D., Ball, K., Miller, R., Roenker, D. L., White, D., & Griggs, D. S. (1988). Bases for expanded functional visual fields as a result of practice. *Investigative Ophthalmology and Vision Sciences, 27*(Suppl.), 111.

Ball, K., Beard, B. L., Roenker, D. L., Miller, R. L., & Griggs, D. S. (1988). Age and visual search: Expanding the useful field of view. *Journal of the Optometry Society of America, 5,* 2210–2219.

Ball, K., Roenker, D. L., & Bruni, J. R. (1990). Developmental changes in attention and visual search throughout adulthood. In J. Enns (Ed.), *Advances in psychology.* Amsterdam, Netherlands: Elsevier.

Ball, D., Roenker, D. L., Bruni, J., Owsley, C., Sloane, M., Ball, D., & O'Connor, K. (1991). Driving and visual search: Expanding the useful field of view. *Investigative Ophthalmology and Vision Sciences, 32,* 1041.

Ball, K., Owsley, C., Sloane, M., Roenker, D., & Bruni, J. (1993). Visual attention problems as predictor of vehicle crashes in older drivers. *Investigative Ophthalmology and Vision Sciences, 34,* 3110–3123.

Ball, K., Owsley, C., Stalvey, B., Roenker, D., Sloane, M., & Graves, M. (1998). Driving avoidance and functional impairment in older drivers. *Accident Analysis and Prevention, 30,* 313–322.

Barancik, J. I., Chatterjee, B. F., Greene-Cadden, Y. C., Michenzi, E. M., Kramer, C. F., Thode, H. C., Jr., & Fife, D. (1986). Motor vehicle trauma in northeastern Ohio. I. Incidence and outcome by age, sex, road-use category. *American Journal of Epidemiology, 74,* 473–478.

Barberger, G. P., & Fabrigoule, C. (1997). Disability and cognitive impairment in the elderly. *Disability and Rehabilitation, 19,* 175–193.

Brenton, R. S., & Phelps, C. D. (1986). The normal visual field on the Humphrey field analyzer. *Ophthalmologica, 193,* 56–74.

Byrne B. (1989). *A Primer of LISREL.* New York: Springer-Verlag.

Campbell, B. (1966). Driver age and sex related to accident time and type. *Traffic Safety Research Review, 10,* 36–44.

Clark, M. C., Czaja, S. J., & Weber, R. A. (1990). Older adults and daily living task profiles. *Human Factors, 32,* 537–549.

Cummings, S. R., Nevitt, M. C., Browner, W. S., Stone, K., Fox, K. M., Ensrud, K. E., Cauley, J., Black, D., & Vogt, T. M. (1995). Risk factors for hip fracture in white women. *The New England Journal of Medicine, 332,* 767–773.

Ettinger, W. H., Jr. (1994). Immobility. In W. R. Hazzard, E. L. Bieman, J. P. Blass, W. H. Ettinger, Jr., & J. B. Halter (Eds.), *Principles of geriatric medicine and gerontology* (3rd ed., pp. 1307–1311). New York: McGraw-Hill.

Evans, L. (1991). *Traffic Safety and the Driver.* New York: Van Nostrand Reinhold.

Ferris, F. L., III, Kassoff, A., Bresnick, G. H., & Bailey, I. (1982). New visual acuity charts for clinical research. *American Journal of Ophthalmology, 94,* 91–96.

Friedland, R. P., Koss, E., Kumar, A., Gaine, S., Metzler, D., Haxby, J. V., & Moore, A. (1988). Motor vehicle crashes in dementia of the Alzheimer type. *Annals of Neurology, 24,* 782–786.

Guralnik, J. M., & LaCroix, A. Z. (1992). Assessing physical function in old populations. In R. B. Wallace & R. F. Woolson (Eds.), *The epidemiologic study of the elderly* (pp. 159–181). New York: Oxford University Press.

Haley, M. J. (1987). *The Humphrey field analyzer primer.* San Leadro, CA: Allergan Humphrey.

Henderson, R., & Burg, A. (1974). *Vision and Audition in Driving.* Washington, DC: US Department of Transportation; Technical Report No. TM[L]-5297/000/000.

Hennessy, D. E. (1995). *Vision testing of renewal applicants: Crashes predicted when compensation for impairment is inadequate.* Sacramento, CA: Research and Development Section, California Department of Motor Vehicles; Report No. RSS-95-152.

Hills, B. L., & Burg, A. (1977). *A re-analysis of California driver vision data: General findings.* Crowthorne, England: Transport and Road Research Laboratory, Report 768.

Janke, M. (1994). *Age-related disabilities that may impair driving and their assessment: Literature review.* Sacramento, CA: California Department of Motor Vehicles; Report to the National Highway Traffic Safety Administration.

Johnson, C., & Keltner, J. (1986). Incidence of visual field loss in 20,000 eyes and its relationship to driving performance. *Archives of Ophthalmology, 101,* 371–375.

Jöreskog, K. G., & Sörbom, D. (1989). *LISREL VII: A guide to the program and application* (2nd ed.). Chicago: SPSS, Inc.

Kline, D. (1988). *Visual aging and driver performance.* Washington, DC: Transportation Research Board; Report No. 218.

Koepsell, T. D., Wolf, M., McCloskey, L., Buchner, D. M., Louie, D., & Wagner, E. H. (1994). Medical conditions and motor vehicle collision injuries in older adults. *Journal of the American Geriatrics Society, 42,* 695–700.

Kosnick, W., Winslow, L., Kline, D., Rasinski, K., & Sekuler, R. (1988). Vision changes in daily life throughout adulthood. *Journal of Gerontology, 43,* 63–70.

Kovar, M. G., & Lawton, M. P. (1994). Functional disability: Activities and instrumental activities of daily living. *Annual Review of Gerontology and Geriatrics, 14,* 57–75.

Leibowitz, H. M., Krueger, D. E., & Maunder, L. R. (1980). The Framingham Eye Study [Monograph]. *Survey of Ophthalmology, 24,* 335–610.

Lucas-Blaustein, M. J., Filipp, L., Dungan, C., & Tune, L. (1988). Driving in patients with dementia. *Journal of the American Geriatrics Society, 36,* 1087–1091.

Marottoli, R. A., Cooney, Jr., L. M., Wagner, D. R., Doucette, J., & Tinetti, M. E. (1994). Predictors of automobile crashes and moving violations among elderly drivers. *Annals of Internal Medicine, 121,* 842–846.

Marottoli, R. A., Mendes de Leon, C. F., Glass, T. A., Williams, C. S., Cooney, L. M., Berkman, L. F., & Tinetti, M. E. (1997). Driving cessation and increased depressive symptoms: Prospective evidence from the New Haven EPESE. *Journal of the American Geriatric Society, 45,* 202–206.

Marron, J. A., & Bailey, I. L. (1982). Visual factors and orientation-mobility performance. *American Journal of Optometry and Physiological Optics, 94,* 91–96.

Mattis, S. (1976). Mental status examination for organic mental syndrome in the elderly patient. In L. Bella & T. B. Karasu (Eds.), *Geriatric psychiatry,* (2nd ed., pp. 77–121). New York: Oxford University Press.

May, D., Nayak, U. S. L., & Isaacs, B. (1985). The life space diary: A measure of mobility in old people at home. *International Rehabilitation Medicine, 7,* 182–186.

McCoy, G. F., Johnson, R. A., & Duthie, R. B. (1989). Injury to the elderly in road traffic accidents. *Journal of Trauma, 29,* 494–497.

Moore, R., Sedgely, I., & Sabey, B. (1982). Ages of car drivers involved in accidents with special references to junctions. *TRRL report HS-033, 142,* 1–30.

Monestam, E., & Wachtmeister, L. (1997). Impact of cataract surgery on car driving: A population based study in Sweden. *British Journal of Ophthalmology, 81,* 16–22.

National Highway Traffic Safety Administration. (1989). *Conference on Research and Development Needed to Improve Safety and Mobility of Older Drivers.*

Washington, DC: US Department of Transportation; Department of Transportation Report DOT 807 554.

National Safety Council. (1993). *Accident Facts.* Chicago: Author.

Owsley, C., Allman, R., Gossman, M., Kell, S., & Sims, R. (1999). Mobility impairment and its consequences in the elderly. In J. M. Clair & R. Allman (Eds.), *The gerontological prism: Developing interdisciplinary bridges* (pp. 305–310). Amityville, NY: Baywood.

Owsley, C., Ball, K., & Keeton, D. (1995). Relationship between visual sensitivity and target localization in older adults. *Vision Research, 35,* 579–587.

Owsley, C., Ball, K., McGwin, G., Sloane, M. E., Roenker, D. L., White, M. F., & Overley, E. T. (1998). Visual processing impairment and risk of motor vehicle crash among older adults. *Journal of the American Medical Association, 279,* 1083–1088.

Owsley, C., Ball, K., Sloane, M., Roenker, D., & Bruni, J. (1991). Visual perceptual/cognitive correlates of vehicle crashes in older drivers. *Psychology and Aging, 6,* 403–415.

Owsley, C., McGwin., G., & Ball, K. (1998). Vision impairment, eye disease, and injurious motor vehicle crashes in the elderly. *Ophthalmic Epidemiology, 5,* 101–113.

Owsley, C., Stalvey, B., Wells, J., & Sloane, M. E. (1999). Older drivers and cataract: Driving habits and crash risk. *Journal of Gerontology: Medical Sciences, 54,* M203–211.

Pelli, D. G., Robson, J. G., & Wilkins, A. J. (1988). The design of a new letter chart for measuring contrast sensitivity. *Clinical Vision Science, 2,* 187–199.

Persson, D. (1993). The elderly driver: Deciding when to stop. *The Gerontologist, 33,* 88–91.

Planek, T. W., Condon, M. E., & Fowler, R. C. (1968). *An investigation of the problems and opinions of aged drivers.* Chicago: National Safety Council.

Quigley, H. A., & Vitale, S. (1997). Models of open-angle glaucoma prevalence and incidence in the United States. *Investigative Ophthalmology and Vision Sciences, 38,* 83–91.

Rubin, G. S., Roche, K. B., Prasada-Rao, P., & Fried, L. P. (1994). Visual impairment and disability in older adults. *Optometry and Vision Science, 71,* 750–760.

Salive, M. E., Guralnik, J., Glynn, R. J., Christen, W., Wallace, R. B., & Ostfeld, A. M. (1994). Association of visual impairment with mobility and physical function. *Journal of the American Geriatric Society, 42,* 287–292.

Sekuler, R., & Ball, K. K. (1986). Visual localization: Age and practice. *Journal of the Optical Society of America A, 3,* 64–67.

Selikson, S., Damus, K., & Hamerman, D. (1988). Risk factors associated with immobility. *Journal of the American Geriatric Society, 36,* 707–712.

Shinar, D. (1977). *Driver Visual Limitations: Diagnosis and Treatment.* Washington, DC: US Department of Transportation, Contract No DOT-HS-5-1275.

Shinar, D., & Schieber, F. (1991). Visual requirements for safety and mobility of older drivers. *Human Factors, 33,* 507–519.

Sloane, M. E., Owsley, C., & Alvarez, S. L. (1988). Aging, senile miosis, and spatial contrast sensitivity at low luminance. *Vision Research, 28,* 1235–1246.

Stalvey, B., Owsley, C., Sloane, M. E., & Ball, K. (in press). Life space: A questionnaire to measure the extent of mobility in older adults. *Journal of Applied Gerontology.*

Steinberg, E. P., Tielsch, J. M., Schein, O. D., Javitt, J. C., Sharkey, P., Cassard, S. D., Legro, M. W., Diener-West, M., Bass, E. B., Damiano, A. M., Steinwachs, D. M., & Sommer, A. (1994). The VF-14: An index of functional impairment in patients with cataract. *Archives of Ophthalmology, 112,* 630–638.

Tinetti, M. E. (1986.) Performance-oriented assessment of mobility problems in elderly patients. *Journal of the American Geriatrics Society, 34,* 119–126.

Tinetti, M. E., Speechley, M., & Ginter, S. F. (1988). Risk factors for falls among elderly persons living in the community. *New England Journal of Medicine, 319,* 1701–1707.

Tuokko, H., Tallman, K., Beattie, B. L., Cooper, P., & Weir, J. (1995). An examination of driving records in a dementia clinic. *Journal of Gerontology: Social Sciences, 50B,* S173–S181.

Verbrugge, L. M., & Patrick, D. L. (1995). Seven chronic conditions: Their impact on U.S. adults' activity level, and use of medical services. *American Journal of Public Health, 85,* 173–182.

Waller, P. F. (1991). The older driver. *Human Factors, 33,* 499–505.

Waller, J. A. (1965). Chronic medical conditions and traffic safety. *New England Journal of Medicine, 273,* 1413–1420.

West, S. K., Munoz, B., Rubin, G. S., Schein, O. D., Bandden-Roche, K., Zeger, S., German, P. S., Fried, L. P., & SEE Project Team. (1997). Function and visual impairment in a population-based study of older adults. *Investigative Ophthalmology and Vision Sciences, 38,* 72–82.

The Role of Concordance Between Perceived and Real Competence for Mobility Outcomes

Allen R. Dobbs

Reductions in mobility can restrict a person's life space (Ball & Owsley, this volume; May, Nayak, & Isaacs, 1985; Stalvey & Owsley, 1998), sometimes with the negative outcomes of social isolation (Eisenhandler, 1990) and depression (Marottoli, et al., 1997). Because any substantial loss of mobility is always a threat to a person's independence and well-being, there needs to be a concerted effort to keep people mobile. Unfortunately, a wide variety of medical conditions can adversely affect mobility. In these cases, it is especially important to attend to mobility needs and extend personal mobility for as long as possible. At the same time, this effort must be balanced with the knowledge that mobility in the face of competence declines can be a serious threat to the safety of the person, and even to others. Nowhere is this more apparent than in the case of competence declines that can reduce the ability to drive safely.

Driving is one of the common ways in which older adults meet their mobility needs (Hu & Young, 1994). In fact, driving has become so integral to the lives of many North Americans that choices about where they will live and their activities often presume transportation needs can continue to be met through driving. The importance of driving for seniors is reflected by statistics indicating older adults are driving more and driving longer into old age (Barr, 1991; Jette & Branch, 1992). The increased driving, unfortunately, is not without a substantial cost. When the amount of driving is taken into account, older drivers as a group, have more traffic convictions and crashes and suffer more fatalities than any other adult age group (National Highway Traffic Safety Administration, 1989). The consequences for older persons who are in a crash are especially problematic: Injuries are more likely, the injuries are more serious, and the recovery rate is slower and less complete than for younger persons (Barr, 1991; Evans, 1988; Graca, 1986; McCoy, Johnston, & Duthie, 1989; Retchin, Cox, Fox, & Irwin, 1988).

There is an immediate need to reduce older driver crashes, and this need will become increasingly important because of the dramatic increase in the number of older drivers that is projected to occur over the next several decades (Retchin & Annapolle, 1993). This increase is expected because of the combined effects of the increasing numbers of older people and the increasing numbers of women who will be driving when they become seniors. Without effective interventions to reduce older driver crashes, the serious problems of today will continue to escalate. Clearly, discovering ways to increase older driver safety, while minimizing mobility losses, is a pressing challenge.

Ball and Owsley, in their chapter on "Increasing Mobility/Reducing Accidents of Older Drivers" in this book, describe the substantial advancements in knowledge provided by their research regarding two general approaches for enhancing older driver safety and mobility. One approach is to identify and reduce or eliminate the cause of the ability decline. The second is to capitalize on voluntary self-regulation. Much of the past and present research concerned with both approaches presumes and investigates the association between ability level and driving patterns (Campbell, Bush, & Hale, 1993; Forrest, Bunker, Songer, Cohen, & Cauley, 1997; Kington, Reuben, Rogowski, & Lillard, 1994; Marottoli, et al., 1993; Retchin et al.,

1988; Stewart, Moore, Marks, May, & Hale, 1993; Stutts, 1998). The presumption of a direct association between ability levels and voluntary changes in driving patterns is clear in the self-regulation strategy for safety improvement. It also is a factor when interventions designed to alter ability levels are used. In these cases, when abilities are improved, the presumption is that there will be a corresponding change in driving patterns. Although the presumption that there is a direct link between abilities and the person's choice of when, where, and how much they drive is appealing and has been of considerable heuristic value, we suggest that it is at the same time a questionable and limiting assumption. In this chapter we first discuss the limitations of the presumption of a direct association between real competence declines and driving patterns. An alternative hypothesis and new framework will then be described. We conclude the chapter with a reinterpretation of some current findings based on the new framework.

LIMITATIONS

The self-restriction solution for increasing traffic safety is based on the assumption that as people's abilities decline, they will voluntarily restrict their driving so as to reduce exposure to the driving situations and conditions that put them at risk for crashes. To combine both safety and mobility concerns, there must be the additional correlate that drivers will appropriately self-restrict their driving. This entails both minimizing to a safe level their exposure to the conditions or maneuvers that are compromised by their changed sensory, motor, or cognitive abilities, all the while maximizing mobility. There are at least two ways this could happen. One way would presume that people are able to identify their own ability declines (sensory, motor, cognitive) and that they are able to use that information to identify the types of driving situations for which those declines put them at an unacceptable risk for a crash. There is little research that would support this possibility. In fact, the inability of professionals to understand the link between the various types of ability declines and driving problems is what has led to the call for research on procedures to evaluate fitness to drive (Odenheimer, 1993; Schieber, 1994). However, if people could make that link, and assuming they would be willing to adjust their driving patterns to accommodate that knowledge, then this would provide a proactive approach to enhancing safety through self-regulation that compensated for ability declines. A second possibility would be a reactive approach wherein the person recognizes declines in their driving ability and adjusts when, where, and how much they drive according to the recognized difficulties in driving. Importantly, the key to the success of both of these approaches is the question of whether people can accurately perceive their own declines in competence. We will return to this point.

Ball and Owsley (1999) present evidence that persons with cataracts do restrict their driving. However, the absolute amount of restriction is small. Those with cataracts reported they drive 1 day a week and one place a week less than did those drivers without cataracts, but there was no reported reduction between the two groups in the number of trips or miles driven per week. The findings relevant to examining the relationship between declines in other ability domains and driving restrictions also have been disappointing. For example, limitations in activities of daily living were found to be significant predictors of driving restrictions in the research by Marottoli et al. (1993), but insignificant predictors in the research by Kington and colleagues (Kington et al., 1994). Mental abilities failed to predict driving restrictions in the research reported by Marottoli et al. (1993), but were a significant predictor of restrictions in the study reported by Stutts (1998).

None of the studies examining self-restrictions among drivers with ability declines, except the Owsley, Stalvey, Wells, and Sloane (1999) study, investigated the question of whether self-restrictions reduced crash rates to a level comparable to that of unimpaired drivers. It is, however, reasonable to conclude the crash rates would have been found to be elevated above that of unimpaired drivers in studies finding no increase in driving restrictions for persons with compromised abilities. Moreover, even when restrictions were found to be related to disability, the question remains as to whether the driving restrictions were sufficient to reduce crash rates. In the Owsley et al. (1999) investigation, the restrictions by drivers with cataracts were not sufficient in that these drivers still had elevated crash rates. In sum, there is little support for the notion that older drivers, or drivers of any age for that matter, restrict their driving patterns in ways that adequately compensate for declines in competence.

Given the lack of support, it may be tempting to reject the original thesis that voluntary driving restrictions are a key for enhancing the safety of drivers experiencing competence declines. The possibility exists, however, that the original thesis is worthy of retention, but that the presumption of a direct link between ability declines and voluntary self-restrictions in driving is untenable. One approach would be to identify subpopulations that could benefit the most from the self-restriction as a means of reducing crashes. It may be, for example, that voluntary self-restrictions in driving are an appropriate strategy for normal older drivers and those having pathologies that do not affect mental abilities.

Another approach is to search for a different conceptual framework that presented the possibility of evaluating how effective a self-restriction strategy would be at an individual level. In this regard, recall that restricting one's driving may restrict one's mobility. This emphasizes the importance of insuring driving restrictions are appropriate. For this reason, proposing a different framework for conceptualizing self-restrictions in driving would be especially helpful if that framework carried with it the promise of identifying the appropriateness of voluntary driving restrictions. In our examination of the problem, we began by looking at subgroups for which the extent of self-restrictions is, undoubtedly, inappropriate. The reasons for that inappropriateness led us to a different way of conceptualizing the basis for imposing self-restrictions on driving.

THE IMPORTANCE OF SELF-PERCEIVED COMPETENCE

Our own work has been oriented toward evaluating the driving competence of persons who are medically at risk for changes in mental competence[1] (Dobbs, 1997; Dobbs, Heller, & Schopflocher, 1998). A large portion of our sample has been drivers who are in the early stages of a dementing illness. Along with causing impairments in abilities necessary for safe driving, the presence of a dementing illness

---

[1]Procedures for evaluating the driving competence of persons medically at risk for competence changes have been developed, validated, and are currently in use in both Canadian and U.S. jurisdictions. The evaluation is available through DriveABLE Testing Inc. Information is available from the authors.

can cause impairments of awareness into ability declines (Auchus, Goldstein, Green, & Green, 1994; Feher, Mahurin, Inbody, Crook, & Pirozzolo, 1991; Lopez, Becker, Somsak, Dew, & DeKosky, 1994; McDaniel, Edland, Heyman, & the CERAD Clinical Investigators, 1995; McGlynn & Schacter, 1989; Ott, Lafleche, Whelilhan, Buongiorno, Albert, & Fogel, 1996; Reisberg, Gordon, McCarthy, & Ferris, 1985; Sevush & Leve, 1993). In this regard, one of the important lessons learned by everyone who works with dementia patients (and least any of us forget, the lesson is repeated over and over and over again) is that there can be a vast discrepancy between a person's real competence and his or her perception of competence. This point is of special relevance when appraising the voluntary self-restriction approach to increasing traffic safety. This is because the success of the voluntary restriction approach rests on the assumption that the person will have insight into declines in competence and regulate his or her driving patterns accordingly. In view of the obvious shortcomings of this assumption, at least for some subpopulations of drivers, perhaps a better assumption is that the person will regulate his or her driving patterns according to self-perceptions of competence, independent of real competence levels.

The conceptual shift to a framework in which self-perceptions of competence hold a central role has several advantages. First, it provides a rationale (and testable hypotheses) for why declines in real competence are poor predictors of driving patterns. This is because real declines in competence are postulated to be relevant only if they are perceived. In cases for which the nature of the decline in competence is such that it is readily perceived by the person, there may be a good match between competence declines and at least some change in driving patterns. However, if the person's insight is impaired or the ability change is difficult to detect (as might be the case when ability changes are slow with insidious onsets) then there may be little or no relation between the person's real competence and his or her driving patterns. Second, implicit in the framework is the implication that the relationship between real and perceived competence should correspond to the appropriateness (or inappropriateness) of driving restrictions. If there is a mismatch between real competence and self-perceived competence, the person's choices about driving patterns based on self-perceived competence would be inappropriate (too restrictive or too lenient). Third, because the relationship between real competence and self-perceptions of competence underlie the appropriateness of driving restrictions, mismatches in these relationships indicate when, and even the type, of interventions that could improve the appropriateness of a person's driving patterns. Appropriateness of driving restrictions has direct implications for both safety and mobility. These relationships will be explored in the next section.

A PERCEIVED-COMPETENCE FRAMEWORK

Both real and perceived competence are continuous variables, but for simplicity, consider only the extremes of competent and not competent. Considering only these extremes, there are four combinations of the match between real and perceived competence; the two congruent matches of real and perceived competence (competent–competent; not competent–not competent) and the two mismatches (competent–not competent; not competent–competent). These perceived and real competency matches could occur for any ability domain relevant to driving. Table 5.9 shows the competence match/mismatch possibilities for physical/sensory and mental ability domains. These broad category domains are acknowledged to be much too gross to be of utility for empirical projects. They are, however, adequate to provide illustrations of advancements that could come from considering the match between real and perceived competency.

To illustrate some of the potential of this kind of a framework, consider first the physical/sensory domain. In Table 5.9, this domain is shown along with what is tentatively labelled as the outcome of the match between real and perceived physical competence. The reason for this tentativeness will be explained later. For the present, consider the outcome to be the direct result of the match between real and perceived competence. When there is physical competence and the person accurately perceives that competence, as is shown in the top row, then the mobility outcome for driving would be expected to be appropriate. That is, no adverse effects for mobility would be anticipated given the match between real and perceived competence, nor would there be any anticipated necessity for interventions. This cell in the framework most likely represents the major-

TABLE 5.9   The Relationships Among Real and Perceived Competence Matches and Mismatches and Mobility Outcomes

| Domain | Competence | | Outcome |
	Real	Perceived	
Physical/Sensory	Yes	Yes	Appropriate
	Yes	No	Inappropriate restriction
	No	Yes	At-Risk
	No	No	Appropriate restriction
Mental	Yes	Yes	Appropriate
	Yes	No	Inappropriate restriction
	No	Yes	At-Risk
	No	No	Appropriate restriction

There are other domains for which this analysis is appropriate. These would include domains such as fiscal resources. We suggest the same outcomes are appropriate for each of the real and perceived competence matches across domains. In this regard, we have found it to be very instructive that whenever there is a lack of competence, regardless of whether it is in terms of physical, mental, fiscal, or other domains, and the person is unaware of that difficulty, the person is at-risk. We suspect that in many cases these also are situations where the caregivers also are at-risk.

ity of the older driver population. Research suggests that, on a per person basis, most elderly drivers are safe and competent drivers (U.S. Department of Transportation, 1993). A major reason advanced for the safety of older drivers is that the changes associated with normal aging are not likely to make drivers incompetent. Moreover, when there are only these age-associated changes, it is assumed that older drivers make the necessary adjustments. The assumption that the normal effects of aging are perceived and driving is restricted accordingly has, however, not been adequately tested.

For all of the remaining three combinations of real and perceived competence there is something amiss with respect to mobility. The mismatch shown in the second row is the situation where the person is competent but he or she does not perceive that to be the case. This case is one that begins to show the importance of considering the match between real and perceived competence. This kind of mismatch is likely to result in the person having inappropriately restricted his or her driving patterns. They would have restricted their driving because they perceived themselves to be incompetent. The restriction is inappropriate because, despite the perception of not having the physical competence to drive, the person has, in fact, the physical capabilities to be competent drivers. What is important to note is that it is not that the person severely restricts his or her driving that signals a problem. Nor would the evaluation of the person as competent have been sufficient to signal a problem. It is the mismatch between real and perceived competence that signals an inappropriate mobility outcome. Many older female drivers may provide a good example of inappropriate driving restriction or cessation based on perceived incompetence in the presence of real competence (U.S. DOT, 1993). Interventions, in this instance, would need to focus on increasing the person's awareness of his or her abilities.

If there is an interest in mobility, then a consideration of rows one and two show why it may be important to look beyond assessments of real competence. If only the real competence had been considered, no mobility problem would have been anticipated for those who misperceived that competence, and the need for interventions would not have been evident. Including an examination of the relationship between real and perceived competence may well resolve the puzzle of why, in some cases, individuals who are competent to drive restrict their driving inappropriately, while others with the same level of competence continue driving without restrictions.

When there is the mismatch between real competence and perceived competence as shown in the second row (real competence–perceived incompetence) the outcome is restricted mobility. This also is the outcome when there is a match between real and perceived lack of competence (bottom row, incompetent–incompetent). Interventions to increase mobility may well be needed in both cases, but because the restriction is inappropriate in the incongruent case (second row), but may well be appropriate in the congruent case (bottom row), the types of interventions for the two cases, undoubtedly, would be very different. When there is competence but the person does not perceive himself or herself to be competent, the intervention is likely to be some instrument to bring about attitude change. When there is physical/sensory impairment and it is appropriately recognized by the person, then it may be appropriate to consider an ameliorative intervention to restore the ability. The Owsley, et al. (1999) study reported by Ball and Owsley (this volume) of the effect of cataract surgery on mobility provides an effective example of that kind of intervention. In an earlier study, Monestam and Wachtmesiter (1997) examined the impact of cataract surgery on car driving in Sweden. Eighty-two percent of their sample reported visual functional problems with driving before surgery, with driving in darkness and twilight the most common visual problem specified. Of relevance to this discussion, 25% of the nondrivers before surgery started to drive after surgery and 40% of all drivers reported that they drove more frequently after surgery. Clearly, changes in real competency presurgery (deficits in visual functioning) and the resulting restrictions in mobility suggest there was an awareness of those deficits. This interpretation is strengthened by the fact that changes in real competency after surgery (improvements in visual functioning) resulted in apparently appropriate reductions in driving restrictions for a substantial portion of this population.

Thus far we have considered three of the four combinations. The remaining mismatch combination is when real competence is lacking but the person's belief is that competence remains (third row). With regard to driving, this kind of incongruence places the person at risk for vehicle crashes. This may well be a case where the person retains his or her mobility through continued driving, but the advisability of that mobility in this case is in doubt, at least without one or more interventions. This is not trivial to point out, in that continued driving without compensation for the disability could place the well-being or even the life of that person and others in jeopardy.

Although the research is not abundant, this cell is, undoubtedly, the most researched of the framework presented here. A number of studies suggest that a substantial number of older drivers with medical conditions or disabilities that would be expected to affect driving competency do not restrict or discontinue driving. Research by Monestam and Wachtmesiter (1997) revealed that almost one quarter of the individuals sampled who had cataracts drove with a visual acuity below the requirements for driving in Sweden. Similar findings have been reported by Campbell et al. (1993). Although certain highly disabling health conditions were found to be strongly related to decisions to stop driving, many of those still driving also had the same highly disabling conditions.

As one way of exploring the generality of the framework, consider the mental ability domain (Table 5.9). When mental competence is considered, again a match of real and perceived competence (first row) is likely to be associated with an appropriate outcome for mobility. Perceiving oneself to be incompetent when competence reigns (second row) would be associated with inappropriate mobility restrictions. The third situation is where mental competence is wanting but the person is unaware of this (third row). As mentioned earlier, this situation represents the classic case seen when evaluating drivers with early dementia. Results from our research and that of others (Dobbs & Dobbs, 1999; Hunt, Morris, Edwards, & Wilson, 1993) reveal that the majority of individuals with a dementing illness fail to recognize their declines in competence. This is shown by the lack of congruence between self-ratings of driving ability and objective measures of performance (e.g., road test performance). In general, self-ratings reflect an overestimation of driving competence. These results are reinforced by a recent review of our videotapes of on-road evaluations that show the reaction of these drivers to their own severe driving errors (Osborne & Dobbs, 1997). In the majority of cases, individuals with dementia who made serious driving errors (e.g., wrong-way on the freeway, head-on collisions avoided by evaluator intervention) showed no evidence of awareness of the error, even if the driving evaluator's intervention was extreme. It is no wonder then that many patients with dementia do not appropriately restrict their driving: They simply are not aware of their competence declines and driving errors. The lack of appropriate restrictions in their driving patterns is consistent with their perception that they remain competent and do not need to alter their driving. The high crash rates are not consistent with safety goals. Perhaps no other subgroup of the driver population so empathically underscores the need to shift to a framework that includes self-perceptions of competence as a central variable for determining driving patterns.

A review of the literature indicates that many drivers with a dementia have stopped driving, although not necessarily through voluntary actions. However, many continue to drive. As with other medical conditions, this again indicates that a change in status on a factor (mental competence) is not sufficient to predict changes in driving status. Recent studies, utilizing outpatient surveys from dementia or geriatric clinics, indicate that prevalence rates for active drivers with a dementing illness range from 23 to 30% (Carr, Jackson, & Alquire, 1990; Drachman & Swearer, 1993; Dubinsky, Williamson, Gray, & Glatt, 1992; Gilley, et al., 1991; Logsdon, Teri, & Larson, 1992; Lucas-Blaustein, Filipp, Dungan, & Tune, 1988; Odenheimer, 1993; Trobe, Waller, Cook-Flannagan, Teshima, & Bieliauskas, 1996). Although a number of studies report that a minority of dementia patients have been found competent to drive in the early stages of their illness (Dobbs, 1997; Fitten, et al., 1995), many dementia patients continue to drive despite a significant deterioration in skill. Fifty-six of the caregivers in the Gilley et al. (1991) study reported that the patient's ability to operate a motor vehicle had significantly deteriorated since the onset of Alzheimer's disease. In that study, 11 of the patients with severe dementia (Mini Mental State Exam scores of less than 14: Folstein, Folstein, & McHugh, 1975) were still driving. Results from Dobbs, Dobbs, Schopflocher, and Heller (1996) reveal that 70% of a large sample of actively driving dementia patients referred for an on-road driving evaluation were found to be incompetent to drive.

Returning to the consideration of Table 5.9, the final situation shown in the last row is where the person lacks mental competence and that person is aware of this diminished competence. In this case, the driving of the person is likely to be restricted, and restriction is appropriate with mobility alternatives introduced, unless interventions that alter both real competence and self-perceived competence are possible.

THE SELF-PERCEIVED COMPETENCE FRAMEWORK AND MOBILITY

To this point, the framework has been discussed only in terms of driving, but we believe that it can be applied to other domains of mobility to provide a different approach that could redirect and advance research. Walking provides one such mobility area. Again using Table 5.9 but now thinking of it in terms of physical/sensory domain and walking, when there is real competence and that competence is appropriately perceived, the outcome is appropriate mobility through walking. Here the person would not be at-risk for inappropriately restricted mobility nor for an abnormally high risk of adverse outcomes such as falls. However, congruent with the driving example, the remaining mismatch combinations signal a need for interventions. When the person is physically competent but does not perceive himself or herself to be competent, then an intervention is needed because the person's mobility is inappropriately limited. The mismatch of real and perceived competence targets intervention tools that would promote understanding and appropriate recognition of the disability.

The risk for falls would be expected to be high when real competence is lacking but the person's belief is that competence remains. This competence–perceived competence mismatch is again a case where the person is mobile, but the advisability of that mobility is in doubt, at least without one or more interventions. In the case of falls, a new direction for interventions might be possible if incongruence between real and perceived competence was investigated and found to be associated with falls. The final case is where the lack of competence is rightly perceived, mobility is appropriately restricted, and substitute mobility options are exercised.

ONE FINAL POINT

Thus far, the outcomes have been discussed as only the tentative result of the match or mismatch between real and perceived competence. This is because there is another important variable that should be considered. That variable is what we call the mobility initiators. Mobility initiators are the reasons for mobility requirements: They are the needs and interests that are to be satisfied through mobility. The role of these initiators has not been given the serious consideration that they probably deserve. They can be very important determiners of mobility or immobility. As an illustration, a person may be competent in the abilities necessary for a particular type of mobility, for example driving, and know they are competent, but if the person does not have interests that would take them out of the home, mobility will not occur. In some cases this may be fine, but if the initiators are suppressed by a presence of an adverse condition such as a depression, then clearly this is not a healthy situation. In this situation, the condition that is suppressing the initiator needs to be addressed.

Sometimes the situation may be such that the most effective intervention would be to alter the initiators. In this regard, we have been struck by the success of the World Wide Web in satisfying some people's social affiliation needs, needs that may otherwise need to be accommodated through transportation. Perhaps some innovative thinking about how initiators could be altered would provide important steps toward maintaining personal independence and for achieving personal goals, even when mobility is restricted.

ACKNOWLEDGMENTS

The support of the Alberta Heritage Foundation for Medical Research, the Alberta Health Service Research and Innovation Fund, and the Alberta Mental Health Research Fund are gratefully acknowledged.

REFERENCES

Auchus, A. P., Goldstein, F. C., Green, J., & Green, R. C. (1994). Unawareness of cognitive impairments in Alzheimer's disease. *Neuropsychiatry, Neuropsychology, and Behavioral Neurology, 7*, 25–29.

Barr, R. A. (1991). Recent changes in driving among older adults. *Human Factors, 33*(5), 597–600.

Campbell, M. K., Bush, T. L., & Hale, W. E. (1993). Medical conditions associated with driving cessation in community-dwelling, ambulatory elders. *Journal of Gerontology: Social Sciences, 48*(4), S230–S234.

Carr, D., Jackson, T., & Alquire, P. (1990). Characteristics of an elderly driving population referred to a geriatric assessment clinic. *Journal of the American Geriatrics Society, 38*, 1145–1150.

Dobbs, A. R. (1997). Evaluating the driving competence of dementia patients. *Alzheimer Disease and Associated Disorder, 11*(Suppl. 1), 8–12.

Dobbs, A. R., Heller, R. B., & Schopflocher, D. (1998). A comparative approach to identify unsafe older drivers. *Accident Analysis and Prevention, 30*, 363–370.

Dobbs, B. M., & Dobbs, A. R. (1999, January). Gender differences in driving patterns among persons with dementia. Paper presented at the Transportation Research Board 78th Annual Meeting, Washington, DC.

Dobbs, B. M., Dobbs, A. R., Schopflocher, D., & Heller, R. (1996, October). *The impact of suspended driving privileges on dementia patients and their caregivers.* Paper Presented at the Canadian Association on Gerontology's 25th Annual Scientific and Educational Meeting, Quebec City, Quebec, Canada.

Drachman, D. A., & Swearer, J. M. (1993). Driving and Alzheimer's disease: The risk of crashes. *Neurology, 43,* 2348–2456.

Dubinsky, R. M., Williamson, A., Gray, C. S., & Glatt, S. L. (1992). Driving in Alzheimer's disease. *Journal of the American Geriatrics Society, 40,* 1112–1116.

Eisenhandler, S. A. (1990). The asphalt identikit: Old age and the driver's license. *International Journal of Aging & Human Development, 30*(1), 1–14.

Evans, L. (1988). Older driver involvement in fatal and severe car crashes. *Journal of Gerontology: Social Sciences, 43,* S186–193.

Feher, E. P., Mahurin, R. K., Inbody, S. B., Crook, T. H., & Pirozzolo, F. J. (1991). Anosognosia in Alzheimer's disease. *Neuropsychiatry, Neuropsychology, and Behavioral Neurology, 4,* 136–146.

Fitten, L. J., Perryman, K. M., Wilkinson, C. J., Little, R. J., Burns, M. M., Pachana, N., Mervis, J. R., Malmgen, R., Siembieda, D. W., & Ganzeil, S. (1995). Alzheimer and vascular dementias and driving: A prospective road and laboratory study. *Journal of the American Medical Association, 273*(17), 1360–1365.

Folstein, M. F., Folstein, S. E., & McHugh, P. R. (1975). Mini-mental state: A practical method for grading the psychiatric status of patients for the clinician. *Journal of Psychiatric Research, 12,* 189–198.

Forrest, K. Y. Z., Bunker, C. H., Songer, T. J., Cohen, J. H., & Cauley, J. A. (1997). Driving patterns and medical conditions in older women. *Journal of the American Geriatrics Society, 45,* 1214–1218.

Gilley, D. W., Wilson, R. S., Bennett, D. A., Stebbins, G. T., Bernard, B. A., Whalen, M. E., & Fos, J. H. (1991). Cessation of driving and unsafe motor vehicle operation by dementia patients. *Archives of Internal Medicine, 151,* 941–946.

Graca, J. L. (1986). Driving and aging. *Clinics in Geriatric Medicine, 2,* 577–589.

Hunt, L., Morris, J. C., Edwards, D., & Wilson, B. S. (1993). Driving performance in persons with mild senile dementia of the Alzheimer type. *Journal of the American Geriatric Society, 41,* 747–753.

Hu, P. S., & Young, J. (1994). 1990 Nationwide personal transportation survey: Demographic special reports. Oak Ridge, TN: Oak Ridge National Laboratories report: FHWA-Pl-94-019.

Jette, A. M., & Branch, L. G. (1992). A ten year follow-up of driving patterns among the community-dwelling elderly. *Human Factors, 34*(1), 25–31.

Kington, R., Reuben, D., Rogowski, J., & Lillard, L. (1994). Sociodemographic and health factors in driving patterns after 50 years of age. *American Journal of Public Health, 84*(8), 1327–1329.

Logsdon, R. G., Teri, L., & Larson, E. B. (1992). Driving and Alzheimer's disease. *Journal of General Internal Medicine, 7,* 583–588.

Lopez, O. L., Becker, J. T., Somsak, D., Dew, M. A., & DeKosky, S. T. (1994). Awareness of cognitive deficits and anosognosia in probable Alzheimer's disease. *European Neurology, 34,* 277–282.

Lucas-Blaustein, M. J., Filipp, L., Dungan, C., & Tune, L. (1988). Driving in patients with dementia. *Journal of the American Geriatrics Society, 36*(12), 1087–1091.

Marottoli, R. A., de Leon, C. F., Glass, T. A., Williams, C. S., Cooney, L. M., Berkman, L. F., & Tinetti, M. E. (1997). Driving cessation and increased depressive symptoms: Prospective evidence from the New Haven EPESE. *Journal of the American Geriatrics Society, 45,* 202–206.

Marottoli, R. A., Ostfeld, A. M., Merrill, S. S., Perlman, G. D., Foley, D. J., & Cooney, L. M. Jr. (1993). Driving cessation and changes in mileage driven among elderly individuals. *Journal of Gerontology: Social Sciences, 48*(5), S255–S260.

May, D., Nayak, U.S.L., & Issacs, B. (1985). The life space diary: A measure of mobility in old people at home. *International Rehabilitation Medicine, 7,* 182–186.

McCoy, G. F., Johnston, R. A., & Duthie, R. B. (1989). Injury to the elderly in road traffic accidents. *Journal of Trauma, 29,* 494–497.

McDaniel, K. D., Edland, S. D., Heyman, A., and the CERAD Clinical Investigators. (1995). Relationship between level of insight and severity of dementia in Alzheimer disease. *Alzheimer Disease and Associated Disorders, 9,* 101–104.

McGlynn, S. M., & Schacter, D. L. (1989). Unawareness of deficits in neuropsychological syndromes. *Journal of Clinical and Consulting Neuropsychology, 11,* 143–205.

Monestam, E., & Wachtmeister, L. (1997). Impact of cataract surgery on car driving: A population based study in Sweden. *British Journal of Opthamology, 81*(1), 16–22.

National Highway Traffic Safety Administration. (1989). *Conference on Research and Development Needed to Improve the Safety and Mobility of Older Driver.* Washington, DC: US Department of Transportation, Department of Transportation Report DOT 807 554.

Odenheimer, G. L. (1993). Dementia and the older driver. *Clinics in Geriatric Medicine, 9,* 349–364.

Osborne, T. J., & Dobbs, A. R. (1997). *Driving and dementia: Awareness of errors during in-car evaluations.* Unpublished honors thesis, University of Alberta, Edmonton, Alberta, Canada.

Ott, B. R., Lafleche, G., Whelilhan, W. M., Buongiorno, G. W., Albert, M. S., & Fogel, B. S. (1996). Impaired awareness of deficits in Alzheimer disease. *Alzheimer Disease and Associated Disorders, 10,* 68–76.

Owsley, C., Stalvey, B., Wells, J., & Sloane, M.E. (1999). Older drivers and cataract: Driving habits and crash risk. *Journals of Gerontology: Medical Sciences, 54,* M203–211.

Reisberg, B., Gordon, B., McCarthy, M., & Ferris, S. H. (1985). Clinical symptoms accompanying progressive cognitive decline and Alzheimer's disease. In V. L. Melynk, & N. N. Dubler (Eds.), *Alzheimer's dementia* (pp. 19–39). Clifton, CA: Humana.

Retchin, S. M., & Anapolle, J. (1993). An overview of the older driver. *Clinics in Geriatric Medicine, 9,* 279–296.

Retchin, S. M., Cox, J., Fox, M., & Irwin, L. (1988). Performance-based measurements among elderly drivers and nondrivers. *Journal of the American Geriatrics Society, 36*(9), 813–819.

Schieber, F. (1994). High-priority research and development needs for maintaining the safety and mobility of older drivers. *Experimental Aging Research, 20,* 35–43.

Sevush, S., & Leve, N. (1993). Denial of memory deficit in Alzheimer's disease. *American Journal of Psychiatry, 150,* 748–751.

Stalvey, B. T., & Owsley, C. (1998). Life space: Developing a measure of the magnitude of mobility. Manuscript submitted for publication.

Stewart, R. B., Moore, M. T., Marks, R. G., May, F. E., & Hale, W. E. (1993). *Driving cessation and accidents in the elderly: An analysis of symptoms, diseases, cognitive dysfunction and medications.* Washington, DC: AAA Foundation for Traffic Safety.

Stutts, J. (1998). Do older drivers with visual and cognitive impairments drive less? *Journal of the American Geriatrics Association, 46,* 854–861.

Trobe, J. D., Waller, P. F., Cook-Flannagan, C. A., Teshima, S. M., & Bieliauskas, L. A. (1996). Crashes and violations among drivers with Alzheimer disease. *Archives of Neurology, 53,* 411–416.

U.S. Department of Transportation. (1993). Addressing the safety issues related to younger and older drivers. *A report to Congress January 19, 1993 on the Research Agenda of the National Highway Traffic Safety Administration.* Washington, DC: U.S. Department of Transportation.

Driving Competence: The Person × Environment Fit

Sherry L. Willis

A major question that Dr. Ball and her colleagues (Ball & Owsley, this volume) have been investigating is: "What are the Risk Factors for Involvement in Crashes among Older Drivers?" This discussion will focus on two issues that were part of the Ball presentation: (a) conceptualization of driving competence; and (b) the measurement of cognitive functioning as a risk factor and driving performance as the criterion variable of interest.

Psychologists studying driving behavior are often primarily concerned with the characteristics of the older driver—age, cognitive status, health, driving experience, and so forth. Secondarily, there is consideration of the demands of the environment or context in which driving occurs. For researchers who are engineers or human factors specialists, the primary focus is on these contextual factors with secondary consideration of the driver in relation to these factors.

DRIVING COMPETENCE: THE FIT OF THE PERSON AND THE ENVIRONMENT

Driving competence is best defined as the congruence or fit between the driver and the environment. Driving competence does not reside solely in the person nor in the environment or context, but in the interaction between the two factors. The need to define competence in terms of a person × environment interaction has been reinforced in the ongoing research at Penn State on the older driver's ability to make left turns. Competence to make a left turn cannot be studied in the absence of the traffic environment, particularly in the absence of oncoming traffic. Most drivers can execute a safe left turn if there is no traffic. Judgment of gap and rate of closure only becomes critical when there are approaching vehicles.

CONGRUENCE OF INDIVIDUAL SKILLS AND ENVIRONMENTAL DEMANDS

Competence can be conceptualized in terms of the congruence between the individual's capabilities and the demands and resources of the environment. This concept can be illustrated by different types of triangles (Figure 5.5). In the equilateral triangle, there is a balance or congruity between the individual's abilities and skills and the complexity of a particular environmental context.

Incongruity and thus incompetence can occur either when the individual's skill level is inadequate or when more challenging environmental conditions occur. There may be a decrease in competence when the individual's skills decline (due to health, cognitive, or sensory limitations), even though the environmental demands do not change. Alternatively, there may be a decrease in competence when there are more challenging environmental demands, for example an intersection with heavy traffic flow or an intersection with no traffic signal, even though the skills and abilities of the individual have not declined. A decrease in competence can of course occur due to a decline in both the individual and increased environmental demands.

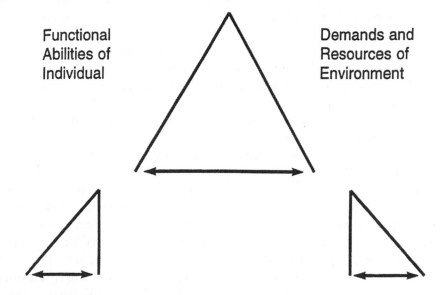

Functional
Abilities of
Individual

Demands and
Resources of
Environment

Figure 5.5   Incongruence in person-environment interaction: Three types.

Environmental Factors in the Study of Driving

Although much of this paper will focus on driver characteristics, at least five domains of environmental factors are important to consider when studying driving.

First, there is the physical environment including the weather. As Ball reported, weather conditions are an important factor in the driver's avoidance behaviors. They are also implicated in accidents and fatalities.

Second, there is the environment within the automobile. This includes placement of equipment (e.g., turn signals, mirrors), structural features of the car that facilitate or limit visibility, and warning devices.

Third, there are the structural features of the roadway, including type of intersection, whether there is a signal and type of signal, number of lanes, and presence or absence of turn lanes.

Fourth, there are the dynamic aspects of the roadway, including traffic flow, size of oncoming vehicles, contrast between oncoming vehicles and road.

Finally, there are the social aspects of the driving context. Ball has found that the mental status of the driver is significantly related to whether the driver avoids driving alone, suggesting the issue of copiloting.

The aggressive or hostile behavior of other drivers on the roadway would be another instance of social factors.

These environmental factors are of interest in their own right. From a psychological approach, however, these environmental factors are important to the extent that they increase or decrease the mental load required of the driver. For example, with respect to making a left turn, features of the roadway such as turn lanes and traffic signals at an intersection can reduce the memory load, speed of processing demands, and vigilance required of the driver. Reduction in mental load is particularly important when a driving situation involves what in psychology is known as a *dual task*—the driver must attend and make decisions based on multiple sources of information simultaneously.

DRIVING COMPETENCE VERSUS DRIVING PERFORMANCE

In studying the everyday functioning of older adults, it is useful to distinguish between *competence* and *performance*. Everyday *competence* has been defined as the adult's ability or potential to perform adequately those activities considered essential in a given domain, such as driving (Willis, 1991, 1996). Competence must be differentiated from everyday *performance*—what the individual actually does routinely in daily life. Competence represents ability to carry out, when necessary, a broad array of activities considered essential of a task such as driving, even though in daily life the adult may not perform these activities or only performs a subset of these activities.

With respect to mobility, an older adult may be capable (physically and cognitively) of going outside one's home or neighborhood but may not choose to do so for any number of reasons—depression, lack of interest, or an idiosyncratic reason such as they can't take their pet to certain public places. An older driver may be competent to make left turns or to drive at night but may choose in daily life to avoid these activities.

This distinction between competence and performance is important for a number of reasons. First, legal judgments regarding whether a guardian or conservator should be appointed for an individual are usually based on the competence of the individual rather than their daily behavior, unless their behavior is endangering other individuals (Smyer, Schaie, & Kapp, 1996; Grisso, 1986). Secondly, the traditional manner in which the individual's ability to live independently, involving ADLs (Activities of Daily Living) and IADLs (Instrumental Activities of Daily Living) is based on capability not routine performance (Lawton & Brody, 1969). The question is asked "Can the individual carry out an activity" not "Does the individual routinely perform an activity." The assessment of IADLs often serves as the basis for determining the capability of the older adult to live independently and for determining eligibility for health and social services.

Dynamic Nature of Competence

Research on driving performance is often studied on a single occasion or over very short time intervals. In real life, competence is dynamic. It changes across time as the individual ages and also as the demands of the environment increase or decrease. Thus, if competence to drive is seen as the congruence of the person's ability and the demands of the environment, both aspects of the equation must be continually monitored across the individual's driving lifespan.

STUDY OF RISK FACTORS IN DRIVING

In considering risk factors related to the driving performance of older adults, three broad domains of variables are often studied. These include: (a) the characteristics of the older driver; (b) a measure of driving performance; and (c) outcome measures, such as involvement in a crash or fatality. Two of these three factors will now be considered in more detail.

In studying risk factors, social scientists often use a structural modeling approach in which the characteristics of the individual are viewed as correlates or predictor variables. Whether individual characteristics account for differences among persons in their driving performance is examined. Driving performance is the criterion variable of interest. What aspects of driving performance are related to outcome measures such as crash involvement is also examined. Finally, whether individual variables influence outcome measures directly or indirectly through their impact on driving performance is considered.

The risk factor domains of vision and cognition have been of primary interest to those in cognitive aging research that study older drivers. Consideration of the measures used to assess vision and cognition suggests that a broader and more diverse array of vision or perception variables may have been considered than cognitive measures.

Often cognition has been assessed by a global or general measure rather than by a battery of tests assessing different dimensions of intelligence. Use of a global measure such as the MMSE (Mini-Mental State Examination) (Folstein, Folstein, & McHugh, 1975) or MATTIS (Mattis, 1976) is quick and efficient and provides the investigator with information on whether the individual is within the normal range of functioning. These measures are often used in assessment of dementia, and thus the investigator can compare the older driver's score to cutoff scores or norms used in clinical investigations.

These global cognitive measures, however, have serious limitations when the focus is on understanding what aspects of cognition are associated with driving behavior. First, these global measures involve test items representing a number of different mental abilities. A global measure often involves measures of verbal ability, memory, and reasoning or executive functioning. These different abilities have different developmental trajectories in adulthood (Schaie, 1996). The very different developmental trajectories for various abilities are masked when cognitive functioning is represented as a single score from a global measure.

Why is a focus on distinct mental abilities, rather than global functioning, important in studying risk factors in driving performance? There are at least two reasons. In the study of vision, it has been useful to examine distinct factors such as acuity, contrast sensitivity, and central and peripheral vision and to determine whether they are significant predictors of outcomes such as involvement in crashes. Similarly, examining the relation of distinct abilities to driving behaviors and outcome measures should be useful. It is important to understand the relative contribution to driving performance of those abilities that show early age-related decline and those exhibiting later decline. It should be very useful to clinicians and rehabilitation therapists if the relationship between specific abilities and particular driving skills were examined more carefully.

It seems likely that different driving tasks involve different constellations of mental abilities. This leads to the final topic dealing with the measurement of driving performance. Assessment of driving performance, particularly of an older adult, in a safe, reliable, and objective manner is a major challenge to research in this area. Given this challenge, several distinct approaches to obtaining some index of driving performance have evolved.

One major dimension is whether the assessment is direct and objective or indirect and subjective. There is obviously a continuum from indirect to direct approaches. Objective, direct assessment involves on-road driving performance while indirect approaches involve a proxy rating or self-report of driving behavior without direct on-road performance. The older adult's report of avoidance behaviors discussed by Ball is an indirect measure of driving performance. Performance on a simulator falls somewhere along this continuum.

Another dimension along which measurement of driving performance varies is the specificity of the driving task. Some assessments focus on a global or summary rating, while others focus on specific driving tasks/behaviors (driving at night, making a left turn).

Figure 5.6 presents a hierarchical approach to studying the relationship between distinct mental abilities and specific driving tasks. There are a subset of mental abilities that are probably involved in most driving tasks. These may include the speed of processing aspects of the useful field of view (UFOV) task discussed by Ball, complex reaction time, and working memory ability.

When considering particular driving behaviors, however, the role of specific abilities becomes more evident. For example, wayfinding and some parking tasks (e.g., parallel parking) are likely to involve spatial ability—the ability to mentally rotate and visualize automo-

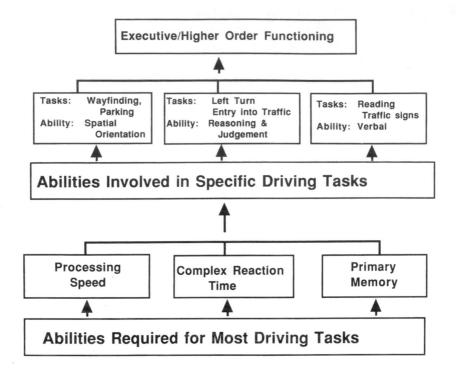

Figure 5.6 A hierarchical approach to studying the relationship between mental abilities and specific driving tasks.

biles and roadway structures in two- and three-dimensional space. One the other hand, interpreting road signs may be influenced significantly by verbal ability and experiential knowledge. Executing a left turn in traffic involves skills such as inductive reasoning and judgment of gap and rate of closure. At the top of the hierarchy are what psychologists call executive functioning—the ability to make decisions in complex situations. For example, planning a route through a new environment or dealing with a demanding traffic situation involves executive functioning. Executive functioning is represented by a constellation of higher-order cognitive skills.

An important next step in research is examining the relationship between specific mental abilities and particular driving tasks for the older driver. Specifying these relationships are important in their own right and as a precursor to developing targeted behavioral interventions with the older driver.

REFERENCES

Folstein, M. F., Folstein, S. E., & McHugh, P. R. (1975). Mini-Mental State: A practical method for grading the cognitive state of patients for the clinician. *Journal of Psychiatric Research, 12,* 189–198.

Grisso, T. (1986). *Evaluating competencies: Forensic assessments and instruments.* New York: Plenum.

Lawton, M. P., & Brody, J. (1969). Assessment of older people: Self-maintaining and instrumental activities of daily living. *The Gerontologist, 9,* 179–185.

Mattis, S. (1976). Mental status examination for organic mental syndrome in the elderly patient. In L. Bellak, & T. B. Karaasu (Eds.), *Geriatric psychiatry: A handbook for psychiatrists and primary care physicians* (pp. 79–121). New York: Grune & Stratton.

Schaie, K. W. (1996). *Intellectual development in adulthood: The Seattle Longitudinal Study.* New York: Cambridge University Press.

Smyer, M., Schaie, K. W., & Kapp, M. B. (1996). *Older adults' decision making and the law.* New York: Springer.

Willis, S. L. (1991). Cognition and everyday competence. In K. W. Schaie, & M. P. Lawton (Eds.), *Annual review of gerontology and geriatrics, Vol. 11.* New York: Springer.

Willis, S. L. (1996). Everyday cognitive competence in elderly persons: Conceptual issues and empirical findings. *The Gerontologist, 36*(5), 595–601.

CHAPTER 6

Will Intelligent Transportation Systems Improve Older Driver Mobility?

Richard J. Hanowski and Thomas A. Dingus

With the U.S. population steadily aging, interest concerning older driver mobility is likely to intensify. To address issues pertaining to older drivers and to be mindful of the public's safety needs, industry and government agencies are supporting research to maximize safety for all drivers. Intelligent transportation systems (ITS) are aimed at improving motor vehicle safety and efficiency. Three systems under the umbrella of ITS are described that may impact older driver performance. Research is presented that addresses issues pertaining to in-vehicle routing and navigation systems (IRANS), in-vehicle safety advisory and warning systems (IV-SAWS), and collision warning systems (CWS). Results indicate that selective systems, which target limitations associated with aging, can be effective in improving older driver behavior and performance.

Mobility is an important issue for elderly persons. For younger people, the concepts of independence and self-sufficiency are often

taken for granted. However, as Waller (1991) points out, independence and self-sufficiency "become increasingly important as the
older person is faced with joining the ranks of the 'elderly' with all
of the stereotypes associated with that term. Although it is obvious
that health can affect mobility, it may often be overlooked that
mobility can affect health and well-being" (p. 501).

The U.S. population is steadily aging. The Transportation Research Board (1988) indicates that those over 65 years of age constituted 8.2% of the population in 1950 and 12.6% in 1990. Projected
growth rates suggest that the over-65 population will grow to 13.9%
in 2010 and to 21.1% in 2030. Data on licensed drivers show a similar
trend. Drivers over 65 years of age accounted for 7.6% of licensed
drivers in 1965, 11.9% in 1985, and 14% in 1993 (National Safety
Council, 1994; Stamatiadis, Taylor, & McKelvey, 1988). Based on
the increasing number of older drivers, we can expect older driver
mobility issues and safety concerns to intensify over the coming
decades.

As a driver ages, that driver is likely to spend less time driving
(Transportation Research Board, 1988). Given this reduced exposure, one would expect that the frequency of crashes and fatalities
for older drivers would be less than that for younger drivers. Indeed,
this is the case. An examination of National Safety Council (1994)
data shows that older drivers are underrepresented in crashes and
fatalities relative to their numbers in the U.S. population. In 1993,
drivers aged 65 and above constituted 14% of licensed drivers, but
represented only 7.8% of drivers involved in crashes and 10.8% of
drivers involved in fatal crashes. The problem with older driver
crash involvement becomes apparent when one looks at crashes and
fatalities in terms of rates per mile driven. For example, Cerelli
(1992) found that beginning at about age 60, the rate of crash
involvement per mile traveled increases and continues to increase
markedly for drivers in their seventies.

Without a doubt, prolonging the mobility of older drivers is an
important issue and a desirable goal, particularly for the elderly
community. However, it is a goal that must be weighed against the
safety needs of the general public. If, through the act of operating
a vehicle, elderly persons become a danger to themselves and the
public, prolonging mobility via driving would not be desirable.
Rather, we must consider the implications of operating a vehicle as

a person's visual and cognitive abilities decline. As Tasca (1992) questions, "Do people eventually become too old to drive?" (p. 1).

To address mobility issues of older drivers and to be mindful of the public's safety needs, industry and government agencies are supporting research efforts to maximize safety for all drivers. A number of documents have recommended that studies be conducted in a variety of transportation-related areas. Some of these areas include those related to driver licensing (Ball & Owsley, 1993), driver training (Hunt, 1993), crashworthiness/occupant protection (Mackay, 1988), postcrash medical care (Cifu, 1993), fitness-for-duty (Hanowski, Bittner, Knipling, Byrne, & Parasuraman, 1995), environmental issues (Benekohal, Michaels, Resende, & Shim, 1994), and intelligent transportation systems (Dingus et al., 1996). The focus of the research presented here is in the area of intelligent transportation systems.

INTELLIGENT TRANSPORTATION SYSTEMS

The term intelligent transportation systems (ITS) refers to a group of technologies that might be used to improve motor vehicle safety and efficiency. ITS encompass a wide range of technologies including advanced vehicle control systems (AVCS), automated highway systems (AHS), advanced traffic management systems (ATMS), commercial vehicle operations (CVO), and advanced traveler information systems (ATIS). Under the umbrella of ATIS, in-vehicle information systems (IVIS) provide information to the driver while, as the name implies, the driver is inside the vehicle. This is in contrast to other transportation information systems that might provide traveler information at a kiosk or on the television screen of a hotel room. Currently available IVIS, such as the Oldsmobile Guidestar, are typically mounted in the dashboard area. From the IVIS display, drivers have access to a variety of traveler information, which may include (a) redundant roadway and signing information, (b) routing and navigation information, (c) safety advisory and warning information, and (d) motorist services information.

Perez and Mast (1992) provide a clear description of the four ATIS subsystems. They define in-vehicle signing systems (ISIS) as a subsystem that provides noncommercial routing, warning, regulatory, and advisory information inside the vehicle. This includes information typically found on roadside signs (e.g., speed limit). In-vehicle routing and navigation systems (IRANS) are designed to help guide the driver from one location to another, as well as provide information on traffic operations and congestion. Moving map displays and turn-by-turn driving direction indicators are examples of the guidance provided with IRANS. In-vehicle safety advisory and warning systems (IVSAWS) provide the driver with information about upcoming unsafe conditions or situations to allow the driver time to take remedial action. An example of an IVSAWS message is a warning to the driver that an accident has occurred and is blocking the roadway ahead. In-vehicle motorist services information systems (IMSIS) provide the driver with commercial logos and information about motels, restaurants, and similar traveler facilities.

Optimally presenting information inside the vehicle, so that it is quickly understood and not distracting to the driver, is one ATIS-related design issue outlined by ITS America (1995). This and other ATIS-related design issues can be investigated by collecting behavior and performance measures as the driver interacts with a system while operating a vehicle. Through this type of research, an understanding of driver behavior can be realized and recommendations for system design can be made. The ultimate goal of such investigation is the safe, efficient, and effective design and implementation of ATIS.

Collision warning systems (CWS) also fall under the umbrella of ITS. Although CWS have been deployed to a limited extent in commercial vehicles, they are currently being evaluated for use in noncommercial vehicles. The goal of CWS is to provide safety benefits to drivers. Given that crash statistics are particularly high for rear-end crashes (Dingus, et al., 1997), research has been directed at examining potential benefits of these systems relative to these types of crashes. The purpose of CWS is to determine potential collision scenarios and warn the driver when the criteria for these scenarios are met. CWS have been described that provide the driver with headway information (time separation between vehicles) and closure (relative speed) information (Dingus et al., 1997; Horowitz & Dingus, 1992). With CWS and ATIS, one of the keys to delivering safety benefits is designing an interface between the driver and the system that is easy to understand.

USER-CENTERED DESIGN

The development of safe, efficient, and usable ITS requires the careful application of human factors design principles and guidelines. One such human factors principle prescribes a user-centered approach to design, an approach that focuses on the system's end-users early in the design process (Hancock & Parasuraman, 1992; Norman, 1988).

One of the first steps for the ITS designer employing a user-centered approach is to define and characterize end-users. Defining the population of end-users for in-vehicle ITS applications is relatively straightforward in that it consists of the population of drivers. Characterizing this population, on the other hand, is not so straightforward considering that the age range of drivers is 15 to 75+ years. As part of characterizing end-users, the ITS designer must consider the abilities and limitations of the entire population of anticipated users. One might expect that the abilities and limitations of a 75-year-old driver will differ considerably from that of a typical younger driver.

The challenge for the ITS designer, therefore, is developing systems that improve motor vehicle safety and efficiency for the entire range of the driving population. Given the reduction of sensory, perceptual, cognitive, and motor capabilities that are associated with aging, designing ITS for older drivers is challenging. ITS technology has the potential to be a double-edged sword for the older driver: systems that are designed to assist in safe driving may also add mental and physical workload and confusion to the driving task (Hanowski et al., 1995). Cerelli (1992) notes that older drivers are at a particular crash risk when their attention and other dynamic information-processing capabilities are most challenged (e.g., during left turn maneuvers). Consideration of older driver issues and the utilization of a user-centered design approach may aid in the realization of ITS goals and objectives, making them safe, efficient, and usable for both younger and older drivers.

Human Factors Research

As Kantowitz and Sorkin (1983) note, the first commandment of human factors is "Honor thy user" (p. 13). In this light, an effort is underway to investigate the benefits of ITS so that systems are de-signed and usable by the entire age range of drivers. The research presented here consists of an overview of select issues associated with two of the ATIS subsystems previously described (IRANS and IVSAWS), as well as issues related to collision avoidance systems. Data from research pertaining to each of these systems as they impact older drivers are highlighted. It must be noted that the goal of this paper is not to discuss all of the issues pertaining to these systems. Rather, the goal is to provide a description of several system-related issues that the authors of this paper have investigated and to describe the results of these investigations. In addition, it is hoped that some insight will be provided into whether older driver mobility can be safely improved as a function of each system.

IN-VEHICLE ROUTING AND NAVIGATION SYSTEMS RESEARCH

One of the first examples of in-vehicle routing and navigation systems (IRANS) tested in the United States was TravTek, a system designed to provide navigation information, a services and attractions direc-tory, and roadway incident and traffic information to the driver (Dingus et al., 1995). As noted by Dingus et al. (1995), the primary design objectives of the TravTek Driver Interface were to:

- Save drivers time and money by providing more effective naviga-tion information,
- Alleviate stress and increase driving enjoyment by providing easy access to value and convenient location information,
- Maintain and improve safe driving performance during system use and in emergency response by providing information for avoiding hazards and responding to emergencies, and
- Alleviate traffic congestion by improving roadway efficiency.

To determine if these objectives were met, a camera car study was conducted wherein cameras and other measurement devices were installed in a vehicle equipped with TravTek. This arrangement allowed (a) more precise and detailed measurement and analysis of driving performance and behavior, which was required to assess the usability and safety of the system; and (b) reasonable control over many environmental factors (roadway types, subject demographics, time of day) necessary for interpreting changes in driving performance and behavior. To ensure that a wide range of drivers were included in the study and so that the results could be generalized to the entire population of drivers, drivers ranged in age from under 20 years to over 75 years.

To assess the costs and benefits of TravTek, the camera car study investigated a number of issues including: Did driving performance, navigation performance, and driving safety vary as a function of age? For the purpose of the current paper, selected results pertaining to driver age will be discussed. However, the reader is directed to Dingus et al. (1995) for a complete discussion of the results for all issues.

The method for conducting the camera car study included collecting on-road data over a four-month period. The study was set up in Orlando, Florida, where visitors and area locals drove one of a fleet of cars equipped with a TravTek system. The research design included independent variables that addressed the aforementioned research issues. For example, there were six navigation conditions: (1) turn-by-turn system with voice, (2) turn-by-turn without voice, (3) route map with voice, (4) route map without voice, (5) paper direction, and (6) a paper map. As shown in Figure 6.1, the turn-by-turn systems provided visual information about the next maneuver along a route. The route map, or moving-map display, provided a head-up view on an electronic street map (Figure 6.2). The voice guidance feature provided aural information such as alerts and notices of maneuvers. The paper direction, which was a listing of the route directions, and the paper map were the control conditions in that they are typical of the type of directions currently relied on by most drivers. The research design also included a variable for driver age, where participants were grouped into one of three age categories: 16 to 18 years, 35 to 45 years, and 65 years and over.

Not surprisingly, the results of this research showed that the older driver age group had committed substantially more safety-related errors than both the middle and younger age groups. Older drivers had twice as many errors as the youngest drivers even though the older drivers drove more cautiously. However, older drivers benefitted the most from the turn-by-turn guidance, particularly with voice. This is shown by reduced lane deviations (Figure 6.3) and increased

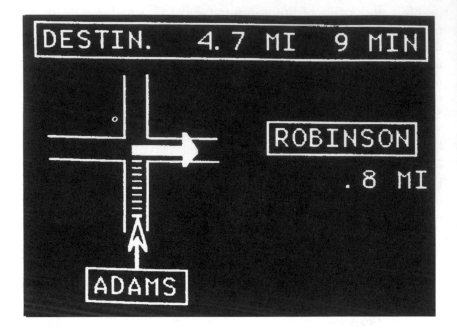

Figure 6.1 TravTek turn-by turn guidance display.

glances to the right and left (Figure 6.4) when compared to control conditions. These results suggest that although older drivers are particularly vulnerable to attention demand during driving, they can benefit from well-designed information systems.

IN-VEHICLE SAFETY ADVISORY AND WARNING SYSTEMS

As outlined by Perez and Mast (1992), in-vehicle safety advisory and warning systems (IVSAWS) provide the driver with information about unsafe conditions and situations to allow the driver enough time to take remedial action. Different sensory modalities are available for providing warning information, including visual (e.g., text message, symbols/icons), auditory (e.g., tones, voice messages), and haptic messages (e.g., vibration). Recommendations for the presentation

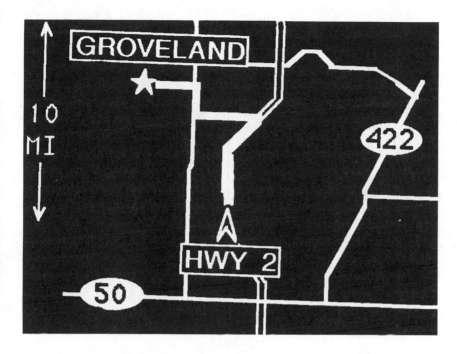

Figure 6.2 TravTek route map display.

of warning messages are well documented (e.g., Campbell, et al., 1996; Lerner, Kotwal, Lyons, & GardnerBonneau, 1993; Wickens, 1992). It is generally accepted that emergency alerts that require immediate attention should be presented aurally (e.g., Lerner et al., 1993), and that redundant communication can improve performance (Wickens, 1992). The results from recent research involving collision warning messages suggest that the redundant presentation of warning information in multiple modalities (auditory and visual) is preferred by drivers (Campbell et al., 1996).

A study was recently conducted at Virginia Polytechnic Institute and State University's Center for Transportation Research that investigated the effectiveness of IVSAWS messages (Hanowski, Dingus, Gallagher, Kieliszewski, & Neale, 1997). The focus of this research was to investigate whether drivers' reliance on cues provided inside the vehicle influenced their observation of unexpected situations,

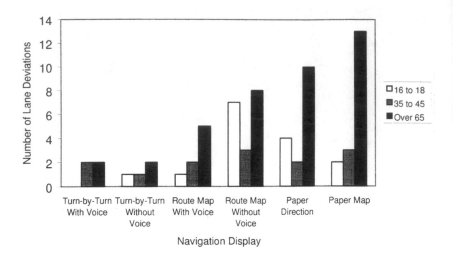

Figure 6.3 Lane deviations for each navigation condition compared across three age groups.

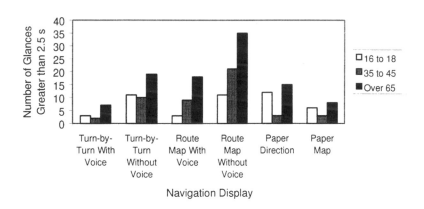

Figure 6.4 Inappropriate glances lasting over 2.5 seconds for each navigation condition compared across three age groups.

as compared to when they relied on cues presented solely outside the vehicle. There were five primary features of this research: (1) the inclusion of unexpected situations, specifically external events and vehicle status warnings, (2) notifying drivers of these unexpected situations via an IVSAWS, (3) the driver's situation awareness when confronted with unexpected situations, (4) the impact of IVIS display density on driver response to unexpected situations, and (5) older driver use of an IVIS when confronted with unexpected situations.

To investigate these areas, three research questions were posed. Each question involved the use of an IVIS and response to unexpected situations:

- Do drivers derive a benefit, when confronted with an unexpected situation, from using an IVIS that has multiple subsystems?
- What impact does IVIS information density have on driver behavior and performance?
- What impact does driver age have on system use and measures related to driver behavior and performance?

As in the previously reported studies, a vehicle was instrumented to collect driver behavior and performance data. Figure 6.5 shows the IVIS display located in the dash area. Within the display, the IVSAWS information was located in the bottom left corner. In Figure 6.5, a warning of an approaching ambulance is represented by an ambulance icon.

Both younger drivers (18–24 years) and older drivers (65–75 years) participated in this study. Participants drove a prescribed route, lasting approximately 2 hours, that took them through Virginia's Montgomery County, including the urban areas of Blacksburg and Christiansburg. The route was divided into three sections. While traversing each section, drivers were presented with a different IVIS display condition: no display, low density display, or high density display.

During the route, drivers were exposed to five scripted external events and one vehicle status warning event. Each of the events was carried out by one or more confederate vehicles (i.e., vehicles that performed staged actions). The list of events consisted of a car

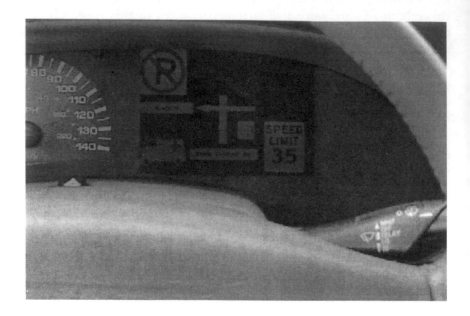

Figure 6.5 IVIS display located in the dash area. The IVSAWS is represented by the ambulance icon in the bottom left corner of the display.

approaching from a hidden entrance, a one-lane tunnel, a disabled vehicle, an open trunk, an ambulance approaching, and a crash ahead.

To measure driver response, a number of dependent measures were collected. These measures were used to evaluate situation awareness, driving performance, and driver preference.

As shown in Figure 6.6, the results indicated that, for both younger and older subjects, drivers received a benefit from the IVIS in terms of reduced mean response time. Drivers were quicker to respond to unexpected events when they were provided with advanced warning information. Based on perception/reaction time data in the literature (e.g., Tasca, 1992), one would expect younger drivers to have faster reaction times. As shown in Figure 6, this finding was apparent

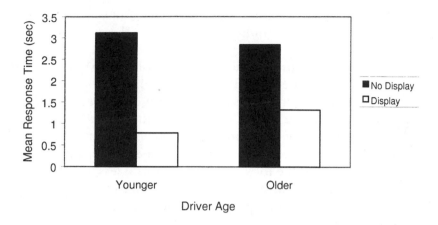

Figure 6.6 Mean response time as a function of driver age and display density.

in the IVIS condition. Caution must be used in assessing the magnitude of the reaction time differences between the younger and older drivers, however, as vehicle speed was not controlled for, and younger drivers typically drove faster than did older drivers.

Drivers were required to follow a predetermined route. Older drivers went off route significantly more frequently, by a factor of three, than did younger drivers. Despite having a more difficult time in navigating the route, this result suggests that older drivers may derive relatively more benefit from a navigation system, provided that the system's design is optimized for them. That is, older drivers may derive relatively greater benefit from a navigation system (i.e., IRANS) because the purpose of such systems is to assist the driver in navigating and prevent the driver from getting lost.

At the conclusion of the driving portion of the study, drivers were administered a preference questionnaire to assess their opinions regarding the IVIS. Of particular interest was the age difference in response to questions concerning system distraction. Note that when a new message was presented on the IVIS, an auditory alert (beep) notified the driver that new information was being presented. Both younger and older drivers seemed to approve of the auditory alert when it accompanied warning information; 70% of younger drivers and 90% of older drivers indicated that they were not distracted. However, when the auditory alert accompanied signing and navigation information (i.e., information that was not urgent), 80% of the younger drivers indicated that the beep was distracting, compared to only 10% of the older drivers. This difference proved reliable. It is hypothesized that the reason for this age difference is that given their more cautious approach to driving, perhaps as a function of slower processing and perception/reaction times, older drivers spent more time focused on the forward road scene and less time scanning the IVIS. Given this scenario, older drivers may have benefitted from the auditory alert, which helped direct their attention to new sign and navigation messages.

As with the TravTek study, the results of this research suggest that older drivers can benefit from well-designed information systems. Slow perception/reaction times to unexpected events and inadvertent divergence from planned routes can both be improved through a well-designed IVIS that incorporates warning and navigation information. In addition, the subjective data from this study support previous research that has suggested that user control of auditory alert intensity is desirable (Campbell et al., 1996; Collins, Biever, Dingus, & Neale, 1997; Lyons, Lerner, & Kotwal, 1994). Based on the results of the present study, we might expect older drivers to prefer auditory alerts and younger drivers to view them as distracting (particularly for nonurgent messages). Allowing users to turn these alerts up or turn them off will be a design feature that may meet the needs of both age groups.

COLLISION WARNING

According to the 1993 General Estimating System (GES), rear-end crashes accounted for 25% of all police-reported accidents and 32% of all crash-caused delays. To address the rear-end crash problem, research and analyses are being conducted to determine causes and potential solutions.

As Carney (1996) notes, three primary factors have been attributed to the rear-end crash problem: following too closely, driver inattention, and perceptual factors. Following too closely, an overtly unsafe driving behavior, involves a relatively low percentage of older drivers. Similarly, driver inattention is not likely to be as big an issue for older drivers as compared to younger drivers because older drivers have been found to be more cautious. For older drivers, it could be argued that systems that target the improvement of perceptual factors might be most successful because older drivers often report problems with visual processing speed, visual search, light sensitivity, and near visual acuity (Kosnik, Sekuler, & Kline, 1990).

Research is being conducted to investigate how ITS might address and ameliorate these three factors to ultimately reduce the rear-end crash problem. In this light, a set of field experiments was conducted to evaluate automotive headway maintenance and collision warning devices. Using an instrumented test car, Dingus et al. (1997) investigated (a) ease of use and behavior and performance effects for several collision warning display designs, (b) the effectiveness of display modalities including visual, auditory, and visual/auditory combination, and (c) the effects of false alarms on driver following behavior.

Across all three studies, 124 drivers participated. Participants included younger (18–24 years) and older (60+ years) drivers. Headway, or the time separation between the participant's vehicle and a lead vehicle, was one of the primary dependent measures. Figure 6.7 shows one of the study results related to driver age. The baseline measure in the figure refers to drivers driving without a collision avoidance system. As can be seen, younger drivers drove closer to a lead vehicle than did older drivers. This result is consistent with previous research that has shown older drivers to be more cautious (e.g., Dingus et al., 1995; Hanowski et al., 1995; Tasca, 1992). Headway for younger drivers was influenced by the number of false alarms generated by the system. Headway for older drivers, on the other hand, was not affected by the system. Older drivers maintained a relatively consistent headway independent of the false alarms generated by the system and independent of the system itself. That is, older drivers maintained a minimum headway of approximately 2.5 seconds with or without use of the collision avoidance system.

The results of this study suggest that headway systems may be more of a benefit for younger drivers than for older drivers. This result is not surprising if one considers the benefits derived from

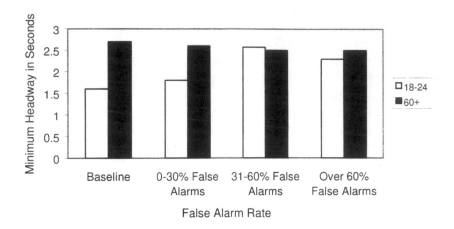

Figure 6.7   Minimum headway as a function of driver age for three false alarm categories and the baseline/no system condition.

headway systems. Using an algorithm that determines optimal headway and safe traveling distance, a headway system indicates to a driver when the driver is too close (unsafe) to a lead vehicle. Younger drivers, who tend to have shorter headways as compared to older drivers, would benefit from a system that provides information that suggests that they increase the time separation between their vehicle and a lead vehicle. Older drivers, on the other hand, do not have the same problem with short headways as do younger drivers. Therefore, the benefits for older drivers from such systems might be expected to be less than that for younger drivers. This result echoes the findings of Mollenhauer, Dingus, and Hulse (1995), who found that a head-up display that presented collision warning information was not helpful to older drivers.

DISCUSSION

The goal of this paper was to provide a brief overview of research being conducted to improve older driver mobility through the implementation of ITS. The answer to the question posed in the title of this paper, "Will Intelligent Transportation Systems improve older driver mobility?" appears to be "Yes, but . . . " where the "but" refers to the ITS application in question. For the navigation system (IRANS) and the warning system (IVSAWS), both displays were well-designed such that the information was easy to comprehend and was presented early enough to allow drivers time to take any required actions. Also, the type of information presented by the IRANS and IVSAWS is synergistic to the typical characteristics displayed by older drivers. For example, data indicate that older drivers are risk-aversive and have a low percentage of involvement in overtly unsafe driving behaviors. Research from different sources has shown that older drivers are cautious drivers (e.g., Dingus et al., 1995; Hanowski et al., 1995; Tasca, 1992). Providing older drivers with information that fits well with these typical characteristics is likely to improve mobility. With the IRANS, the display provided, among other things, navigation information. Field studies have shown that older drivers are more likely to inadvertently go off a desired route as compared to younger drivers (Hanowski et al., 1997). Providing older drivers with navigation information, therefore, seems to be a desirable solution for addressing this problem. With the IVSAWS, the display provided warning information that required the driver to take immediate remedial action. Older drivers have been shown to have slower cognitive processing than younger drivers, along with slower perception/reaction time (Spirduso, 1980). IVSAWS benefit older drivers by providing advanced information and allowing them more time to react to a situation that might require a quick response.

The benefit provided by collision warning systems (CWS), on the other hand, existed for younger drivers, but not for older drivers. Again, the reason for this is believed to be due to the driving characteristics of older drivers. More specifically, older drivers are involved in a low percentage of rear-end crashes as compared to younger drivers. Older drivers are typically more cautious drivers and maintain a greater headway between their vehicle and the vehicle in front of them. One of the benefits of a CWS is that it directs the driver to increase headway when the driver is following too close. For younger drivers who are involved in more rear-end crashes, headway information may be beneficial in increasing the time separation between vehicles. However, for older drivers, this is not a problem to begin with. As such, little or no benefit would be expected.

The research presented here indicates that mobility can be improved through ITS. Systems that are apt to provide the most benefit to older drivers will be those that improve driving skills in elderly persons and ameliorate environmental hazards. In the research described, it was demonstrated that older driver navigational skills and perception/reaction time can be improved by well-designed systems. CWS, on the other hand, presented a solution to a problem not experienced by older drivers. As such, the success of headway maintenance CWS may not be as likely in the older driver population as it may be with younger drivers.

The decrements associated with aging have been well documented, and the effects of these decrements on driving have been identified (e.g., Mollenhauer et al., 1995). The challenge for researchers is to develop technologies to supplement diminished skills while at the same time designing systems with a user-centered approach. The threat of developing ITS for older drivers is the double-edged sword mentioned earlier. That is, systems that are designed to assist in safe driving may add mental and physical workload and confusion to the driving task. The research presented here has shown that select systems that target limitations associated with aging can be effective in improving older driver behavior and performance. As behavior and performance are improved, mobility for older drivers is likely to increase without sacrificing safety for the older drivers themselves or the general public.

REFERENCES

Ball, K., & Owsley, C. (1993). The useful field of view test: A new technique for evaluating age-related declines in visual function. *Journal of the American Optometric Association, 64*, 71–79.

Benekohal, R. F., Michaels, R. M., Resende, P. T. V., & Shim, E. (1994, January). *Highway design and traffic operation needs of older drivers.* Paper presented at the Annual Meeting of the Transportation Research Board, Washington, DC.

Campbell, J. L, Hooey, B. L., Hanowski, R. J., Gore, B. F., Kantowitz, B. H., & Mitchell, E. (1996). *Investigation of alternative displays for side collision avoidance systems* (Final Report DTNH22-92-07001). Seattle, WA: Battelle.

Carney, C. (1996). *The effects of sensor range and timing on drivers ability to use collision warning systems.* Unpublished master's thesis, University of Iowa, Iowa City, Iowa.

Cerelli, E. C. (1992, May). *Crash data and rates for age-sex groups of drivers, 1990.* Research Note, US Department of Transportation, National Highway Traffic Safety Administration. Washington, DC: National Center for Statistics & Analysis-Research & Development.

Cifu, D. X. (1993). Rehabilitation of the elderly crash victim. *Clinics in Geriatric Medicine, 9,* 473–483.

Collins, D. J., Biever, W. J., Dingus, T. A., & Neale, V. L. (1997). *An examination of driver performance under reduced visibility conditions when using an in-vehicle signing and information system (ISIS).*

Dingus T. A., Hulse, M. C., Alves-Foss, J., Confer, S., Jahns, S., Rice, A., Hanowski, R. J., & Sorenson, D. (1996). *Development of human factors guidelines for advanced traveler information systems and commercial vehicles: Literature review* (FHWA-RD-95-153). Washington, DC: Federal Highway Administration.

Dingus, T. A., Hulse, M. C., Mollenhauer, M. A., Fleischman, R. N., McGehee, D. V., & Manakkal, N. (1997). Effects of age, system experience, and navigation technique on driving with an Advanced Traveler Information System. *Human Factors, 39*(2), 177–199.

Dingus, T. A., McGchee, D., Hulse, M., Jahns, S., Manakkal, N., Mollenhauer, M., & Fleischman, R. (1995, June). *Trav'Tek evaluation Task C3— Camera car study* (DTFH61-91-C-00106). Washington, DC: Federal Highway Administration.

Hancock, P. A., & Parasuraman, R. (1992). Human factors and safety in the design of Intelligent Vehicle Highway Systems (IVHS). *Journal of Safety Research, 23,* 181–198.

Hanowski, R. J., Bittner, A. C., Jr., Knipling, R. R., Byrne, E. A., & Parasuraman, R. (1995). Analysis of older driver safety interventions: A human factors taxonomic approach. *Proceedings of the 1995 Annual Meeting of ITS America, Intelligent Transportation: Serving the User Through Deployment, 2,* 955–965.

Hanowski, R. J., Dingus, T. A., Gallagher, J. P., Kieliszewski, C. A., & Neale, V. L. (1997). *Driver response to unexpected situations when using an In-Vehicle Information System.*

Horowitz, A. B., & Dingus, T. A. (1992). Warning signal design: A key human factors issue in an in-vehicle front-to-rear-end collision warning system. *Proceedings of the Human Factors Society 36th Annual Meeting* (pp.

1011–1013). Santa Monica, CA: Human Factors and Ergonomics Society.

Hunt, L. A. (1993). Evaluation and retraining programs for older drivers. *Clinics in Geriatric Medicine, 9*, 439–448.

ITS America. (1995). *Safety and human factors research needs.* Washington, DC: Author.

Kantowitz, B. H., & Sorkin, R. D. (1983). *Human factors: Understanding people-system relationships.* New York: Wiley.

Kosnik, W. D., Sekuler, R., & Kline, D. W. (1990). Self-reported visual problems of older drivers. *Human Factors, 32*(5), 597–608.

Lerner, N. D., Kotwal, B. M., Lyons, R. D., & GardnerBonneau, D. J. (1993). *Preliminary human factors design guidelines for crash avoidance warning devices.* Manuscript in preparation.

Lyons, R. D., Lerner, N. D., & Kotwal, B. M. (1994). Preliminary human factors guidelines for crash warning devices. *Proceedings of the IVHS America 1994 Annual Meeting* (pp. 751–759). Atlanta, GA: IVHS America.

Mackay, M. (1988). Crash protection for older persons. *Transportation Research Board Special Report 218, Transportation in an aging society: Improving mobility and safety for older persons* (Vol. 2). 158–193. Washington, DC: Transportation Research Board.

Mollenhauer, M. A., Dingus, T. A., & Hulse, M. C. (1995, April). *The potential for advanced vehicle systems to increase the mobility of elderly drivers.* (Available from the University of Iowa Public Center for the Midwest Transportation Center). Iowa City.

National Safety Council. (1994). *Accident facts 1994.* Chicago: Author.

Norman, D. A. (1988). *The design of everyday things.* New York: Doubleday Currency.

Perez, W. A., & Mast, T. M. (1992). Human factors and advanced traveler information systems (ATIS). *Proceedings of the Human Factors and Ergonomics Society 36th Annual Meeting* (pp. 1073–1077). Santa Monica, CA: Human Factors and Ergonomics Society.

Spirduso, W. W. (1980). Age differences in motion perception and specific traffic maneuver problems. *Transportation Research Record, 1325*, 23–33.

Stamatiadis, N., Taylor, W. C., & McKelvey, F. X. (1988). Accidents of elderly drivers and intersection traffic control devices. *Journal of Advanced Transportation, 24*(2), 99–112.

Tasca, L. (1992). *Review of the literature on senior driver performance* (RUSO 92107). Ontario, Canada: Ministry of Transportation, User Safety Office, Planning and Policy Branch.

Transportation Research Board. (1988). *Transportation in an aging society: Improving mobility and safety for older persons—TRB Special Report 218 (Vol. 1).* Washington, DC: Author.

Waller, P. F. (1991). The older driver. *Human Factors, 33*(5), 499–505.

Wickens, C. (1992). *Engineering psychology and human performance* (2nd ed.). New York: HarperCollins.

Intelligent Transportation Systems and the Older Driver: An Auto Industry Perspective

Thomas F. Swigart

Research findings of Hanowski and Dingus, and others suggest that intelligent transportation system (ITS) technologies have the potential to safely extend older driver mobility by compensating for the declining capabilities of these drivers. Successful application of such research findings for the benefit of older drivers will depend on their translation into product design. This discussion highlights some of the current activities and challenges of this process. The discussion is organized into three parts: the general issues of aging in relation to technology; research related to ITS and the older driver; and trends impacting automotive design and some of the challenges of implementation of ITS technology for the older driver.

The significance of mobility to the well-being of aging individuals was effectively characterized by Villeneuve (1993) in a presentation at the Transportation Research Board annual meeting in which she presented, from personal experience, stories of success and disappointment of older individuals facing loss of mobility. In this conference, Richard J. Hanowski presented a paper, co-authored with Thomas A. Dingus, in which the results of three studies were considered in relation to the question, "Will intelligent transportation systems (ITS) improve older driver mobility?" This question and the more general question of how technology can be incorporated into vehicle design to benefit aging drivers will depend on the successful collaboration and interface of individuals having diverse roles and perspectives, such as research, policy, infrastructure, and products. The role of the automobile industry is to provide the products that will ultimately bring these technologies to the customer. Analogous to the auto industry belief that knowing its customers is critical to successful product design, this discussion is offered to those interested in the issue of elderly mobility as a perspective on how their contributions might impact the auto industry as the designers and producers of products for all drivers.

This discussion is organized into three sections: Section I: Aging, Technology, and ITS, looks at the general issues of aging and technology and a snapshot of ITS development; Section II: Research Findings Related to ITS Solutions for Aging Drivers, offers a limited review of the Hanowski and Dingus paper and the findings of others; Section III: The Challenge of ITS in Vehicle Design for Older Drivers, provides a look at trends influencing vehicle design and how they might impact the integration of ITS into vehicles.

SECTION I: AGING, TECHNOLOGY, AND ITS

Aging

Data highlighting the increasing number of aging drivers are widely quoted, as are the increases in variability within and between individuals in physical and cognitive capabilities with advancing age. Less commonly stated is a parallel between aging and some issues related to disability suggested by Mitchell (1997a). "Elderly people experience various problems . . . some of which are similar to problems experienced by people with some disabilities." He estimates that by 2025, approximately 20% of Canadian drivers will be over 65 or disabled.

In this same Transport Canada report, Mitchell references a finding of the U.S. National Long Care Survey indicating that the diseases associated with old age are afflicting fewer people and onset occurs at an older age, while there is no evidence of delay in the onset of the physiological effects of aging related to driving (reaction time, vision, attention, and so forth). The implication is that healthy elderly persons may remain in the driving population longer, as their physiological capabilities decline.

In combination, the basic demographic expansion of the elderly driving population and drivers with disabilities constitute a large and growing group of drivers that might benefit from technological systems to enhance their mobility.

Aging and Technology for Drivers

It is proposed that aging drivers can benefit from ITS technology. There is risk, however, that the complexity of these new systems might require capabilities beyond those of aging drivers. Rather than benefitting from ITS, aging drivers could become its casualties. Hanowski and Dingus refer to this as the "double-edged sword" of ITS. To address such concerns, gerontechnologists are working to translate knowledge of aging processes into products and services to benefit elderly persons. The Eindhoven University, Institute for Gerontechnology (Eindhoven U) describes its goal as closing the gap between elderly persons and technology. The gap is characterized as first, adapting existing technologies for elderly users with perceptual, cognitive, and mobility limitations, and second, adapting new technology to solving the unique difficulties of, or providing new opportunities to, those aging, as is proposed in the application of ITS.

In adapting technology for aging drivers, advances in technology that these drivers have experienced in earlier years may be a factor in the aging process. Fozard (1996) describes a developmental view of aging in which he states, " . . . aging cannot be defined independently of the environment in which it occurs. Both technology and the environment of which it is a part are changing over time at the same time a person is aging; hence, personal aging and the epoch in time during which a person ages are interdependent." ITS technologies, while beginning to appear in vehicles, will be developed and implemented gradually. The most sophisticated ITS technologies envisioned today are years away from becoming mainstream vehicle components. The future elderly user is likely to have far more experience with technological devices than today's elderly user and thus may be more prepared to accept them.

Intelligent Transportation System

Highway usage has continuously increased over many years. Annual motor vehicle miles driven more than doubled between 1970 and 1995, and licensed drivers have increased by 58% (American Automobile Manufacturers Association, 1997). It became apparent at a federal level that the traditional solutions to increased usage, such as adding and widening roads, would not be sufficient to handle future demands. In 1991, Congress passed the Intermodal Surface Transportation Efficiency Act (ISTEA). Objectives of this legislation include functional efficiency of the highway system, economic efficiency, and safety. Intelligent transportation systems include a broad range of diverse technologies that are seen as a major contributor to meeting the objectives of ISTEA.

The challenge is massive, requiring the coordination and partnering of many public and private sector interests. ITS America (ITS) was formed by Congressional mandate to coordinate the development and deployment of ITS in the United States.

An aggressive, 20-year strategic plan for ITS was developed in 1992. Much of the early activity has been directed to the drafting of standards that will bring consistency and order to the development of ITS. The Society of Automotive Engineers and the International Standards Organization (ISO) have committees working to develop and deploy consensus standards governing the safety and usability on in-vehicle ITS applications and interfaces. While several projects have been initiated, developing ITS standards for older drivers is not a priority project at this time.

A parallel activity to the development of ITS-related standards is the development and validation of ITS component technologies and hardware, such as those evaluated in the Hanowski and Dingus studies. As ITS implementation proceeds, it is likely that a number of these systems will be adopted for use. Currently, it is not uncommon for individual systems to be developed independently by different organizations. This highlights the importance of the standards effort to aid the independent developers in producing compatible systems.

The Evolution of ITS Implementation

From a chronologic perspective, Mitchell (1997a) anticipates that "near term" ITS developments will include ITS equipment such as vision enhancement, route guidance, and emergency alerts. Intermediate developments would include intelligent cruise control, collision warning, and automated lane following. Finally, would come automated highways. Based on work in progress, intelligent cruise control systems seem closer to implementation than Mitchell suggests, and there are still significant issues to be resolved with vision enhancement. The general progression in ITS evolution, however, is a shift from driver control, where the ITS provide information to the driver, to ITS that assume partial or complete control of the vehicle. These advanced systems would perform both decision tasks and vehicle control tasks, which are now the responsibility of the driver. In relation to Fozard's developmental view of aging, this progression from driver to vehicle control is in reverse order to the development of technological familiarity within the group of aging drivers. The longest vision for ITS, for example, automated highway systems that assume control of the vehicle, require the least of a driver's capability.

An obvious implication of system control (as compared to human control) is that the tasks performed by vehicle systems require little or no operator involvement and are thus transparent to the aging process. Even with the most automated systems envisioned, however, there would be some portions of a trip where the vehicle requires operator control or monitoring. Major issues exist here with respect to the transition from operator to vehicle control, monitoring during vehicle control, and override procedures. An example is assuring that the operator is alert and ready to resume control of the vehicle following periods of operator inactivity where the vehicle is in control.

SECTION II: RESEARCH FINDINGS RELATED TO ITS SOLUTIONS FOR AGING DRIVERS

Hanowski and Dingus Studies

Hanowski and Dingus present the findings of three on-road studies using instrumented vehicles to shed light on the issue of whether these three ITS technologies, by compensating for declining capabilities, can enable the older driver to maintain performance at a safe and functional level. The three ITS technologies that are the focus of the Hanowski paper include in-vehicle routing and navigation systems (IRANS), in-vehicle safety advisory and warning system (IV-SAWS), and collision warning systems (CWS). IRANS provide navigation information, IVSAWS alert drivers to unusual circumstances that may impact their travel, such as an accident ahead, and CWS warns of imminent collision. These systems provide information that the driver must then process. Appropriate vehicle inputs remain the responsibility of the driver. Thus, the three systems considered in the Hanowski and Dingus paper represent only a portion of the potential range of ITS technologies that could be applied to the issue of older drivers.

The first study utilized TravTek and presented route guidance information in varying forms including voice, maps, and so forth. Response measures included number of glances exceeding 2.5 seconds and lane deviations. The conclusion was that older drivers can benefit from well designed IRANS, specifically those providing voice commands.

In the second study, drivers were confronted with unexpected external events (such as a car approaching from hidden entrance, one lane tunnel, disabled vehicle) and asked to respond. Auditory alerts were found to decrease the response time to unexpected events for older drivers. Many younger drivers, however, found the auditory alert to be distracting, especially for nonurgent messages.

Thus, findings of the two studies above support the contention that ITS technologies can provide a relative advantage to mature drivers.

The final study evaluated spacing maintenance (distance between vehicles) and CWS and their potential to reduce rear-end collisions. The experiment was designed with the assumption that perceptual factors were the most likely age-related causal factor in rear-end collisions. Older drivers were found to maintain a cautious 2.5 seconds minimum headway and did not benefit from the system.

While this third study did not show a differential benefit of the CWS for older drivers, rear-end collisions still represent a substantial portion of accidents, approximately 25% of police-reported accidents according to 1993 General Estimating System figures cited by Hanowski. The benefit of the conservative 2.5 second headway maintained by older drivers seems to be supported by the relatively lesser involvement of older drivers in rear-end collisions. Three related points are worth consideration. First, if driver inattention or perceptual errors are the factors contributing to these accidents, the context of the experimental situation may induce the participant to maintain a higher level of attention and more conservative driving behavior. Second, in many contexts, it would seem that high traffic density would limit the discretion to maintain a longer headway and possibly influence the effectiveness of a CWS. Finally, the results of the display modality study were not discussed, however, Horowitz and Dingus (1992) reference a summary of literature on aircraft displays (Stokes, Wickens, & Kite, 1990) that concludes the auditory signal modality is superior (to visual) when immediate action is required. This recommendation would probably apply to CWS as well.

Horowitz and Dingus (1992) comment that "The use of auditory displays in automobiles is limited." The trend, however, is for the proliferation of auditory signals, and, while driving, the auditory environment can be quite complex due to vehicle noise, road and outside noises, and possibly a radio. Findings of at least two of the three Hanowski and Dingus studies recommend the auditory modality for effective information communication, and the same recommendation would most likely apply to an effective CWS as well. The older driver, who may have the greatest potential to benefit from auditory guidance, is the most likely to have degraded auditory capability. There is clearly an opportunity for loss of information due to the masking of one system by another as more systems are implemented in this environment of auditory complexity.

On reviewing the Hanowski and Dingus studies, I would concur that the findings offer encouragement that ITS technologies can mitigate age-related decrement in driving performance and safely extend mobility. The promise in these results also suggests additional challenges to researchers interested in pursuing ITS solutions for older drivers issues. Among these are:

- Evaluate other ITS technologies for differential benefit to older drivers.
- Relate human capabilities to driving performance.
- Conduct usability research to support interface design for older drivers.
- Conduct research to support integration of multiple systems and its impact on older drivers.

Other Studies

While studies targeting elderly persons are relatively few, Mitchell (1997b) reviewed literature on ITS with regard to aging and disabled drivers. The general result of the review supports the Hanowski and Dingus findings that ITS technologies can mitigate some of the difficulties encountered by elderly drivers, if carefully executed. For example, Walker, Alicandri, Sedney, and Roberts (1990), in a simulator study of seven ITS systems reported that increased task difficulty effected older drivers to a greater extent than younger drivers, and audio presentation was thought to be somewhat safer than visual. To assess acceptance of ITS systems, Barkow, Parviainen, and Joly (1993) conducted a study of wants with a small sample of disabled and elderly drivers and found a high level of overall acceptance of ITS technologies. Preferred ITS systems were: advanced vehicle control and safety systems (driver monitoring, control aids, and warnings of failures and advanced traveler information systems, including navigation systems and onboard displays of touring information). Auditory guidance with a visual backup was favored as the display modality for these systems.

The European DRIVE II project EDDIT (Elderly and Disabled Drivers Information Telematics) (Oxley & Mitchell, 1995) evaluated 14 systems representing six ITS applications and two generic issues (head-up display versus dashboard display and complexity). Elderly participants reacted positively to ITS, however, some of the limitations of implementation of the more complex systems were apparent. Simpler intersection displays were preferred to maps for route guidance, touch-screen controls were disliked as were small or complex displays. Again the theme of the results is a preference for large controls and displays, simple systems, and the auditory information modality.

From this review of research findings, Mitchell and Suen (1997) identified impairments associated with age, the problems associated with those impairments, and the ITS technologies that can mitigate those problems. These are summarized in Table 6.1.

The research seems to suggest that ITS technologies have the potential to improve older driver mobility. As new technologies evolve, the research and implementation must include the older driver perspective if mobility of older persons is to be maintained and extended. The next section will present an automotive perspective of industry trends and some implications for design for the elderly population.

SECTION III: THE CHALLENGE OF ITS IN VEHICLE DESIGN FOR OLDER DRIVERS

Is the Older Driver Really Different?

Older drivers exhibit declines in physical and cognitive capabilities, have more concern for safety, and more discretion in their driving patterns, but there is very little that suggests that they are really different in the sense that they can be readily categorized for design purposes. Design recommendations for older drivers are typically directional (larger, simpler, easier). Fozard (1996) points out that bringing the benefits of technology to elderly persons requires advocacy, yet he highlights two issues. The first is the heterogeneity of aging (which could include any variable from visual acuity to lifestyle). The second is the denial of the consequences of aging by most people (old and young). Consistent with the denial issue, some in automotive marketing feel that a vehicle identified as an old person's car will not sell. To summarize these considerations, the challenge becomes to identify and quantify design targets for a diverse group that does not want to acknowledge its own identity and then to design a product, incorporating new technologies, that will be positively perceived in the marketplace.

TABLE 6.1   Impairments, Problems and ITS Equipment for Older Car Drivers

Impairment	Problems	ITS Equipment
Increased reaction time. Difficulty dividing attention between tasks.	Difficulty driving in unfamiliar or congested areas	Navigation/route guidance Traffic information, VMS
Deteriorating vision, particularly at night	Difficulty seeing pedestrians and other objects at night, and reading signs	Night vision enhancement. In-vehicle signs
Difficulty judging speed and distance	Failure to perceive conflicting vehicles. Accidents at junctions	Collision warning. Automated lane changing
Difficulty perceiving and analyzing situations	Failure to comply with yield signs, traffic signals and rail crossings. Slow to appreciate hazards on highway	In-vehicle signs and warnings. Intelligent cruise control
Difficulty turning head, reduced peripheral vision	Failure to notice obstacles while maneuvering. Worries over merging and lane changes	Blind spot/obstacle detection. Automated lane changing and merging
More prone to fatigue	Get tired on long journeys	Intelligent cruise control. Automated lane following
General effects of aging	Worries over inability to cope with a breakdown. Worries about driving to unfamiliar places, at night, in heavy traffic.	Emergency callout (Mayday). Vehicle condition monitoring. ATIS
Some impairments vary in severity from day to day. Prone to tiredness	Concern over fitness to drive	Driver condition monitoring

Reprinted with permission from the Minister of Public Works and Government Services Canada, 1999.

A study, conducted for the Society of Automotive Engineers SAE Mature Drivers Standards Committee (Saunby & Matle, 1994), identified automotive ergonomic characteristics that were significantly different in importance to young drivers and to older drivers. The younger drivers were university students and the older drivers were participants in American Association of Retired Persons driver education classes. Of 34 items, the seven that were found to differ significantly in importance ratings between the young and the older drivers included: glare control, ease of using seat belt, seat belt comfort, ease of exiting, ease of entering, minimize instrument panel clutter, and ease of opening and closing doors. Each of these seem consistent with declines in capabilities and greater concern for safety that would be expected in an older group.

An elderly mobility conference was held in Novi, Michigan (Southeastern Michigan Council of Government, 1994), which attracted representatives from a number of fields, including health care, government, and law enforcement, as well as the automobile industry. A workshop activity, intended to identify automobile features that would aid mobility of elderly persons, produced a shopping list of conventional and technology-related features. The technology-related features included voice activation, image enhancement, obstacle detection, intelligent cruise, and stranded motorist aid. While this list reflects an awareness of older driver issues among the workshop participants, the greater need is for data from the elusive target group of older drivers.

The information referenced above suggests that design for the aging drivers requires products and infrastructures that accommodate evolutionary declines in capabilities rather than paradigm shifts. While younger individuals may visualize the older driver as a member of a distinctly different group, in practice this group is quite difficult to characterize and does not conveniently fit the perceptions of the young.

Vehicle Design Trends and the Older Driver

As aging is a process of change, so is vehicle design. In recent years, vehicles have become smaller and more fuel efficient, while customers are demanding interior comfort and spaciousness. The result is smaller, aerodynamic vehicles, which attempt to maintain a perception of interior spaciousness. Feature content is increasing with phones, advanced entertainment units, and trip computers. ITS systems are being considered.

Improvements in occupant protection have added features and design requirements. The airbag, for example, has provided important safety benefits for vehicle occupants, but in providing this benefit, the airbag reduces visible space available to locate controls and displays. Vehicles must also comply with requirements for structural integrity of the roof of the vehicle in a crash. Today's smaller, aerodynamic vehicles have angled pillars that are closer to the occupants and must be carefully designed and positioned to provide both structural strength and adequate visibility.

The automobile business is now global. The design of vehicles to meet the requirements of worldwide markets involves the accommodation of many considerations that impact successful ergonomic design. Symbols, for example, are replacing words for the labeling of many controls and displays in an effort to overcome language differences. While symbols have been used more extensively in Europe, many older American drivers are more accustomed to English words and have some difficulty interpreting symbols. Redundancy (words and symbols) is seldom used due to limited space for graphics.

The result of the considerations above is that more content is competing for less real estate on the instrument panel. This is with only minimal incorporation of high-tech features in current vehicles. The development of new technology seems to be outpacing our ability to successfully implement new systems. As new systems and features are developed, priority should not only be given to achieving functionality and feature content but also to the usability of the product. In some systems, the feature content is a function of internal software, and additional features can be added at low cost through software modification. While the monetary cost may be low, the result of the increased complexity may be considerable with respect to errors, confusion, delays, and dissatisfaction with the product. Unfortunately, there are limited data to direct us in the effective design and integration of new technologies, especially for older drivers.

Shortage of prime real estate or desire to integrate components have also encouraged the placement of vehicle features where space is available and in locations that may not be optimal for the user. An example is the use of the headliner, above the rear view mirror. Rockwell, Augsburger, Smith, and Freeman (1988) report that approximately 91% of the population use bifocals after age 55. If bifocals are required to read a display located in that area, the observer must tilt the head upward to view the display through the lower portion of the bifocal lens. This could be difficult for many older drivers, especially those with limited neck mobility. While this location may be appropriate for large displays of discretionary information, it may be undesirable for older drivers, who find it harder to access.

Design Targets to Include Aging Driver

Successful vehicle design in today's highly competitive markets can depend on millimeters and pennies. The field of ergonomics, in many areas, is challenged to establish precise design criteria to accommodate the general population of users, and even more challenged for the aging user. Applying handbook and experimental data to vehicle design issues frequently requires extrapolation well beyond the conditions that generated the information. While vehicle engineers are generally able to estimate the consequences of design modifications in terms of weight, time for design, or part cost, ergonomic engineers have difficulty representing the ergonomic benefits in equally tangible metrics.

There seems to be a general feeling that what works for the old, also works for the young. If we can identify design targets that accommodate older drivers, younger drivers will also be accommodated. While probably valid in most cases, the design trends outlined in the previous section suggest the need for creative solutions to meet the needs of the older driver. As the list of features grows longer and with space at a premium, conventional solutions of larger graphics and controls will limit the features that can be offered. In this sense, design for the older driver may, in fact, dissatisfy the younger driving population by limiting feature content.

Despite the challenge, targets must be set if design for older drivers is to proceed and the benefits of the new technologies are to benefit and not hinder the older driver.

Final Comment

The research of Hanowski and Dingus and others suggests that ITS technologies have the potential to safely extend the mobility of older drivers. For these research findings to benefit elderly drivers, they must be translated to product design. This discussion has presented a view of trends and developments that are shaping automotive design as well as some of the challenges of implementing technology in product design. It is hoped that this perspective will be useful to those individuals of diverse backgrounds who are working in this field.

REFERENCES

American Automobile Manufacturers Association. (1997). *Motor Vehicle Facts & Figures 1997.* Detroit, MI: Author.

Barkow, B., Parviainen, J. A., & Joly, R. (1993). Accommodation to the Requirements of Drivers with Disabilities in IVHS. *Proceedings of the IEEE-IEE Vehicle Navigation and Information Systems Conference.* 385–388.

Eindhoven University, Institute for Gerontechnology. Description of university activities and perspective on Gerontechnology. Available: http://www.tue.nl/gerontechnologie.

Fozard, J. L. (1996). Aging and Technology: A Developmental View. *Proceedings of the 40th Annual Meeting of the Human Factors and Ergonomics Society* 138–140.

Horowitz, A. B., & Dingus T. A. (1992). Warning Signal Design: A Key Human Factors Issue in an In-vehicle Front-to-rear-end Collision Warning System. *Proceedings of the 36th Annual Meeting of the Human Factors and Ergonomic Society* 1011–1013.

ITS America. Available: URL: http//www.itsa.org.

Mitchell, C. G. B. (1997a). *Intelligent transportation systems (ITS) applications for improving transportation for elderly and disabled travelers* (TP12925E). Transport Canada.

Mitchell, C. G. B. (1997b). *The potential of intelligent transportation systems to increase accessibility to transport for elderly and disabled people.* (TP12926E). Transport Canada.

Mitchell, C. G. B., & Suen (1997). *IITS Impact on Elderly Drivers.* Paper presented at the XIIIth International Road Federation World Meeting, Toronto, Canada.

Oxley, P. R., & Mitchell, C. G. B. (1995). *Final report on Elderly and Disabled Drivers Information Telematics (Project EDDIT).* Brussels, Belguim: Commission of the European Communities DG XIII, R & D Programme Telematics Systems in the Area of Transport (DRIVE II).

Rockwell, T., Augsburger, A., Smith, S., & Freeman, S. (1988). The older driver—A challenge to the design of automotive electronic displays. *Proceedings of the 32nd Annual Meeting of the Human Factors and Ergonomics Society* 583–587.

Saunby, C. S., & Matle, C. C. (1994). *Assessment of importance of automotive characteristics by older and younger drivers.* Warrensdale, PA: SAE.

Southeastern Michigan Council of Governments. (October, 1994). *Proceedings, Elderly Mobility Conference,* pp. 17–18.

Stokes, A., Wickens, C., & Kite, K. (1990). *Display technology: Human factors concepts.* Warrendale, PA: SAE.

Villeneuve, E. (1993). *Driving decisions for seniors: A cost-effective community-based program for intervention and research with older drivers.* Paper presented at the Meeting of the Transportation Research Board, Washington, DC.

Walker, J., Alicandri, Sedney, C., & Roberts, K. (1990). *In-vehicle navigation devices: Effects on the safety of driver performance.* Washington, DC: Office of Safety and Traffic Operations R&D.

Intelligent Transportation Systems and the Older Traveler: Prospects for Mobility Enhancement

Paul P. Jovanis

I t is a pleasure to comment on the fine chapter by Hanowski and Dingus. My review is in three parts. First are comments on the details of the paper, particularly areas in which additional relevant research findings support or differ from those reported by the authors. Particular attention is paid to in-vehicle route guidance and navigation systems and collision warning systems. Second is a discussion of important mobility implications of a broader set of ITS services aimed at improving older traveler mobility, but not necessarily by driving a personal auto. These systems and services need to be discussed to appreciate the full implications of ITS for mobility of elderly persons. Finally there are conclusions and recommendations.

OVERALL COMMENTS

The authors provide an excellent perspective on Intelligent Transportation Systems (ITS). While the acronyms can be a bit overwhelm-

315

ing for the uninitiated, the authors are clear in differentiating the functionality of the services provided. The introduction of the user-centered perspective on system design is an important conceptual starting point for the presentation of research findings.

Two of the systems selected for detailed review, in-vehicle routing and navigation and collision warning systems, are the subject of substantial research and commercial development. Products are already on the market with some of the functionality described in the paper. Articulating the performance record of these systems and highlighting their challenges for the older driver is particularly important. In-vehicle safety and warning systems have been the subject of more limited experimentation, so the findings are of general interest. The implementation of these systems requires cooperative communication between the roadside and vehicle that is not likely to occur for several years into the next millennium. While interesting and well conducted, the study does not have the immediacy associated with studies of vehicle routing or collision warning systems.

The double-edged sword is an apt metaphor for problems confronting use of ITS in-vehicle technologies for elderly persons. Addition of physical and mental workload is particularly problematic for older persons, who have been particularly challenged in dynamic information processing contexts. It is important to recognize that ITS market research studies indicate that the primary attributes for ITS traffic information is that it be dynamic, accurate, and personalized. While these studies (Kemp & Lappin, 1997) are not focused on elderly persons, they indicate potential directions for broadly available ITS products and services evolving from the private sector. Older drivers, because of mobility needs that differ somewhat from the general population, may demand different attributes from their ITS systems. Nevertheless, it is not clear if customized systems will evolve from the marketplace, where virtually all ITS systems will be developed. The authors thus raise the appropriate cautions about the implications of attentional demand for older driver safety.

IN-VEHICLE ROUTING AND NAVIGATION SYSTEMS

The authors provide an excellent overview of the TravTek experiment conducted in Orlando, Florida. TravTek is probably the most significant and successful ITS field experiment in terms of the thoroughness of the evaluation and the safety and human factors lessons learned. Dingus was one of the lead researchers in the evaluation effort, so the description of the findings from this study comes from first-hand experience. Older drivers (65 years and older) performed very well with turn-by-turn navigation supplemented by voice, virtually identically to the 35- to 45-year-old subject group. This finding demonstrates that systems can be designed for safe operation by older drivers in the highly complex and dynamic urban traffic environment.

Caution is advised concerning dismissing other generic designs (e.g., all electronic maps) as unsafe. Simulator studies conducted in California (Srinivasan & Jovanis, 1997) indicated that a turn-by-turn navigation display performed significantly worse than an electronic map, located at identical points in the instrument panel. The identical turn-by-turn display located head-up on the windshield produced nearly comparable performance to voice-only guidance. The electronic map performed nearly as well as voice-only guidance as well. Importantly, the turn-by-turn and map systems in this study were not supplement by aural prompts, and the study was conducted in a more restrictive driving simulator environment, not on the road.

While not focused on older drivers, this study cautions against too negative an evaluation of the electronic map. User exit interviews after the California study revealed that drivers like the electronic map for its ability to orient them spatially, particularly with respect to the number of intersections remaining until the next turn. The California study also confirmed the positive benefits of voice-only navigation, as did earlier research (Srinivasan & Jovanis, 1997).

IN-VEHICLE SAFETY AND WARNING SYSTEMS

The findings reported by Hanowski and Dingus are among the first for in-vehicle safety and warning systems. The driver's ability to respond more quickly with the information display (illustrated in Figure 6.6 of the chapter) is impressive and shows substantial potential of improved road safety. The concluding comments concerning the value of auditory alerts and the ability of subjects to tune and adjust intensity are particularly important. While testing digitized voice alerts as part of perception studies of collision warning systems (Jovanis, Campbell, Klaver, & Chen, 1997), older subjects expressed difficulty in comprehending many voice-based alerts, particularly those using a female speaker. Younger subjects expressed no difficulty under identical test conditions. These findings further reinforce the recommendation for on-off switches and intensity controls.

COLLISION WARNING SYSTEMS

Hanowski and Dingus present interesting findings concerning rear-end crash avoidance through in-vehicle systems. It is important to note that this is only one type of potential collision, and the system requirements of a more comprehensive system may evolve from these early systems with more restrictive functionality. Warnings about other types of collisions, such as blind zone during lane changing and conflicts at intersections may be more helpful to older drivers who have difficulty in these driving contexts. Provision of the additional functionality raises important questions about how to manage multiple alerts and warnings from multiple systems. This is an important design consideration for any user group, but particularly for the older driver who may be more distracted by contemporaneous alerts.

Research undertaken in California (Jovanis, et al., 1997) has indicated that older drivers have different perceptions of the comprehensibility of collision warning alerts. A set of 67 subjects, 11 of which were over the age of 60, rated the comprehensibility of 50 collision warning alerts on seven dimensions: urgency, annoyance, understandability, command attention, ability to convey the type of collision, ability to convey what to do, and overall utility. Each subject rated each of 50 alerts on each of the dimensions using a 7-point Likert-type scale. Groups of 6 to 12 subjects were tested with randomized order of presentation of the alerts.

Older subjects much more strongly preferred text messages supplemented by auditory alerts. They expressed significant difficulty in comprehending icon-based alerts without supplemental text. They also had difficulty discerning the message content of aural messages conveyed using a female digitized voice that younger subjects understood readily.

While the subjects were not task loaded or in a given driven context, these studies indicate that older subjects have different patterns of comprehension of collision alerts. It is potentially problematic that the older subjects could not clearly discern the nature of the alerts when text was not provided. Route guidance studies have consistently shown that reading text is distracting and results in longer glance times and greater difficulty in reacting to external events. Further tests are needed in driving contexts and under task-loaded conditions to determine if these results are generalizable.

ITS SYSTEMS AND SERVICES TO ENHANCE OLDER TRAVELER MOBILITY

An important issue not directly addressed by the authors is the prospects offered by ITS services for enhancing older traveler mobility. The focus is not on user safety while traveling so much as the ability of ITS to identify and support mobility options for those who seek alternatives to driving (Schweigert & McGrane, 1994). Consistent with a user-centered perspective, a focus group-based laboratory experiment was conducted followed by a series of telephone and mail surveys to assess travelers current mobility needs and how the unmet or problematic needs may be addressed by ITS services (Klaver, et al., 1996; Abdel-Aty, Jovanis, Chen, & Klaver, 1997). The findings of these experiments are summarized to provide insights concerning services and systems that users state they need to support their travel.

A set of laboratory experiments were conducted in which a computer emulation of ITS systems and services was demonstrated to small groups of older (and some disabled) travelers in the Davis, California area. Reactions to and perceptions of the systems were solicited in a focus group interactive discussion. A series of travel scenarios were described to the subjects using familiar local landmarks and common trip purposes. Issues of discussion with the subjects included whether a particular service or system was useful and comprehensible to them and whether it would increase their mobility by facilitating the trip. Nine of the 11 subjects were over 60 with six aged 70 or older.

The systems and services tested included three advanced information systems: an interactive kiosk information system (described as being located at a transit station or terminal); a bus signing system on-board the vehicle informing travelers of the next stop location and possible bus transfer locations; and an interactive in-home information system. In addition, traditional paratransit services were discussed along with two possible enhancements: real-time paratransit in which the user could schedule a ride an hour or 2 in advance, and real-time ridesharing in which personal vehicles are used and scheduled to provide mobility to riders on an hour or so basis. Details of the design of the interfaces and systems were explored along with the services and travel niches that the systems were intended to serve. All the service concepts have been subjects of field testing in the United States and Europe.

The subjects responded very positively to the information systems and were able to readily understand the information provided. Subjects particularly mentioned the improved utility and comprehensibility of the electronic information compared to paper maps and transit schedules. Subjects responded most positively to the in-home systems and recommended that additional services be provided concerning activities of interest to seniors and disabled persons along with phone numbers and other information to access service providers. In some discussions, these nontransportation services seem viewed as more important and valued than transportation information.

Real-time paratransit services were viewed very positively, with many subjects commenting on the improved convenience offered by the shorter schedule requirements. While most senior participants currently drove, they stated that real-time paratransit would be a viable option for them when a car was not available. It is important to note that Davis is a small community of about 50,000 well served by transit, but with high affluence and levels of auto availability. While preferred, real-time ridesharing was seen mostly as a backup to the personal auto for travel.

Method of access to information and services was an issue, and most participants expressed strong preference for telephone access with an operator. Any automated system, particularly using a computer, would face serious obstacles. Most of our subjects, as well as those in a follow-up survey strongly preferred personal operator interaction (Chen, Klaver, Uwaine, & Jovanis, 1998).

Real-time ridesharing was not perceived positively at all. Subjects were concerned about their personal security and the safety of the drivers and vehicles in which they were passengers. Subjects were concerned that a transportation agency would not be able to provide sufficient background checks and system monitoring to allay their fears in these areas. They suggested that a well-respected public institution (such as the university) would be more credible in this role and help assure security. While the mobility benefits of the service were recognized, it was clear that the service would have to be carefully designed, operated, and marketed to achieve acceptance by the public.

The services and systems explored in this research do not possess the inherent safety risks of the in-vehicle systems discussed by Hanowski and Dingus. They can provide useful mobility enhancements, but are focused more on nonauto travel. Given the tremendous auto mobility of elderly persons, this may condemn such services to a relatively small market share. Nevertheless, providing easy, clear, convenient alternatives to the automobile should be part of any strategy that seeks to maintain older subjects' lifestyles and mobility, while judiciously restricting their access to driving if they pose a risk to themselves and others.

SUMMARY

ITS systems offer many opportunities to enhance the mobility of older drivers and travelers. Safety and distraction issues remain challenges for in-vehicle devices for both older and younger travelers. Hanowski and Dingus have done an excellent job reviewing critical issues in safe operation of in-vehicle devices. It is also important that ITS services and systems be encouraged that assist the nondriving traveler. Preliminary research on these systems shows great promise as well.

REFERENCES

Abdel-Aty, M. A., Jovanis, P. P., Chen, W. H., & Klaver, K. (1997). *A survey of elderly travelers: Initial results from California and their implications for ITS.* University of California, Davis. Institute of Transportation Studies.

Chen, W. H., Klaver, K., Uwaine, R., & Jovanis, P. P. (1998). *Importance of transit information, information system attributes, and transportation service attributes on public transit use by the elderly and disabled.* The Pennsylvania State University, Department of Civil and Environmental Engineering, University Park.

Jovanis, P. P., Campbell, J., Klaver, K., & Chen, W. H. (1997). Driver Preferences for Visual and Auditory Collision Warning Alerts, *4th World Congress, Intelligent Transportation Systems, Mobility for Everyone,* Paper 1076, Berlin, Germany, 8 pages.

Kemp, M. A., & Lappin, J. E. (1997). ATIS focus groups in the USA - Phase 1 of the US DOT User Acceptance Research Project [CD-ROM]. *Proceedings, 4th World Congress on Intelligent Transportation Systems.*

Klaver, K., Chen, W. H., Reddy, P., Kurani, K., Uwaine, R., & Jovanis, P. P. (1996). *Innovative transportation systems and services for the elderly and disabled: A prototype experiment.* University of California, Davis: Institute of Transportation Studies.

Schweigert, C., & McGrane. (1994). The challenge for developing and implementing advanced public transportation systems for elderly and disabled customers. *Proceedings of the 1st World Congress on Applications of Transport Telematics and Intelligent Vehicle-Highway Systems.*

Srinivasan, R., & Jovanis, P. P. (1997). Effect of selected in-vehicle route guidance systems on driver reaction times. *Human Factors, 39,* 200–215.

Author Index

Subject Index

Page numbers followed by f indicate figure and pages numbers followed by t indicate table.

Travel patterns
of elderly, 98–100, 100t, 101t
mobility loss and, 108
Travel resources,
of elderly, 100, 101t
TravTek
in-vehicle routing and navigation systems, 284–286, 286f, 287f, 304
study overview, 316–317
Turano, K. et al,
visual environment, 29–30
Two vehicle accidents
by age group, 164, 166t–168t
causes of, 203t
fatalities, 164, 171t–172t
Tzankoff, S. et al,
energy metabolism in elderly, 77

UFOV. *See* Useful field of view
(UFOV)
UFOV Visual Attention Analyser,
assessment tool, 216–217
Urban accidents,
by age group, 177, 181t–182t
Useful Field Of View test (UFOV), 47
Useful field of view (UFOV)
assessment tools, 47, 216–217
cutpoints for impairment, 219–220,
219t
effect on life space, 231–232, 231t
injurious accident factor, 238–240
interventions for, 241
relation to crash frequency, 234–
238, 234f
training for, 241–244
User-centered design
intelligent transportation systems
(ITS), 283–284
for public transportation, 319–321

Vehicle, multiple
accident fatalities, 164, 173t
accidents, by age group, 169t
accidents by age group, 164, 169t
Vehicle, single

accidents, causes of, 190, 202t
accidents by age group, 164, 165t
Vehicle, two
accident fatalities, 164, 171t–172t
accidents, causes of, 203t
accidents by age group, 164,
166t–168t
Vehicle design
as environmental factor, 271
older drivers and, 309–311
Villeneuve, E.,
older drivers, 299–300
Virginia Polytechnic Institute,
in-vehicle safety advisory and warning systems, 287, 288–292,
290f, 291f
Vision
ambient vision, 45–59
defined, 49
night driving and, 54–55, 55f
role of, 48–50
assessment tools, 215–216
cataracts
mobility loss and, 244–230
self-restriction and, 254
surgery for, 229–230
cutpoints for impairment, 219–220,
219t
driving, 30–33, 32f
relation to crash frequency, 234–
238, 234f
Visual acuity
assessment tools, 215–216
effect on life space, 231–232, 231t
Visual environment,
personal mobility and, 27–33, 32f
Visual field sensitivity,
assessment tools, 215–216
Visual impairments
cataracts, 244–230
effect on life space, 231–232, 231t
role in mobility loss, 214–233
role in motor vehicle accidents,
233–245
Visual information processing
accident location, 208–210, 209f